TOMMY'S ARK

*Soldiers and Their Animals
in the Great War*

Richard van Emden

BLOOMSBURY

LONDON · NEW DELHI · NEW YORK · SYDNEY

First published in Great Britain 2010

This paperback edition published 2011

Copyright © 2010 by Richard van Emden

The moral right of the author has been asserted

Bloomsbury Publishing Plc
50 Bedford Square
London WC1B 3DP

www.bloomsbury.com

Bloomsbury Publishing, London, New Delhi, New York and Sydney

A CIP catalogue record for this book is available from the British Library

ISBN 978 1 4088 1007 1

10 9 8 7 6 5 4 3 2

Typeset by Hewer Text UK Ltd, Edinburgh
Printed in Great Britain by Clays Limited, St Ives plc

Dedicated to Paul and Lucy Averley and their daughters,
Martha, Alice and Madeleine

CONTENTS

ABBREVIATIONS

The following abbreviations are used throughout the text:

Ranks	Units
Acting Captain – A/Capt.	Army Service Corps – ASC
Brigadier – Brig.	Battalion – Bttn
Captain – Capt.	Battery – Batt.
Company Sergeant Major – CSM	Company – Coy
Corporal – Cpl	Division – Div.
Gunner – Gnr	Machine Gun Corps – MGC
Lance Corporal – L/Cpl	Regiment – Rgt
Lieutenant – Lt	Royal Army Medical Corps – RAMC
Lieutenant Colonel – Lt Col	Royal Engineers – RE
Major – Maj.	Royal Field Artillery – RFA
Private – Pte	Royal Garrison Artillery – RGA
Quarter Master Sergeant – QMS	Royal Horse Artillery – RHA
Reverend – Rev.	Royal Marine Light Infantry – RMLI
Second Lieutenant – 2/Lt	Royal Naval Division – RND
Sergeant – Sgt	Yeomanry – Yeo.
Sergeant Major – Sgt Maj.	
Trooper – Trp.	

INTRODUCTION

In mid-1915, a medical officer, Lieutenant Philip Gosse, was making his way forward through a communication trench to the front line. Gosse had just been drafted out to France and was being guided to a dugout in which a captain of the Royal Army Medical Corps was sitting on an upturned box. He was working intently at a table but as Gosse and his guide entered the dimly lit room they were at first unclear just what the man was doing.

> When we drew near and I saw what that occupation was, I knew at once that he was a man after my own heart, for he was attentively engaged in skinning a field vole. From this I wrongly jumped to the conclusion that, like myself, he was an amateur taxidermist and collector, but he repudiated any such claims and confessed that all he was doing was skinning a field vole to make a muff for his little daughter's doll to wear when it took perambulator exercise.

A few months later and another part of the line: an irregular and hastily convened court martial was under way; two lives were at stake. The trial had been set up with all the attributes of a military court with its appointed judge, prosecution and defence. Witnesses were on standby as the two defendants waited impatiently in the wings, as it were. Jimmy and Jane, a gander and a goose belonging to A Battery, 52nd Brigade, Royal Field Artillery, had been purchased in early December 1915 and were being rapidly fattened up for Christmas Day lunch. However, their 'personalities' had captured the imagination of some men in the unit who suggested that instead of being eaten they might make excellent battery mascots. After due deliberation, the jury 'acquitted' Jimmy and Jane and the pair took up their new role, travelling in the mess cart, heads hanging over the side, to general amusement. They subsequently went everywhere with the unit, enduring not only counter-battery fire but also a brief kidnapping by an acquisitive farmer. Rescued, the pair survived the war and were sent to England and a zoo. Jimmy died in 1920 while Jane lived in retirement on a Berkshire farm until 1931.

Voles and geese: not the animals one first associates with the Western Front at a time when horses provided the quickest and most reliable form of transport for officers – including the Commander-in-Chief – and when, with mules and donkeys, they remained the primary source of power needed to haul guns and transport to and from the front line. Film and photographs reinforce the view that it was not so much an animals' war as an equine war, with a few messenger dogs and pigeons thrown in for good measure.

Nevertheless, look more closely at the images, explore widely the vast photo libraries, and another world becomes apparent, a world in which animals were not just utilised for immediate military requirements but kept as pets or mascots, providing comfort to men who rarely received leave and who were consequently starved of affection. These men, often cautious about making close friends for fear of losing them in battle, could heap attention on a creature. Images of men holding chickens, goats, dogs, cats, rabbits, even hedgehogs, have survived and in greater numbers than might have been expected.

Many animals were found wandering the battlefield or taken from abandoned farms to be treasured by the men. One officer, killed with his dog on the Western Front, was buried with his faithful friend, while another went on to commission a post-war sculpture of his dog Timmy in honour of the occasion, in May 1916, that it had warned him and his men of a German gas attack. In time a few pets became legendary, going on to receive dedicated burial spots with appropriate headstones, while others were stuffed to 'live on' in regimental museums.

And then, all around the fighting men, there was nature, surviving, finding ways to adapt to the rapidly altering conditions. There were of course the ubiquitous rats and mice that plagued soldiers' lives, but there were dozens of other smaller mammals and insects forgotten by history, indigenous to the land, that burrowed underground, scurried through the uncultivated fields, or flew, hovered or buzzed around the trenches, creatures that inevitably caught the eye of soldiers as they sat bored in a trench or which were uncovered as saps were dug or trench lines improved.

This book tells the story of all the creatures, great and small, that inhabited the strip of murdered earth that snaked hundreds of miles from the Belgian coast to the Swiss Alps. In all, sixty-one species are included here and within a few species, such as birds and butterflies, there are also a number of varieties: for example, forty-three kinds of bird are noted. Some species are mentioned once, others on a number of occasions: these include spiders, maggots, canaries, chickens, owls, lions, turkeys, fish, horses, cats, ferrets, wasps and worms. However, just as importantly, this is not a book about wildlife in isolation from man. On the contrary, it is about the human condition in war, explored through the soldiers' relationship with the natural world around them.

On the whole, trench warfare was a grind in which time was turned upside-down. Night time was used for work. Darkness obscured the patrols in no-man's-land; it provided cover for the men repairing the protective barbed-wire belt in front of the trench, and it masked the work of the limber drivers bringing up supplies. Daytime was for sleep, rest and relaxation. It was a chance to enjoy the sun's rays and to look around. Letters were written, and, in looking for inspiration, a soldier needed to see no further than the sparrow that rested on the parapet, or the bees that darted from one trench-top flower to the next.

Some men had little interest in wildlife and eyed lazily the spider spinning and respinning a thread, persevering while the ground trembled with distant shell explosions. Conversely, others, perhaps keen gardeners at home, men who appreciated town parks and the countryside, could become momentarily absorbed by the trials and tribulations of a mouse trapped in a sump or the clumsy passage of a beetle through a tuft of grass. A few erstwhile bird-watchers, pigeon fanciers or more general amateur naturalists were captivated by the world around them and wrote at length in diaries and letters about what they saw. And then there were a few, like Philip Gosse, who went on to write war memoirs in which the recollection of war became an adjunct to the preferred memory of wildlife in the middle of conflict.

'Some of my readers may find fault with me for having comparatively so little to say about the "horrors" of war and so much about the beasts and the birds,' he wrote in the introduction to his book, *The Memoirs of a Camp Follower*.

> The title might well have been, 'A Solace of Birds', for without the birds I dare not think how I should have got through the war at all. One friend, after reading my manuscript, asked if I could not include 'more horrors', even at the expense of some of the birds, but I told him that in any case I could remember no more 'horrors', though of birds I remembered so much.

It was not just the birds he recorded in his memoirs, for in his possibly unique service he toured the front line officially, capturing and stuffing mammals of all kinds to be shipped back to the Natural History Museum in London, where his exhibits remain to this day.

It occurred to Gosse and to many others who served and stopped to think, that, while men on both sides of the line daily bludgeoned each other in the vainglorious pursuit of battlefield mastery, it was in fact the animal kingdom that remained in over-all control of the Western Front. For while man hid himself away, digging for his very existence into the ground, wildlife carried on as normal, seemingly adapting without fuss to its altered environment. Corporal Hector Munro, better known as the author Saki, referred to such a state in an article:

> The magpie, wary and suspicious in his wild state,' he wrote, 'must be rather intrigued at the change that has come over the erstwhile fearsome not-to-be-avoided human, stalking every-where over the earth as its possessor, who now creeps about in screened and sheltered ways, as chary of showing himself in the open as the shyest of wild creatures.

Walking in Ploegsteert Wood in Belgium, the scene of heavy fighting in 1914, Norman Edwards, a private in the Gloucestershire Regiment, discovered a scene that provided proof of nature's adaptation as well as some solace for the soul:

> In a jagged hole, rent in the base of an oak by a shell, I found a thrush quietly and sanely carrying on its life work. I peeped into the nest and the flawless perfection of those four blue eggs, warm and pregnant with life, diverted my thoughts as perhaps nothing else could have done.

By their very existence, these creatures performed a vital function. They gave men a temporary reprieve, a brief 'leave' that reminded them of home. They also reassured many soldiers that there still existed, in all the surrounding madness, a sane order to life that would always override the temporal carnage. Such feelings were never better exemplified than in the last minutes of the classic film *All Quiet on the Western Front*, based on the book by the German Great War veteran Erich Maria

Remarque. The German soldier, the last survivor of his class, stretches his hand out to a butterfly and is shot by a sniper. On both sides of the line it was easy to become transfixed by a moment of beauty.

Melville Hastings, a pre-war British émigré to Canada, noted in his letters before he was mortally wounded:

> Our abode is amongst the roots of a once beautiful wood. The beeches and elms are hopelessly mutilated, and the beheaded pines are gradually suffocating unto death. Their amputated limbs are everywhere, trunks are riven from head to foot, even the ground itself is twisted and torn. But, thank God, a man can cast his eyes up above this desolation to the sun and the blue sky, indestructible by us puny sinners. The little birds also defy defacement, and their music is the contribution of animate nature to the joyful fact that God's handiwork can never be utterly marred by man.

Wildlife and nature gave men peace and comfort in their otherwise tumultuous lives but, as importantly, it gave them an escape from the pressures of living constantly with each other. The poet and author Siegfried Sassoon expressed such feelings when, during the Battle of the Somme, he found himself alone standing on a rough wooden bridge staring down into the swirling reeds of a river. Away from his comrades, for once undisturbed by their 'mechanical chatter', he wrote: 'How seldom I get free from them, good people as they are.'

This natural world would inevitably affect the vocabulary of war. Locations were given official designations such as 'Dead Mule Corner', a site close to the Somme village of Martinpuich, and unofficial names too, such as an abandoned trench near another Somme village, Flers, where 120 Germans had been hastily buried. It became known by the men as Bluebottle Alley, for obvious reasons. In the same vein, informal directions used to cross the battlefields noted, as a guide, the salient landmarks: 'bear half left to dead pig, cross stream 25 yards below dead horse'; even a certain familiar stench could be noted: 'then follow the smell of three dead cows . . .'

Wildlife gave men an outlet by which to communicate to their loved ones something of the world in which they lived and their emotions. Fearful of frightening families at home, they could escape by describing the flora and fauna on the trench parapet, as well as the animals that shared their dugout. Many of these descriptions by articulate young officers are beautifully observed and have provided a rich source of material for this book. Equally, the otherwise indescribable world in which they existed could be 'translated' to the civilian through words they all knew. One man, portraying one of the first tanks in action, noted how 'slowly it rolled and swayed towards us; its motion was not that of a snake, nor of an elephant, but an indescribable blend of the two'. Bullets were described as 'humming like a hive of bees', or sounding like 'cats sneezing', soldiers reported; rifle-grenades 'made a noise like an enormous hornet'. Even ghastly events, if they needed to be told, could be illustrated by reference to the natural world: 'to see men suffering from shock, flopping about the trenches like grassed fish, is enough to sicken one', wrote an officer to his family.

The story of animals in war has been described in books before, entirely thematically and drawing on tales from conflicts throughout the ages, and not focusing solely on the Great War. These publications are heavily weighted towards animals utilised for the service of man, and the stories told are in an overwhelmingly author-led narrative with an occasional short, pithy quote from the serving soldier. My passion for the 1914–18 conflict has always been rooted in understanding how soldiers withstood the extraordinary pressures of serving in one of history's toughest crucibles of war. Any under-researched aspect of life, any nuance that affected their experience, is of immediate and profound interest to me.

One anecdote found in the memoirs of an officer, Lieutenant Fildes, is such an example. It is a small but nevertheless illuminating insight into an aspect of life in the wild that I had never thought of before or attributed to the life led by soldiers. Men's antipathy towards vermin, rats in particular, is taken for granted, but how about the dislike, even the phobic fear, of other creatures, fears that were naturally prevalent among civilians? His is a rare example in that he noted his hypersensitivity to insects, an instinctive response to 'creepy-crawlies' that must have existed to a greater or lesser extent among other soldiers but which has gone largely unrecorded:

> Four in the morning, a chilly damp one too – this was a pretty dismal start for a day in May. Where was I this time last year? In a comfortable bed, wherever it was. Something tickled my neck, and with a quick motion I carried my hand to the spot. I hated insects, always had; this I disliked above all others as I was unable to see it . . . Ten minutes later I crawled into my shanty, reflecting that for one night at least the rain would have driven the spiders away.

Tommy's Ark takes an entirely different approach from any other book on the subject of animals in war. First, it is chronological in character. This establishes the animal kingdom firmly within the context of the human war, showing how the animal world was changed and shaped by the conflict that itself altered dramatically as time passed. This has certain strengths. As the war changed, so did the position of animals, irrespective of whether they were servants of the war effort or no more than inadvertent bystanders. The battlefield of the Somme, for example, to the men who arrived there in the summer of 1915, when the area was little more than a backwater, looked entirely different from the landscape witnessed a year later, after the battle. Likewise the Ypres Salient in 1914 and 1915, with its untended farmland and abundance of wildlife, was profoundly altered once the Allies and the Germans both unleashed the heavy and sustained bombardments to which the ground around the town was subjected in 1917.

Secondly, the animals' stories are described by the soldiers through their letters, diaries and memoirs. The diversity and richness of the quotations used is testament to the fact that wildlife was never eradicated from the battlefield, no matter how muddy or how pitted the ground appeared to be. Soldiers remained ever conscious of its presence so that, even in the act of going over the top, men wondered at the song of the skylark overhead or became excited at a hare zigzagging through the shell-holes.

Although a simple chronology is at the heart of this book, I have nevertheless sought to highlight a number of themes and ideas. For example, soldiers sometimes took animal life senselessly and then repented, reflecting often bitterly on their actions. They themselves drew the appropriate comment. On the spur of the moment, Private Thomas Hope killed a mole. 'Poor little inoffensive mole, its life was as precious to it as mine is to me,' he wrote, after 'tapping' the mole over the head with a stick. 'I must be a bloodthirsty brute,' he decided.

Other stories are grouped together because dates and the passage of time are irrelevant. An interesting snapshot of one creature's predicament in war can result, such as that of frogs: frogs squashed on the communication trench duckboards; frogs heard croaking in the night air as the guns temporarily fell silent; frogs gently carried out of harm's way by a commanding officer, or eaten as a novelty.

Wherever possible, I have tried to keep the stories broadly within the time frame in which they were written although, as with all anthologies, the stories are not necessarily chronologically sequential. Nevertheless, no memories of times before the soldiers concerned arrived in France or after they were removed from the fighting by injury are used. Likewise, references to animals and insects are aligned as closely as possible to the seasons in which they appear; it would not do to have bees or butterflies in winter.

The quotations used are taken from various sources, primarily the Imperial War Museum, the Liddle Archive at Leeds University and archives housed in regimental museums. Other stories were taken from published books, many long out of print but full of relevant anecdotes. Especially productive was the little-accessed goldmine of officers' memorial books, most published during or very shortly after the war. These were privately published in small numbers by grieving families who sought to come to terms with their loss by saving for posterity the letters sent home from France and Flanders.

These letters and diaries, along with those of other officers fortunate enough to survive, are numerically out of proportion to those written by other ranks, at least in relation to their serving numbers – around one officer for every forty men served in a battalion. However, in the preparation of this book, seventy-four officers are cited, seventy-two other ranks, with officers' quotes, on the whole, being the more substantial in literary quality and length. Literacy rates among pre-war soldiers were poor, much as they were among the civilian population that volunteered or were conscripted. This is especially clear when their writing skills are contrasted with those of the young university undergraduates who applied to serve in the officer corps. These young officers' powers of description were often excellent, and furthermore they had more time and more opportunities to write. They worked in dugouts that were reasonably dry compared with frequently wet and windy trenches, and access to paper was easier for officers than for other ranks.

Fortunately, where a quotation comes from is largely irrelevant. If an earwig happens to pass across the hand of an officer or other rank as he writes, the description is what is important; it does not affect the understanding of the war, how it was fought, how it was won, how that war is now judged and interpreted by historians.

Everyman saw the weasel scampering along the trench parapet, the cow trapped in the barbed wire, the kitten stuck in the rubble of a house; it is just that not Everyman chose to make a physical note of the observation.

During my research, many books were 'mined' by speed-reading the text looking for appropriate stories. This was an entirely scattergun approach, inevitably fruitless in many cases but productive in others, sometimes exceptionally so. It was a necessarily slow process. 'Weasels' or 'sparrows' were rarely logged as searchable words in an index even if the author had a particularly interesting story to recall. Some exceptional memoirs made almost no reference to wildlife, in part as a result of when they were written. A memoir produced fifty years after the event is unlikely to contain the minutiae of animal life, simply because such stories would inevitably remain unlogged in the mind whereas the loss of friends, or injuries, barrages, gas attacks and going over the top were seared into the consciousness. Letters written at the time were always a better source for 'here and now' stories.

Most of the illustrations in this book come from the archives of the Imperial War Museum, and from friends within the Great War fraternity who have generously lent me images to reproduce here. All remaining photographs are taken from my own collection. Few have been published before. While gathering images for the plate sections, I was aware that many stories would be almost impossible to illustrate. Fishing by means of a hand grenade thrown into a lake or river appeared to be one such story. However, since the advent of online auction sites almost anything is obtainable with perseverance, and a recently acquired set of original photographs taken by an officer in France yielded the only example I have ever seen of a grenade-induced fountain of water. The original caption, 'Obtaining a variety of food by bombing fish at Potijze!', established the veracity of the image.

As this book complements my previous work, *The Soldier's War*, it seemed sensible to follow a broadly similar format. This, in

effect, is the animals' war. The book is divided into five chap-
ters, each covering one year of the conflict and beginning with a
short overview of the current military situation. This is followed
by a description of how, each year, wildlife adapted itself within
the zone of conflict and how soldiers' perceptions of animals and
wildlife changed. There are a few German photographs, reflecting the shared relationship to wildlife; indeed, there are several
instances of animals, particularly dogs, crossing no-man's-land to
be looked after by both sides, as well as another occasion when
both British and German soldiers shot at the same flock of geese
flying overhead.

The natural world in France and Belgium was not unlike that
at home in Britain. Nevertheless, the copious horrors of war threw
nature's beauty and complexity into the sharpest relief imaginable and therefore it has its own unique validity. The soldiers who
understood that stark contrast left records which, when collected
and distilled, have given us an insight into the Great War that has
not been explored before.

A week since, I was lying out in no-man's-land. A little German
dog trotted up and licked my British face. I pulled his German
ears and stroked his German back. He wagged his German tail.
My little friend abolished no-man's-land, and so in time can
we.

Lt Melville Hastings, killed in action, 3 October 1918

1914

The War in 1914

By the standards of the Great War, the Battle of Mons was little more than a skirmish. The small Belgian town had, simply by chance, become the place where British forces, moving north-east from the Channel ports, met the German army marching south-west. In fact, it was one German army, one of three that had ignored Belgium's sovereignty by using her territory as a back door to an invasion of northern France. It was partly to uphold the rule of international law that Britain had gone to war, or so it was claimed. However, in a series of secret pre-war agreements and informal understandings between the different European nations, Britain had privately agreed, in principle, to support France in a conflict against Germany. Germany was the rising European power with interests in Empire-building that threatened Britain's long-term pre-eminence in Europe and her colonies.

War between Britain and Germany had long been expected and it was perhaps the fulfilment of this 'expectation', rather than Belgian neutrality, that had excited Britain's declaration of war in those first days of August. France had already declared war on Germany as a result of a military agreement she had with Russia. Russia, in turn, had supported Serbia when the ailing Austro-Hungarian Empire, backed by her ally, Germany, had threatened Serbia. It was all very complicated and stemmed back to the assassination in June 1914 of the heir to the Austro-Hungarian throne by a young Serb nationalist – not that the British soldiers marching to Mons cared much about that. Germany required a short, sharp corrective to its international misbehaviour and these boys were going to hand it out in spades and be home for Christmas.

The British Army was tiny by international standards as, traditionally, Britain had had the navy to protect her shores and overseas interests. Many British battalions were stationed overseas in countries such as India, so that the number of men available to go to the aid of France was initially just 80,000 men, collectively known as the British Expeditionary Force (BEF). On the morning of 23 August, forward elements of this small force had taken up positions alongside a canal that separated them, and the town of Mons, from the Germans. The fighting that took place there that day taught both sides a couple of swift lessons. The Germans received a rude awakening to the remarkable professionalism of the small British army. This army had been tuned to a level of efficiency most other countries, with their large conscript armies, could not hope to match. Equally, the British learnt that, no matter how good a professional soldier might be, vastly overwhelming numbers of enemy soldiers will, in the end, overwhelm. Appeals in Britain by the new Secretary of State for War, Lord Kitchener, for a civilian army were already under way when news of the Battle of Mons and the subsequent retreat reached the national press; the news stimulated the greatest surge in voluntary enlistment the country has ever known.

The British retreat from Mons was a remarkable feat of arms. The British soldiers, a third of whom were reservists softened by civilian life, tramped as much as 175 miles in two weeks, carrying arms, clothing and equipment weighing 66lb. The weather was hot, rations were scant, supplies of drinking water were thin. At any time they could expect to halt and fight, then move on again. Sleep or rest were always at a premium. In the end the BEF escaped destruction by a narrow margin, helped in part by the failures of the enemy to press home their clear advantage.

The retreat took the British Army close to Paris and beyond to the Marne where the rot was stopped and the German advance turned, with the aid of a new French army formed in the capital and driven to the front in taxis. The German lines of communication and supply were overextended, her men perhaps as exhausted as those they were chasing. In the end, the Germans were forced to fall back and dig in on the first high ground that could be defended, the Chemin des Dames. Stalemate. And so began a race for the coast as each side sought to gain an advantage by outflanking the other. The sand dunes on the edge of the coastal town of Nieuport in Belgium were reached in October by both sides, and the first tentative 'front-line' trench system began to emerge that would eventually stretch from this insignificant town all the way to the French Alps.

Throughout October and November, the Germans threw battalion after battalion against British positions, first around the northern French town of La Bassée, then against forces positioned in a tight salient around the Belgian town of Ypres. Despite the Germans having the ascendancy in men and munitions, the British Army held their ground – just – and at great cost. The old regular army of which Britain had been so proud was badly shaken, many surviving battalions losing 80 or 90 per cent of their original strength. It was only the onset of winter that brought a close to major hostilities, while in Britain the training of the new civilian army continued apace.

The Natural World in 1914

The first weeks of the war were a time of rapid movement, of glorious withdrawal some might argue, others would say of an ignominious and chaotic retreat. This was a time when the cavalry was able to fulfil its new role, acting as a fast-moving screen to protect the infantry, a time of classic mounted charges and short, dismounted action. All light artillery, all limbers and wagons were pulled by horses or mules; it was, at least at this moment, an overwhelmingly equine war. For the men who took part, it was on these four-legged friends that their survival depended.

This was not a time to take stock of the autumnal countryside but rather to survive punishing marches before eventually digging in and holding off the enemy's best attempts to force a decisive victory within the year. As British soldiers marched first south towards Paris, then north-west in the direction of Ypres, they felt enormous sympathy for the local families driven from their homes. These civilians had their world stacked on top of a horse- or bullock-drawn cart; precious possessions were piled high on prams, or carried in shawls. Pets not already pressed into service, pulling or carrying, padded alongside their owners in the general tide of misery. It was open warfare where villages and farms were swept up briefly into the fighting and when livestock were abandoned to their fate. The soldiers pitied these animals almost as much as the civilians, for livestock were often left locked and unfed in sheds or abandoned to wander aimlessly. Cows were clearly distressed for want of being milked, dogs remained chained up to their kennels. Other animals, chickens, pigs and geese, were greedily spied by famished men for whom army rations in no way compensated for the energies they expended in marching, digging and fighting. These animals were seized and eaten, although a very few, usually abandoned dogs, were taken on as impromptu mascots.

By the time the British Army had settled to the trench life more normally associated with the Great War, most wildlife had departed: dead, flown to sunnier climes or safely hibernating. There was not much to see and even less to worry about when the men, ill-equipped for that first winter, shivered and froze in their hastily dug ditches, feet stuck in cloying mud.

The men of 1914 were far fewer in number than those who served in every other year of the war, less than 10 per cent of the numbers found serving on the Western Front two years later. The timescale was shorter too, just four and a half months, and most of this was autumn or winter. As a result, the variety of animals recorded is far smaller than in any other year. And there may have been another reason, too. The regular soldier, used to the more exotic wildlife of postings in Africa or on the North West Frontier, was perhaps unimpressed by the animals of northern France and Belgium and less inclined to write, as well as less capable of writing, the keen observational prose of his better-educated territorial and Kitchener counterpart, for whom war on the Western Front was such a novelty in the spring and summer of 1915.

Soldiers' Memories

The speed at which the British Army mobilised on the outbreak of war was quite breathtaking. Within twenty-four hours of the order, reservists began to arrive at their depots to join units they had left as long as nine years before. These old soldiers would have to be kitted out; feet unused to brand new boots would have to be hardened for marching once more. However, the knowledge of soldiering had never left them and they slotted back into the old routine with serving soldiers as if they had never left. For those joining the Army Service Corps, the artillery and cavalry, quick reacquaintance with horses and mules was important; a good mutual understanding was always critical in times of war.

In August 1914 the British Army had 25,000 serving horses and mules. However, many more would be needed to go overseas or to replace the inevitable casualties. The army paid an annual fee to civilians such as farmers and landowners, and to civilian businesses, for the right to call on their horses and mules in the event of war. Some of these were hunting horses required for the cavalry, others were light or heavy draught animals for limbers and guns. In the event, the government immediately ordered that another 140,000 were requisitioned and these were handed over or rounded up following 4 August.

On 13 August, the first units of the BEF set sail for France. Horses and mules made up almost the entire contingent of animals taken overseas, although a number of other creatures, usually favoured dogs, were also stowed on board. Many of these were regimental mascots but only one animal would go on to receive formal recognition after the war and be awarded a medal for its service overseas, the coveted 1914 Star.

Taffy the IV was the 2nd Welsh Regiment's goat and he served with the regiment throughout the early campaigns before dying in January 1915.

Trp. Benjamin Clouting, 4th (Royal Irish) Dragoon Guards

Two days after the outbreak of war, I was detailed to travel with six other troopers and two veterinary officers to Birmingham's R. White's mineral water factory, commandeering heavy draught horses, not for us, but for the artillery and Army Service Corps. Our job was simply to wait around until the veterinary officers had passed each horse fit and healthy, and, once each was numbered, ride one and lead another to the local train station. These mammoth horses had never had anyone on their backs before and didn't understand our spurs' commands. Each time we dug them in, they stepped backwards as if to get away. We soon tumbled to the fact that if we wanted them to move we would have to give verbal commands. At the station a train was waiting, and once loaded, off it went.

Cpl Robert Lloyd, 1st Life Guards

Darkness had begun to set in while the horses were being run into the trucks. This proved to be an exciting job. Our regiment alone had six hundred to entrain, and they stood on a narrow platform waiting their turn. There was a line running behind them, on which trains kept continually passing, and it was a miracle nobody got dragged on to the rails and run over.

It was here I first made the acquaintance of Herbert. He was the tallest horse in the unit, and he had a dislike amounting to violent hatred for trains, buses, steam-engines, and all huge things which moved mechanically and made strange noises in their insides. He absolutely refused to enter his truck, but there was no time for ceremony, so half a dozen hefty soldiers slipped a surcingle [band] round his hindquarters and gave him a lift. This decided him to make a plunge through the door of the truck, but being so tall his saddle caught in the roof, and he bounced back amongst us, more obstinate than ever. We then turned him round, removed his saddle, and backed him in without more ado.

The British Army went to France with 40,000 horses and mules. It was a major logistical operation leading or hoisting aboard hundreds of thoroughbred cavalry horses, as well as shires, and by no means all of them were willing travellers. Although veterinary officers did their best to stable animals properly on board, a number died of heart attacks en route and others went berserk in the fetid and cramped conditions. The smell of the horses was almost unbearable for the men who travelled with them.

2/Lt Arnold Gyde, 2nd South Staffordshire Rgt

There was plenty of excitement on deck while the horses of the regimental transport were being shipped into the hold. To induce 'Light Draft', 'Heavy Draft' horses and 'Officers' Chargers' – in all some sixty animals – to trust themselves to be lowered into a dark and evil-smelling cavern, was no easy matter. Some shied from the gangway, neighing; others walked peaceably on to it, and, with a 'thus far and no farther' expression in every line of their bodies, took up a firm stand, and had to be pushed into the hold with the combined weight of many men. Several of the transport section narrowly escaped death and mutilation at the hands, or rather hooves, of the Officers' Chargers.

Maj. Patrick Butler, 2nd Royal Irish Rgt

Arrived at the Docks, we had about three hours of frenzied work. We were told that Divisional Headquarters would go in the third ship, the *Armenian*, and accordingly we went on board and started to settle down. I began to try to collect the various component parts of the mess cooks, food baskets, etc, and to search in the bowels of the ship for my servant, groom and horses. Only accommodation, not food, was to be provided for us, and very elementary at that.

I went below to look for my belongings. The dim and stuffy vistas swarmed with men, and down both sides the horses were jammed in long, uneasy rows. This was the lowest deck of all. Just above it there were more men, and an assortment of loose boxes in which were tied the huge, heavy draught horses allotted to our transport. One of these poor animals was behaving like a mad thing, and threatened to smash his way out of his pen, secured by the head as he was, by sheer weight and violence. Every now and then he would rear aloft, and get a leg over the side of the box in a sort of paroxysm of fear and rage. Poor brute! There was a crowd of men round him, and at first I could not see what was taking place; but soon I heard the drip, drip of blood, and a trickle began to make its way through the planks on to the deck below, close to the companion at the foot of which I was standing. The sight was not pleasant. After an interminable delay the cooks, groom and servant all reported to me, and I located my three chargers. As I escaped up to the light and air I had to pass again near the monster draught horse. I could see his huge bulk filling the stall, but he seemed strangely quiet now. I noticed that the men still crowded round, but they were more intent and reassured, and with a sort of curiosity in their faces. There were horror and pity in their looks, not cruelty. The drip, drip was now a steady outpouring of blood. It flooded the deck. They were bleeding him to death, a man told me. He had already staggered once, and would fall now at any moment. As I gained the deck I fancied I heard the thud. The 'merciful bullet' was impracticable here, on account of the congested state of the decks. Poor beast, his troubles were over early.

Cpl William Watson, RE, 5th Div.
Towards evening we dropped anchor off Le Havre. On either side of the narrow entrance to the docks there were cheering crowds, and we cheered back, thrilled, occasionally breaking into the soldiers' anthem, 'It's a long, long way to Tipperary'. We disembarked at a

secluded wharf, and after waiting about for a couple of hours or so – we had not then learned to wait – we were marched off to a huge dim warehouse, where we were given gallons of the most delicious hot coffee, and bought scrumptious little cakes.

It was now quite dark, and, for what seemed whole nights, we sat wearily waiting while the horses were taken off the transport. We made one vain dash for our quarters, but found only another enormous warehouse, strangely lit, full of clattering wagons and restive horses. We watched with wonder a battery clank out into the night, and then returned sleepily to the wharf-side. Very late we found where we were to sleep, a gigantic series of wool warehouses. The warehouses were full of wool and the wool was full of fleas. I feared the fleas, and spread a waterproof sheet on the bare stones outside. I thought I should not get a wink of sleep on such a Jacobean resting-place, but, as a matter of fact, I slept like a top, and woke in the morning without even an ache. But those who had risked the wool . . . !

Driver Charles Keller, RHA

The horses had been packed below deck, side by side and so close that they couldn't move. It was probably the only way that so many could be transported. They suffered terribly. Those that could staggered down the gangplank, but many had to be lifted off with slings. It was a relief to see them on the dock where they had a chance to move around. Lines were strung out on the dock for them to be tied while being watered and fed, and after that had been attended to we got something to eat ourselves. We spent the night behind the horses with our saddles for a pillow and during the next four years most of our nights were spent in this manner.

When the brigade was ready to move, the horses were loaded on to box cars: eight to a car, four at each end with their heads to the centre and the centre space was filled with hay, oats, harness and four drivers' equipment and blankets. This left hardly any room for the drivers who had to sit in the door openings. We sat there the whole journey.

The infantry had disembarked with far less theatre and had marched into camp and under canvas. From there, battalions left by train towards the border with Belgium where they detrained and were introduced to the stone pavé roads that were to prove so hard on men's feet. Rest, at the end of the day, was most welcome though not always easy.

L/Cpl Alfred Vivian, 4th Middlesex Rgt

Our journey eventually finished up in front of a rickety barn, adjoining a promising looking building. This barn was minus a door, and quite a good portion of its ceiling. On the wall outside was chalked '10 Hommes'.

'Where does the 10 homes come in?' inquired one of the men. 'There ain't enough of this to make one; all I can say is, the other ten families must be damned thankful we have turned them out.'

'You take another look around, my friend, and you will discover that the eviction of the former inhabitants has still to be proceeded with,' I pointed out.

Indeed a veritable riot was in progress in the darkness of the barn now we had entered, our appearance being greeted by a lively chorus of animal sounds, registering distinct anger and annoyance. A herd of little pigs gambolling about two old sows, some cows and dozens of farmyard fowl, and a various assortment of other animals, strenuously contested our right of admittance, and they were only got rid of after a hot and lengthy engagement.

Cpl William Watson, RE, 5th Div.

The people crowded into the streets and cheered us. The girls, with tears in their eyes, handed us flowers. Three of us went to the Mairie. The Maire, a courtly little fellow in top-hat and frock-coat, welcomed us in charming terms. Two fat old women rushed up to us and besought us to allow them to do something for us. We set one to make us tea, and the other to bring us hot water and soap. A small girl of about eight brought me her kitten and wanted to give it me. I explained to her that it would not be very comfortable tied with pink ribbons to my carrier. She gravely assented, sat on my knee, told me I was very dirty, and commanded me to kill heaps and heaps of Germans.

The French nation may have welcomed the British soldiers but their animals were of a different mindset altogether. After a visit to the local town in search of tobacco, Alfred Vivian and his comrades returned to discover they had been evicted.

L/Cpl Alfred Vivian, 4th Middlesex Rgt

Taking advantage of our absence, the animals had carried out a raid which had successfully restored them to their original habitation. What chaos they had produced in the quarters that we had so industriously made spick-and-span! Pigs grunted their defiance at us, while chickens filled the air with their derisive and triumphant cacklings. An old sow stood looking a pathetic picture of absolute boredom, while she slowly disposed of the last mouthful of my bed. An aged and decrepit old roué of a donkey, possessed of only one blasé eye, which he fixed on us disdainfully, leaned carelessly, with an air of utmost abandon and indifference, against the billet wall, ruminating on the doubtful flavour of a lump of the material torn from a haversack.

A wild melee ensued, which resulted in the invaders being driven from the position, and we worked hard repairing the ravages our struggle had caused, and eventually arranged things more or less shipshape once again.

On the morning of 22 August, a squadron of cavalry sent forward to reconnoitre the ground ahead had come back with unmistakable and worrying news. Tens of thousands of enemy soldiers were converging on the lightly defended Belgian town of Mons. The last hours of peace were ebbing away.

As a precaution, Lance Corporal Vivian was sent with six men to a cottage a hundred yards ahead of his battalion. There, early the following morning, he finally saw the enemy.

L/Cpl Alfred Vivian, 4th Middlesex Rgt

Coming carelessly along the road towards us was a Uhlan patrol consisting of seven or eight men, then a scanty eighty yards away. The surprising nature of the sight robbed us of our breath and wits, and left us standing in a row gasping and looking like a lot of codfish. The scene impressed me so strongly that it will always remain vividly engraved on my memory.

A short and vicious burst of rapid fire from us completely anni- hilated that little group with an ease that was staggering. In a second, the only living survivors were five poor chargers, that, rendered riderless and being unharmed, turned and galloped back with snorts of terror towards the direction from whence they had appeared, until they gained the sanctuary of a wood, and disap- peared from our view.

Immediately the excitement abated, and we stood aghast, over- come with horror by the enormity of the thing we had done.

Lt Malcolm Hay, 1st Gordon Highlanders

Somewhere hidden in the memory of all who have taken part in the war there is the remembrance of a moment which marked the first realisation of the great change – the moment when material common things took on in real earnest their military significance, when, with the full comprehension of the mind, a wood became cover for the enemy, a house a possible machine-gun position, and every field a battlefield.

Such an awakening came to me when sitting on the roadside by the White Estaminet. The sound of a horse galloping and the sight of horse and rider, the sweat and mud and the tense face of the rider bending low by the horse's neck, bending as if to avoid bullets. The single rider, perhaps bearing a dispatch, followed after a short space by a dozen cavalrymen, not galloping these, but trotting hard down the centre of the road, mud-stained, and also with tense faces.

L/Cpl Alfred Vivian, 4th Middlesex Rgt

Church bells chimed sweetly in the towns and hamlets about us, and dimly, from the distance, we discerned faint strains of music being poured out at the service being held in the convent in our rear.

A lark hovering immediately above our hole in the roof [of the cottage] trilled out a glorious burst of song, and we craned our necks the better to view it. A strange and indefinable sense of unreality stole over me and, for some extraordinary reason, I became attacked by a strong desire to cry. I endeavoured to impart my sensations to my colleague, and I said to him: 'There is something so extraordinary hanging in the air, that I feel that the thing I would most enjoy would be to visit a church. I don't like this quietness and –'

'Smack!' the tile within two inches of our heads was shattered into a thousand fragments, and the two of us flopped simultaneously to the floor. I arose with an effort and continued in a quavering voice: 'I was about to add that I harboured a feeling that something startling was bound to happen to break the spell!' We did not need telling that the violent blow sustained by the tile above us was the result of a direct hit by a well-directed bullet.

That 'something startling' was the Battle of Mons, which would rage around the town throughout the rest of the day. Then, fearing that the British soldiers in the town were about to be enveloped by the overwhelmingly larger German force, the vanguard of the BEF was ordered to pull back, taking the first steps of what would become an epic retreat south. To many men on the fringes of the fighting, the day may well have looked like manoeuvres on Salisbury Plain, although the general atmosphere of nervousness would have told them otherwise.

Lt Malcolm Hay, 1st Gordon Highlanders

The situation in front of the trenches had not yet changed, as far as one could see, since the first shot was fired. An occasional bullet still flicked by, evidently fired at very long range.

The corner house of the hamlet six to seven hundred yards to our left front was partly hidden from view by a hedge. The cover afforded by this house, the hedge and the ditch which ran along-side it, began to be a cause of anxiety. If the enemy succeeded in obtaining a footing either in the house itself or the ditch behind the hedge, our position would be enfiladed.

One of my men who had been peering over the trench through two cabbage stalks, proclaimed that he saw something crawling along behind this hedge. A prolonged inspection with the field glasses revealed that the slow-moving, dark-grey body belonged to an old donkey carelessly and lazily grazing along the side of the ditch. The section of A platoon who were in a small trench to our left rear, being farther away and not provided with very good field glasses, suddenly opened rapid fire on the hedge and the donkey disappeared from view. This little incident caused great amuse-ment in my trench, the exploit of No. 4 section in successfully dispatching the donkey was greeted with roars of laughter and cries of 'Bravo the donkey killers', all of which helped to relieve the tension.

It was really the donkey that made the situation normal again. Just before there had been some look of anxiety in men's faces and much unnecessary crouching in the bottom of the trench. Now the men were smoking, watching the shells, arguing as to the height at which they burst over our heads, and scrambling for shrapnel bullets.

Capt. Aubrey Herbert, 1st Irish Guards

The order to move came about 5.30, I suppose. We went down through the fields rather footsore and came to a number of wire fences which kept in cattle. These fences we were ordered to cut. My agricultural instinct revolted at this destruction. We marched on through a dark wood to the foot of some cliffs and, skirting them, came to the open fields, on the flank of the wood, sloping steeply upwards. Here we found our first wounded man, though I believe as we moved through the wood an officer had been reported missing.

The first stretch was easy. Some rifle bullets hummed and buzzed round and over us, but nothing to matter. We almost began to vote war a dull thing. We took up our position under a natural earthwork. We had been there a couple of minutes when a really terrific fire opened.

The men behaved very well. A good many of them were praying and crossing themselves. A man next to me said: 'It's hellfire we're going into.' It seemed inevitable that any man who went over the bank must be cut neatly in two. Then, in a lull, Tom gave the word and we scrambled over and dashed on to the next bank. Bullets were singing round us like a swarm of bees, but we had only a short way to go, and got, all of us, I think, safely to the next shelter, where we lay and gasped and thought hard.

Our next rush was worse, for we had a long way to go through turnips. The prospect was extremely unattractive. The turnips seemed to offer a sort of cover, and I thought of the feelings of the partridges, a covey of which rose as we sank. Tom gave us a minute in which to get our wind – we lay gasping in the heat, while the shrapnel splashed about . . . As we rose, with a number of partridges, the shooting began again.

The following day, as the position on the left flank of the BEF deteriorated, the cavalry was ordered forward to take part in one of the great charges against both infantry and artillery. The 4th (Royal Irish) Dragoon Guards was one of three regiments, including the 9th Lancers and 18th Hussars, ordered to attack across largely open fields to stop the advance of German troops and to give the hard-pressed British infantry time to get away.

2/Lt Roger Chance, 4th (Royal Irish) Dragoon Guards

The regiment waits, dismounted, in a field behind the village.
I have slipped the reins over my charger's head and he crops the
lucerne. A remount, drafted from a hunting stable, he has not
worked off a summer's ease and sweat darkens his bay coat. Cleg
flies, out for blood, pester him. A lark sings out to me in a pause
in the boom of the guns . . . 'Get girthed up,' says [Captain]
Oldrey, 'stand by your horses, prepare to mount, mount.' The
commands are rapped from troop to troop and 'walk-march'
follows. There is a whee-thump of shells and a crash of house
tiles from the village ahead. I see Colonel Mullens halted on
the bank above, grimly watching us go. The order given to our
Major Hunter will become a hasty squadron order yelled to me
from those in front but all I can hear is the wholesale crack of
shrapnel.

We span the unmetalled road which runs straight, unfenced,
through a stubble field dotted with corn stooks. I endeavour one-
handed to control my almost runaway steed. Talbot has gone
down in a crashing somersault. Then I'm among the ranks of those
who, halted by wire, veer right in disorder like a flock of sheep. A
trooper crouched on his saddle is blasted to glory by a direct hit
whose fragments patter to earth. We follow the 9th Lancers to a
heap of slag which affords cover. Sergeant Talbot appears mounted
again, with Captain Sewell whose chestnut horse coughs foam and
blood at me.

Trp. Benjamin Clouting, 4th (Royal Irish) Dragoon Guards

It was a proper melee, with shell, machine-gun and rifle fire
forming a terrific barrage of noise. Each troop was closely packed
together and dense volumes of dust were kicked up, choking us
and making it impossible to see beyond the man in front. We were
galloping into carnage, for nobody knew what we were supposed
to be doing and there was utter confusion from the start. All
around me, horses and men were brought hurtling to the ground

amidst fountains of earth, or plummeting forwards as a machine gunner caught them with a burst of fire.

Ahead, the leading troops were brought up by agricultural barbed wire strung across the line of advance, so that horses were beginning to be pulled up when I heard for the one and only time in the war a bugle sounding 'troops right wheel'. I pulled my horse round, then with a crash down she went.

I hit the ground at full tilt and with my sword still firmly attached by a lanyard to my hand, was lucky not to impale myself. Dazed, I struggled to my feet and can now recall only an odd assortment of fleeting thoughts and sights – a single image of chaos. A riderless horse came careering in my direction and, collecting myself, I raised my hand in the air and shouted 'Halt!' at the top of my voice. It was a 9th Lancers' horse, a shoeing smith's mount and wonderfully trained, for despite the pandemonium, it stopped on a sixpence.

Running through the field to my right was a single-track railway, and mounting, I rode off in that direction.

Cpl William Hardy, 4th (Royal Irish) Dragoon Guards

We galloped right across the enemy's firing line, absolutely galloping to death. The noise of the firing was deafening, being mingled with the death shouts and screams of men. Corporal Murphy, riding by my side, was shot through the chest and I had to take him out of the saddle and undress and tie him down to dress his wound. Men were shaking hands with each other, thankful they were still alive.

Tracking all night. It was sickening to see the wounded horses that were trying to follow us, but the majority were shot.

In this magnificent but desperate charge, the three regiments had been broken up by enemy fire, leaving small groups of surviving cavalrymen to make their own way from the carnage in the hope of finding their units later that day. The charge delayed the Germans, many of whom were terrified by the spectacle, and it was not until several hours later that the enemy pressed forward, during which time many of the British infantrymen had slipped away. One of those who saw the aftermath of the charge was a young private, John Lucy.

Pte John Lucy, 2nd Royal Irish Rgt

These mounted men were only six in number, and they led in other horses beside their own. On approaching them, I was surprised to learn that they had been in action, and were all wounded, slight wounds, bullets through arms and muscles, and that kind of thing. They were hussars. We were full of admiration for these heroes. They told us that some of their regiment had been killed, hence the led horses, and we looked on them and the riderless horses with increased respect. There is something poignant in a riderless horse coming out of battle. For the moment we thought them even greater beings than the cavalrymen. The mildness in their eyes and the grace of their bodies as they pawed the ground warmed us towards them. We patted their sleek necks.

The retreat from Mons would cause the horses as well as the men an immense amount of suffering. For the civilians, the German advance was nothing short of catastrophic. As the British regiments retreated, the soldiers became caught up in a huge civilian exodus, people abandoning everything but what they could carry.

Capt. Arthur Osburn,
Medical Officer attd. 4th (Royal Irish) Dragoon Guards

The refugees were driving their cattle, sheep, pigs, geese and poultry and bringing, in every kind and form of vehicle, all they possessed from their babies in arms to their grandfather clocks. Tired old women with their aprons full of ornaments and silver forks gesticulated and wept and fainted. There were men carrying mattresses and women dragging children. Cart-horses and bullocks, hay-carts, dog-carts, wagonettes and decrepit and reluctant motor cars were all jammed together in the most extraordinary confusion.

2/Lt Arnold Gyde, 2nd South Staffordshire Rgt

How miserable they were, these helpless, hopeless people, trailing sadly along the road, the majority with all they had saved from the wreckage of their homes tied in a sheet, and carried on their backs. Some were leading a cow, others riding a horse, a few were in oxen-driven wagons. They looked as if they had lost faith in everything, even in God. They had the air of people calmly trying to realise the magnitude of the calamity which had befallen them.

Cpl William Watson, RE, 5th Div.

We found the company encamped in a schoolhouse, our fat signal sergeant doing dominie at the desk. I made him a comfortable sleeping-place with straw, then went out on the road to watch the refugees pass. I don't know what it was. It may have been the bright and clear evening glow, but – you will laugh – the refugees seemed to me absurdly beautiful. A dolorous, patriarchal procession of old men with white beards leading their asthmatic horses that drew huge country carts piled with clothes, furniture, food, and pets. Frightened cows with heavy swinging udders were being piloted by lithe middle-aged women. There was one girl demurely leading goats.

Capt. Arthur Corbett-Smith, RFA

No man in the world is more tender to helpless or dumb creatures than the British soldier or sailor; no man more cheerful. And no man in the Force but felt his heart wrung by the infinite pathos of the folk of Mons and round it. History will never record how many soldiers lost their lives that day in succouring the people who had put such trust in their presence.

And how many won such a distinction as no king can bestow – the love and gratitude of little children? One man, at least,

I knew (I never learned his name) who, at the tears of two tiny mites, clambered into the ruins of a burning outhouse, then being shelled, to fetch something they wanted, he could not understand what. He found a terror-stricken cat and brought it out safely. No, not pussy, something else as well. Back he went again, and after a little search discovered on the floor in a corner a wicker cage, in it a blackbird. Yes, that was it. And, oh, the joy of the girl mite at finding it still alive!

'Well, you see, sir,' he said afterwards, 'I've got two kiddies the image of them. And it was no trouble, anyway.'

Pte John Lucy, 2nd Royal Irish Rgt

Our own cheerful platoon commander, he who was so keen on bayonet charges, now limps badly, and commandeers a heavy Belgian carthorse – a vile animal, a stink factory that gasses the whole platoon and adds to our misery. Another horse, an officer's charger, is found by a corporal, who rides it all day and only late in the evening discovers that the saddlebags are stuffed with chocolate. There is a scramble for the chocolate, and the artillery come and claim the charger to take the menial place of a draught horse gone lame in a gun team.

Many artillery horses fall out, lame and fatigued. The men outmarch the horses. Some horses have been shot, others stripped of harness and left alive, standing or limping, along the line of retreat.

One of our signallers stops to repair a puncture and is left behind. He returns on his bicycle waving the busby of a German hussar who was closely following us up. He has shot the enemy cavalryman, but what about the horse? He has shot the horse too, in his excitement. He is damned for his stupidity by the officers.

2/Lt Arnold Gyde, 2nd South Staffordshire Rgt

Horses have been slaughtered by the score. They looked like toy horses, nursery things of wood. Their faces were so unreal, their expressions so glassy. They lay in such odd postures, with their hoofs sticking so stiffly in the air. It seemed as if they were toys, and were lying just as children had upset them. Even their dimensions seemed absurd. Their bodies had swollen to tremendous sizes, destroying the symmetry of life, confirming the illusion of unreality.

The sight of these carcasses burning in the sun, with buzzing myriads of flies scintillating duskily over their unshod hides, excited a pity that was almost as deep as pity for slain human beings. After all, men came to the war with few illusions and a very complete knowledge of the price to be paid. They knew why they were there, what they were doing, and what they might expect. They could be buoyed up by victory, downcast by defeat. Above all, they had a Cause, something to fight for, and if Fate should so decree, something to die for. But these horses were different: they could neither know nor understand these things. Poor, dumb animals, a few weeks ago they had been drawing their carts, eating their oats, and grazing contentedly in their fields. And then suddenly they were seized by masters they did not know, raced away to places foreign to them, made to draw loads too great for them, tended irregularly, or not at all, and when their strength failed, and they could no longer do their work, a bullet through the brain ended their misery. Their lot was almost worse than the soldiers'!

It seemed an added indictment of war that these wretched animals should be flung into that vortex of slaughter. We pitied them intensely, the sight of them hurt and the smell of them nauseated us. Every memory is saturated with that odour. It was pungent, vigorous, demoralising. It filled the air, and one's lungs shrank before it. Once, when a man drove his pick through the crisp, inflated side, a gas spurted out that was positively asphyxiating and intolerable.

Trp. Benjamin Clouting, 4th (Royal Irish) Dragoon Guards
We retreated south through village after village, mostly small grubby affairs, surrounded by coal mines and slag heaps, a feature

of the region. It was hot, dry and dusty, and very quickly the horses began to look exhausted and dishevelled. Where we could, we rode along the road's soft, unmetalled edges, for the oval stones were very hard on their legs, but our horses soon began to drop their heads and wouldn't shake themselves like they normally did. Many were so tired they fell asleep standing up, their legs buckling, as they stumbled forward, taking the skin off their knees.

To ease the horses' burden, excess kit was dumped. Shirts, spare socks and other laundry were all thrown away along with our greatcoats. It helped, but the horses really needed a good rest and this was an impossibility. The best we could do for them was to halt, dismount and lead on, a short-lived order to walk that usually lasted for no more than a mile or so. As a result, the horses' shoe nails wore down at a terrific rate, each lasting little more than a week or ten days, before the chink, chink sound of a loose shoe meant falling back to find the farrier. It was sad to see our horses, so coveted and closeted at home, go unkempt. Saddles, once removed after every ride, now remained on for several days and nights with only the girths being slackened. The horses became very sore, their backs raw from over-riding, although they tended to suffer less than the French horses, which were simply ridden into the ground. The French cavalry never walked anywhere, and when they finally halted to give their horses a breather, it was not unknown for part of the horse's back to come away with the saddle. One horse went mad, banging its head against a wall, before it was finally put out of its misery. It was appalling to see. For our part, we did the best we could, bandaging our horses' grazed knees with rags or bits of puttee, but the majority could consider themselves lucky if they got a rub down with a bit of straw, or a pat on the back to bring back the circulation.

Lt Eric Anderson, 108th Batt., RFA
We only lost two horses through exhaustion. They had been turned loose to look after themselves. All our old peacetime horses

were looking really fit, though a little thin. The horses given us on mobilisation had not, as a rule, done so well, as we had not had time to harden them properly before going over to France and they had been plunged straight into the middle of real hard work. They had hardly had 1lb of oats issued to them but had done well on unthrashed oat straw. This was given them at every possible opportunity so they did not do so badly.

Capt. Charles Norman, 9th (Queen's Royal) Lancers

When horses fell sick or were wounded, the men had to ride or lead them with the transport. When men were killed or wounded, their horses had to be led with the troop or with the sick horses. A troop after action was therefore always hampered by an excess or a shortage of horses. Very seldom indeed was it in the desired condition of having one man to one horse. This greatly reduced its efficiency. At regular intervals, sometimes on the eve of an important action, 30 or 40 men were withdrawn from the squadron to go away and bring up a draft of horses. When these fresh horses arrived, generally after 48 hours, many of them were fat and soft, and quite unfit for hard work. It was always better to keep a hard horse, though wounded and sore, if he were going on well and fit for work, than to take a soft one in his place, though he had a whole skin. Unfit horses with soft backs and girths were useless, and seldom lasted two days of hard work.

Driver Charles Keller, RHA

A horse cannot rest properly when it has to wear its harness all the time, travelling most of the twenty-four hours each day. Even at Le Château [26 August] where we were for more than a day we didn't risk removing the harness. On the march, we would find ourselves dropping off to sleep as we travelled along and it was the same with the horses. When that happened we would dismount and walk along beside the teams to keep awake. Most nights we would walk more than we would ride. Whenever we stopped to give the teams a rest and some food we would sit in front and lean against their front legs to take a nap, then if the horse started to move it would wake us up.

In the confusion of the retreat, both horses and men became ravenously hungry. The Army Service Corps did what it could, dumping food by the side of the road to be picked up by whoever happened to pass that way. When it was possible to stop, the infantry automatically posted men to watch out for the enemy. It gave some men and horses a few hours' rest at most.

L/Cpl Alfred Vivian, 4th Middlesex Rgt

Early in the morning, just before dawn, a slight contretemps occurred which resulted in the loss of two perfectly innocent and gentle lives.

One of the sentinels, peering into the gloom, suddenly espied figures stealthily moving in his direction. Failing to elicit a response to his challenges, he opened fire, the sound of his outburst creating the wildest excitement and apprehension in the camp.

The discovery of the corpses of two cows testified to the watchfulness of our guard, and we relaxed our excited vigilance with expressions of relief.

When daylight enabled us to look round, I sought a view of these unfortunate victims of circumstance, and was forced to rub my eyes and pinch myself at the peculiar sight they presented. It appeared that the bullets of that sentry had possessed the uncanny and unusual power of flaying the beasts and removing the greater part of the flesh thus exposed. I rightly guessed, after reflection, that some of the starving men had felt too hungry to allow such a unique gift of food to go begging.

Daylight found me absolutely raging with hunger, and I eagerly watched for signs that would reveal to me the identity of the 'butchers', in the hope of being able to secure a titbit to allay the pangs of emptiness that assailed me, but all in vain, and I surmised that they must have devoured the meat raw and warm as they hacked it away from the carcasses.

A large farmhouse lay a short distance in front of us, and on the pretext of obtaining drinking water I sought permission to take a party to it, which was granted. To our great disappointment, it was found deserted, and the most minute search failed to reveal anything in the nature of food. This almost broke our hearts, and we returned miserably to our unit.

To the exhausted infantry, it might have looked a much better bet to have been a cavalryman or limber driver, sitting as they were on horses or wagons rather than toiling all day on foot. Yet infantrymen only had themselves to worry about; those with horses had an onerous responsibility to their animals, a fact not always appreciated by the infantry.

Lt Eric Anderson, 108th Batt., RFA

We had the greatest difficulty getting water. One battery was billeted at each farmhouse, the only places where water was to be had from wells and they [the infantry] were rather naturally afraid the water supply might run short. The sight of a couple of hundred thirsty horses used to produce all sorts of tales about staff orders having been given that no horses were to be watered there. As the staff never troubled to find *us* water, we generally disregarded such efforts till some irate one in authority could be found to drive us away. By this time, with any luck, we had watered quite a lot of horses, then we'd try elsewhere and finish up before getting pushed off again. No infantryman can understand why horses want to drink, apparently. It is the great grouse we had against them at the beginning.

Capt. Charles Norman, 9th (Queen's Royal) Lancers

One and a half or two hours were required to get the horses finished for the night. Watering a squadron was a long business if only one pump was available and no troughs. Sometimes a squadron had to water half a mile from billets at a pond. Barns had to be emptied of cattle, carts and farm rubbish before horses could be got under cover.

In the morning, watering, feeding, packing saddles and saddling up occupied another hour and a half. This had to be completed before daylight. Thus from time actually spent in billets, three hours at least must be deducted to find the actual amount of rest obtained. Thus if a force reach billets at 10 p.m. and received orders to be ready for move at 5 a.m., the period of actual rest was only four hours. The amount of rest obtained was of course very much less than this.

Trp. Benjamin Clouting, 4th (Royal Irish) Dragoon Guards

Clean water was of great importance to a regiment on the move, and whenever possible, water bottles were kept topped up. On one occasion, the squadron turned into a stream, and the horses, tired and thirsty, went to drink, but we were told to 'Ride on', so on we went. The water was less than a foot deep, clear and inviting, and it seemed such a waste. Several troopers did try to get water into their enamelled bottles, removing the cork and slinging them over into the stream as they rode. But most bottles were already too light, and despite tipping and dipping them in the water, most failed to collect much before reaching the other side.

2/Lt Arnold Gyde, 2nd South Staffordshire Rgt

During a few minutes' halt, a cow near the road stood gazing, with that apathetic interest peculiar to cows, at the thirsty men. It was not for nothing, as the French say, that one of the reservists had been a farm hand. He went up to the cow, unfastening his empty water bottle as he went, and calmly leant down and began to milk the neglected animal until his bottle was full. It was not in itself a funny proceeding, but there was something about the calmness of both the cow and the man, and something about the queerness of the occasion, that appealed to the sense of humour of the dourest old Puritan of them all. They laughed, they roared, they shouted, in a way that reminded the men of the last 'soccer' season. The noise must have mystified the pursuing Uhlans not a little.

The days in late August were hot and sultry with the odd thunder-storm to relieve the misery. Even so, the retreating cavalrymen were glad of the coolness evening brought. But with the onset of night, other unexpected problems were encountered.

Capt. Charles Norman, 9th (Queen's Royal) Lancers

At night it was very difficult for the rear units of a brigade or regiment to keep closed up. When the order to trot was given from a walk, it reached the rear of the column so late that the rear troops had often to gallop in order to keep touch, and when a walk was ordered from a trot, the rear troops unavoidably crashed into those in front. The darker the night, the more difficult was the marching. On one very dark night I felt much gratitude to a light grey horse in the rear of the troop in front of me as it served as a beacon.

Lt Eric Anderson, 108th Batt., RFA

It was now 11 p.m. and we heard we were to have two hours' rest. We managed with much difficulty, and in the pitch dark, to clear the road and with still greater difficulty to get the horses fed. The men were simply foolish from fatigue and lack of sleep and just dropped off to sleep in the middle of whatever they were doing. Going round in inky darkness to feel whether horses have their feeds or not is no jest and then all the men had to be kicked up again to take the nosebags off. It may sound unnecessary but if horses aren't looked after they just crock up, and you had much better have stayed in England.

QMS W.W. Finch, 1st Royal Scots Fusiliers

How the Army Service Corps managed to keep the moving masses of men supplied with rations day by day could only be appreciated by those who understood it. By hook or by crook they kept the regimental wagons filled and named places where biscuits and beef, and cheese and jam, could be dumped down in time for the retiring troops to gather up supplies as they passed.

There were farm horses in the battalion wagons, and owing to the incessant work they showed chafings and raw places innumerable, but no sooner was a sore place spotted than the driver was down from his seat with a tin of Vaseline and a pad of rifle flannelette until the trappings looked more like bandages than harness.

Trp. Benjamin Clouting, 4th (Royal Irish) Dragoon Guards
The horses were so hungry, they were barely able to wait for their food, and impulsively strained forward in the horse lines at meal times, mouths open, hoping to get a mouthful of corn. As soon as a nosebag was on, they bolted the food, throwing their heads up into the air to get as much corn as possible into their mouths. The problem was that whole oats passed through the horses' digestive system and straight out again in the manure, doing no good at all. To slow down the rate at which they ate, pebbles were put in the nosebags with the corn, although, strictly speaking, we were not supposed to do this. As the horses bit down hard, they received a salutary shock, ensuring that they chewed their food more gingerly.

The regiment had just come back to a village and I was detailed to help feed the troop's horses, so I went to pick up a couple of feed bags and walked over to the horse lines. The horses had become noticeably agitated, but one, overexcited at the prospect of food, shot forward and in one movement bit my stomach, dragging me slightly across him before letting go. I had just a shirt on and the pain was excruciating. When I pulled my shirt up my stomach oozed blood from a wound.

Cpl William Watson, RE, 5th Div.
Finally, we halted at a tiny cottage. We tried to make ourselves comfortable in the wet by hiding under damp straw and

putting on all available bits of clothing. But soon we were all soaked to the skin, and it was so dark that horses wandered perilously near. One hungry mare started eating the straw that was covering my chest. That was enough. Desperately we got up to look round for some shelter, and George, our champion 'scrounger', discovered a chicken house. It is true there were nineteen fowls in it. They died a silent and, I hope, a painless death.

The order came round that the motorcyclists were to spend the night at the cottage – the roads were utterly and hopelessly impassable – while the rest of the company was to go on. So we presented the company with a few fowls and investigated the cottage. It was a startling place. In one bedroom was a lunatic hag with some food by her side. We left her severely alone. Poor soul, we could not move her! In the kitchen we discovered coffee, sugar, salt and onions. With the aid of our old post sergeant we plucked some of the chickens and put on a great stew. I made a huge basin full of coffee.

For understandable reasons of maintaining discipline in friendly countries, the army had introduced strict rules forbidding looting in France or Belgium. However, when it came to food many officers and men were uncertain where they stood when livestock roamed free on abandoned farms. Justifiable scrounging or stealing? It was a difficult call.

2/Lt Arnold Gyde, 2nd South Staffordshire Rgt
The men's nerves were tried to breaking point, and a little detail, small and of no consequence in itself, opened the lock, as it were, to a perfect river of growing anger and discontent.

This was how it happened. The colonel had repeated the previous night the order about looting, and the men were under the impression that if any of them took so much as a green apple he would be liable to 'death or some such less punishment as the

Act shall provide'. They talk about it and grumble, and then suddenly, without any warning except a clucking and scratching, the mess sergeant is seen by the greater part of the battalion to issue triumphantly from a farm gate with two or three fat hens under his arms. Smiling broadly, totally ignorant of the enormity of his conduct, he deposits his load in the [officers'] mess cart drawn up to receive the loot! The men did not let the opportunity slip by without giving vent to a lot of criticism.

Pte Harold Harvey, 2nd Royal Fusiliers

The farm was deserted, its lawful owners having found the situation too hot for them. Cows roamed about at random, and so did pigs. But after we had dug ourselves in and made our position secure, the chickens were what interested us most. There were two hundred and fifty of these at the least. Catching them was good sport, but eating them was something finer. What a nice change from bully beef and biscuits. Cooking was not quite à la Carlton or Ritz, but more on prehistoric principles. So many fowls were caught, killed and plucked for cooking and eating that the wet mud was completely covered with feathers and resembled a feather bank. As for ourselves, the feathers sticking to the wet mud on our uniforms and equipment turned us into Zulus, or wild men of the woods. The enemy presumably did fairly well also, with a poultry farm in the distance. They appeared to have a portable kitchen.

Maj. Patrick Butler, 2nd Royal Irish Rgt

There was a dense belt of wood between us and the firing line, and over this the shells came screaming, bursting to the right and left, short and beyond. The enemy's guns systematically searched up and down and across, and every now and then they would concentrate a crushing fire on some particular spot, generally where there were neither troops nor animals, punching craters in the fields,

setting barns and ricks instantaneously alight, and sending up
dense clouds of evil, acrid smoke.

Animals that had been left behind when the people of the farm
departed so hurriedly were still grazing all over the place, until
every now and then a shell would come and send them scampering off to some fresh spot. Pigs and chickens were enjoying a most
unwonted degree of freedom, and not being confined within any
limits were able to fend for themselves for food. The unfortunate
watchdogs were the most to be pitied, for in a great number of
cases they had been left to starve on the chain. Our men often
tried to release them, but in many cases they had become so fierce
that nobody dared approach them.

I remember witnessing an amusing encounter between two
diminutive pullets which, quite oblivious of the battle that was
taking place all around them, were engrossed in a fight on their
own account, gazing into each other's eyes in that intent way they
have when fighting. Perhaps each blamed the other for the noise
that was going on.

Trp. Benjamin Clouting, 4th (Royal Irish) Dragoon Guards
On many farms we found a mess, with abandoned animals roaming around, some in a bad state. On one farm, we came across
sheds containing several dozen cows all blowing their heads off,
desperate to be milked. In their anxiety to clear out, the owners
had loaded up their carts and left the animals locked up and
unmilked. We were told to go and unchain them and let them
out into a field, otherwise they would starve. They were in obvious pain as they came into the yard, their swinging bags so full
that milk was actually squirting out.

Maj. Patrick Butler, 2nd Royal Irish Rgt
A shell landed full in the middle of a small circle of piglets. It
scattered them in all directions, but not one of them was hurt. I
could hear their concerted squeal high above the roar of battle.

But we did not like pigs. They roamed at large everywhere, very hungry, and there were stories of their gnawing dead bodies, and even attacking the wounded.

Ravenously hungry, Lance Corporal Vivian had already visited one farm in search of food. At the time, he and his comrades discovered nothing, or so Vivian had thought.

L/Cpl Alfred Vivian, 4th Middlesex Rgt

I had noticed this sack being carried slung on his back during the march, and it had excited my curiosity, especially as I thought I could observe movement within it. I had also been slightly puzzled by mysterious smothered screams, coming from somewhere within my vicinity, which I vainly suspected originated from that sack, but I had lacked the energy to ask questions on the subject.

As he now, therefore, showed sign of revealing his secret unasked, I watched him intently as he gently manipulated the fastenings. The string removed, he pulled it gently open, and peered into its depth, making an encouraging sound with his mouth the while.

A great commotion in the interior of the bag answered his efforts, and, to my unbounded amazement, a small and perky head of a little white pig, a couple of weeks old, appeared. Smiling happily, the soldier tenderly drew it forth, and sitting it upright, dangled it upon his knee. As proud as a father with his firstborn, he fondled that little beast, calling it by most absurd terms of endearment that would have caused an elderly spinster's pet poodle to turn bilious with envy.

This little pig, however, had other ideas, and appeared to be hunting for something which claimed its attention to the exclusion of all else. Not being able to discover the object of its frantic search, it set up a terrifying squealing that soon brought everybody alert with frightful curses. This almost caused a fight between the owner of the pig and the remainder, until the atom of potential pork, finding by a lucky chance its owner's finger, sucked at that digit voraciously, and immediately became quiet. The man then laid himself down, with the piglet snuggled down on one of his arms, with the finger of his other hand deputising as a mother, to the animal's huge contentment.

This presented a most laughable picture, the man of war lying there crooning and making mother noises to his adopted baby, while the latter rested with great confidence against him, his bright little eyes sparkling with childlike mischief. I asked him how and where he had obtained it, for I was curious, as he was one of the men that had accompanied me to the farm to get water and incidentally to search for food on the morning of the 24th. He told me that he had found it hidden in the manger of an empty horsebox on that morning, and took it at first with the intention of converting it into food. The fact that we had been able to obtain the means of staving off our hunger had bought a reprieve to the little mite, which now lay complacently ignorant of the vile and untimely fate which at one time threatened it.

I asked him if he had any intention of killing and eating it later on, in the event of a repetition of the failure of food supplies, and his furious reply: 'Whatcher take me for, a blinkin' cannibal?' both flabbergasted and amused me.

Anonymous soldier, 1st Gloucestershire Rgt

A young pig had strayed, from goodness knows where, and found itself wandering between the front and support lines. Immediately every rifle in B Company was directed at this new and more than welcome type of target. Bully beef and biscuits had been the staple diet, and here was pork to be had for the hitting. Yet no one could hit it! The animal either bore a charmed life, or the much vaunted marksmanship of the Glosters existed only in name. Then the enemy gunners joined in the same game. Their shooting became more intense, and, very reluctantly, B Company crouched down. Their mouths turned dry with disappointment and renewed thoughts of iron rations.

The shelling ceased. Up bobbed one head; then another; and soon the whole company was peering eagerly across the flat space which separated them from the front line. Extraordinary thing! That pig, which had survived the shooting of the finest infantry in the British Army, had been scuppered by a spare shrapnel bullet, and an enemy one at that.

Hearts were now high. Quickly two volunteers went out and brought in the pig. It was small and emaciated, but nevertheless a pig; and, as such, was duly quartered, each platoon receiving a quarter.

That night the battalion was relieved, moving back to where No. 8 platoon found itself in a sunken road near a clump of trees. About two hundred yards further back could be seen some dilapidated farm buildings. The members of Sergeant Bray's platoon were hungry and tired. Yet were they happy. Their portion of pig was fastened to a high branch of a tree, and, while the older soldiers discussed ways and means of cooking it on the morrow, the younger ones fell asleep.

L/Cpl Alfred Vivian, 4th Middlesex Rgt

My sleeping companion, the 'pigman', sat on his haunches, his little pig perched on his knee, feeding it carefully with army biscuit laboriously brought to the required moisture and softness by the process of chewing. As each morsel became ready, he conveyed it on one of his fingers, to the mouth of the pig (which had been unanimously accorded the name of 'Percy') which eagerly awaited its arrival, and devoured it with avidity.

We all took Percy to our hearts, in spite of his funny little drawbacks, and were all most anxious to keep him with us, and most of us were prepared to increase our affection to the extent of taking him to our stomachs, in the event of certain emergencies arising. Fortunately for his peace of mind dear little Percy did not suspect our hungry love for him. Any attempt on the part of the remainder of us to pay some little attention to Percy was resentfully rebuffed by his nurse in no uncertain manner. This resulted in him being subjected to a great deal of ragging.

Anonymous soldier, 1st Gloucestershire Rgt

The next morning, about 5 a.m., the platoon 'stood-to'. At once, as though he knew, the enemy began a very heavy bombardment. Things and men moved quickly, and the hindquarter of a pig was left swinging in the air. Very fortunately, before the enemy artillery barrage lifted and moved towards them, the men were able to occupy a bend in the sunken road about two hundred yards in the rear of their original support position. Soon bruised and battered men of the Guards began to trickle back. The enemy had broken the line. The Glosters were now heavily shelled, but the stolid West Countrymen pressed themselves flatter against the parapet, gripped their rifles, with right forefinger curled round the trigger, and looked keenly into the mist. Forms began to move out in front. The lines of singularly grotesque figures, with hunched backs, staring eyes, and stiff arms thrusting out their rifles, came through the mist towards the road. A peculiar lull; then the 'mad minute'. The marksmanship of the old army was no myth. The German attack petered out.

At dusk the Glosters were once again moving back to reserve. In his imagination everyone in Sergeant Bray's platoon could see the quarter of a pig swinging on a certain tree. Hope springs eternal even in the heart of an old soldier. They reached the end of the sunken road near a clump of trees. The quarter of the pig had gone!

A raucous voice from somewhere along the road started to sing: 'Old Soldiers never die, never die . . . They simply fade away.'

L/Cpl Alfred Vivian, 4th Middlesex Rgt

The bombardment had become intense, when, above the din, arose a plaintive voice raised in a pitiful appeal. 'Piggy! Piggy!

Come back 'ere or you'll get 'urt', seconded by a stentorian chorus urging Percy to show good sense and return to his 'father'.

This extra vocal uproar drew my attention to a spot where I perceived poor little Percy rushing to and fro in utmost bewilderment, scared out of his senses by the shells that burst around him, while his owner stood with his arms thrown out entreatingly, tearfully pleading with Percy to return to the comparative safety of the trench.

Finding that his appeals were unavailing, the owner suddenly sprang out into the open and ran forward to secure his charge from harm. After a short and exciting skirmish, he succeeded in catching him and, gathering him up, turned to regain shelter. Alas! That was poor little Percy's swansong, for before the trench was regained, a splinter from a shell raked him through, and wrote finis to his young life.

The end of our potential mascot, which had every opportunity of becoming famous, cast gloom over all, and sad glances were bent on its erstwhile owner while he reverently placed the little corpse in the bottom of the trench.

Lance Corporal Vivian did not record whether they now ate their erstwhile companion. Percy, the 'potential' mascot, was one of the first of many such animals that would be taken to the hearts of soldiers throughout the war.

The BEF had helped to hold the German onslaught and in September the first trenches were dug as both sides stopped to catch breath. If neither side could beat the other front-on, then an outflanking manoeuvre would be needed. The race to the sea begat the Western Front and in October and November the fighting raged in the villages and fields of northern France and around a beautiful but slowly disintegrating Belgian city: the name of Ypres entered the British consciousness.

Elsewhere, in early October, an ill-advised attempt to halt the German advance on Antwerp saw the embarkation from England of the Royal Naval Division to Belgium. It was a short-lived and costly campaign. British Marines were forced into a hasty retreat and civilians were once more ousted from their homes, as one British nurse recalled.

Staff Nurse Clara Holland, Territorial Force Nursing Service
My heart bled at the pathetic sight of the many dogs and cats that refused to leave the piles of what had once been their homes. Many of them were mad with starvation and snarled when we approached them. It seemed so terrible that these faithful dumb pets of scattered families should also have to suffer in such an awful way.

The next day I returned, borrowed a rifle from a soldier, and another soldier and myself went around shooting these miserable, howling and starving things. We had very nearly finished our gruesome job, when we had to stop suddenly as the Germans began to answer our rifle shots from a wood beyond.

I saw a small kitten, frightened by our firing, rush out of the remains of a house, and I was just about to shoot it when it ran towards me and sat down at my feet. I hate cats, but this little poor wee thing looked so pathetic as it stared up at me with its little mouth open, that I stooped and picked it up, and it was then I saw that it had but three feet, one of its back ones having been shot off, and the stump was bleeding. I carried it to the hospital and dressed its wound, and that night it went back to Antwerp with me as the smallest and youngest 'blessé' and the mascot of our hospital.

Would you have believed that a cat would have eaten chocolate? No, no one would and yet this little starving thing eagerly ate chocolate, all that I had in the food line with me, and swore over it as if it had been the most delicious of 'catty' meals.

It was not just domestic pets and farm animals that became tangled up in the war. In towns and cities, public zoos and privately owned collections of exotic animals were overtaken by the fighting. Keepers were forced to leave and the animals were abandoned to their fate.

Staff Nurse Clara Holland, Territorial Force Nursing Service
All the beautiful animals in the zoological gardens were shot. Lions, tigers, elephants, monkeys, in fact every animal in the building was killed in case they got out and added to the terrors.

Not all animals ended up dead, however. In time, a few elephants were used by the German army in northern France for ploughing, pulling and heavy lifting, while the odd lemur and a few lion cubs ended up as mascots on both sides of the line.

As for farm animals, the outlook remained almost uniformly bleak. From 1914 until the end of the conflict, the total number of farm livestock within the war zone would fall by nearly 95 per cent.

Staff Nurse Clara Holland, Territorial Force Nursing Service
On a quiet day, of which there were a few, when no vigorous fighting was going on, we went on a hunting expedition to a village to replenish the larder of the hospital. It was a big bag consisting of a fine fat pig, a sheep and many fowls. We had great fun and a good run, for the pig's squeals outdid the scream of shells. The fowls gave us a lot of trouble; some of them got on to the top of some haystacks and it was a hot job getting them, but we caught them all in time and put them, pig and all, into a motor. It seemed such a pity to leave them for German consumption when we were in need of these so badly at Malines Hospital and they were only roaming about amongst the ruined farmyards.

At Ypres the fighting was the fiercest of the war to date. The Germans, sensing that they could force the issue in the west, launched attack after attack on the beleaguered British infantry. Hand-to-hand fighting often resulted as last-ditch efforts were made to hold a trench line. In the midst of the fighting, bemused animals roamed free while, further back, civilians who had bolted occasionally returned to pick up any remaining possessions that might still be at home.

Pte Frederick Bolwell, 1st Loyal North Lancashire Rgt

Just in front of the King's Royal Rifles' trenches was a huge German officer waving with one hand to the retiring Rifles to surrender and with the other waving his troops on. It did not seem much good for us to attempt to fight that dense mass of Germans, but we did. Out of the thousand [men in the battalion], or thereabouts, that we lined up with a couple of nights before very few got away, the enemy taking about four hundred of my regiment prisoners and our casualties being about the same number.

I had a run for my life that day. A chum of mine who was with us had a cock-fowl in his valise that morning from the farm; he had wrung its neck but he had not quite succeeded in killing him; and, as we ran, this bird began to crow. As for myself, I had no equipment; I had run having left it in the bottom of the trench. It is quite funny as I come to think of it now, the old cock crowing as we ran; but it was really terrible at the time. We were absolutely overwhelmed, not only in our particular spot but all along the line, and had to concede nearly one thousand yards to the enemy.

L/Cpl Arthur Cook, 1st Somerset Light Infantry

There was a terrific rattle of musketry as we advanced into the village, but we were not wanted so we retired about two miles where we remained till 5 p.m. We have been greatly praised for yesterday's work. The Germans have set fire to many houses and ricks in the vicinity by shellfire. Most of the houses have been hit, places that had been vacated only a few hours previously by peaceful inhabitants. Birds were singing in their cages as if nothing unusual was going on; pigs were grunting for food in their sties; horses were neighing for fodder; remains of a hasty meal are left on the table and hot embers are still burning in the grate. The furniture is still orderly except where a hostile shell has penetrated the room and disturbed it. The houses have the appearance of being hastily abandoned with the hope of returning again in a few hours. God only knows if they will ever see their homes again, or what is left of them.

Pte Frank Richards, 2nd Royal Welsh Fusiliers
There were plenty of ducks and chickens about, pigeons in the toilet of the house we were staying in, and vegetables in the gardens. We also scrounged a lot of bottles of champagne and other wines and made up for the starvation diet we had been on for some time. Our usual rations were also more plentiful now and we were getting a bread ration. One morning a man came up with a permit. He had formerly occupied the house we were staying in and he told us he wanted to take two pigeons away. We had killed some pigeons the day before and only that morning I had killed another four which were boiling merrily away with a couple of chickens in a dixie. He went up to the toilet and came down crying. He made us understand, by pointing to the photographs of two pigeons hanging up on the wall, that they were the two finest pigeons in the whole of northern France and that they had pedigrees as long as ships' cables. But we also made him understand by pointing to our bellies that they were as empty as drums.

Pte Frederick Bolwell, 1st Loyal North Lancashire Rgt
Most of my regiment being gone and the remainder mixed up with other brigades which had formed another line, two chums and myself went to a farmhouse fifty yards behind this newly made line. There we had a field battery; and, after getting a little rest, we started out to find the remnants of the regiment. The enemy was still shelling, and the battle was still going on; but by nightfall, not finding any of them, we came back to the old house and found the battery gone. That night we slept on beds in the farmhouse, and next morning, 1 November, after a hurried breakfast of biscuits and beef, we all set out to join our respective

regiments; but, after wandering about for an hour and seeing no signs of any of ours, my two chums decided to go back to the farmhouse and make a dinner.

There were plenty of vegetables in the garden and an outhouse full of potatoes; and we found a spirit-lamp and a pot; so we commenced to prepare our meal. In a short time it was all in the pot, when alas!, the Germans began to shell our house, sending over incendiary shells. They let us have it battery fire. The first lot took off the foreleg of a cow, which along with some others was grazing at the back of the house; the poor thing hopped around on three legs for a second or two and then dropped, the other cows running up to lick the blood from its wound. The next lot hit the top of the house, one shell taking away the roof of the scullery, behind which one of my chums was standing; the other had already run into the trenches fifty yards away. I was the last to go, the other two having thought that I had been hit. I did not leave the place until the house was well alight; and three hours after, when the enemy's guns had died down and the fire had burnt out the house, I went over to see how the dinner had got on, and found it done to a turn, cooked by the heat from the burning house. Needless to say, we did full justice to that dinner, all three of us.

Pte Frank Richards, 2nd Royal Welsh Fusiliers
There was a decent orchard in the farm at the back of our trench, and Stevens and I used to slip over in the night and fill his pack full of apples. We had to fill our bellies with *something*. There was one cow and one pig left in the farm. Buffalo Bill [nickname of A Company's CO, Major Clifton Stockwell] had the pig killed and sent back to the company cooks with instructions to melt a lot of the fat down and cook the remainder; the pork came up the following night and we enjoyed it greatly although we had no bread to eat it with. The fat that was melted down we used for greasing our rifles with . . .

One morning the officers were about to have breakfast at the end of the trench leading to their bay, from where it was possible by stooping low in a ditch to get into the farm by daylight. One of the officers' servants, whose duty it was to milk the cow so that the officers could have milk in their tea, reported that the cow had broken loose and that they would have to do without milk that morning. Buffalo Bill jumped to his feet, revolver out, and roared at the man: 'My God, you'll catch that cow and milk her or I'll blow your ruddy brains out!' The cow was grazing about twenty yards away where there was a dip in the ground. The man ran after her, the cow ran up the slope to the rear, the man following; if they kept on they would be in full view of the enemy. Buffalo Bill saw the danger the man would soon be in. He shouted: 'Come back, you ruddy fool, and never mind the cow!' The man evidently did not hear him, but kept on. One or two bullets hit up the dirt around him. The enemy had been sending over a few light shells that morning, and now they sent over one or two more. One burst quite close to the cow. The cow got killed and the man received a nice wound in the leg which took him back to Blighty. I expect when he got home he blessed Buffalo Bill, also the cow and the German who shot him: even at this time we used to reckon that anyone who got a clean wound through the leg or arm was an extremely fortunate man.

Cpl John Lucy, 2nd Royal Irish Rgt

The first great battle of Ypres was drawing to its climax. Such were the conditions in which I took my small part one afternoon, assisted by a comedian of a militiaman whom I had posted on observation duty. He was put on guard at the forward corner of a wood overlooking the ground between our reserve trench and the weakly held front line. His task was to give the alarm in case of a breakthrough, so that we might get ready to counter-attack without wasting time.

He deserted his post, and left his sector unobserved.

The adjutant came fuming at me, his section commander. I hurriedly turned out another man, gave him his orders, and showed him the small funk hole I had shown his predecessor, in which to take shelter if shelling became intense near the observation post . . .

I quartered the country behind, and as I was doing this a rifle bullet fired at close range spurted earth a few yards from me. Good Lord, I thought, is my sentry turned assassin, or have the Germans broken right through? I automatically hit the ground, rolled into a depression, and released the safety catch. A squealing pig topped a little crest to my front, and bounced about bewildered, flopping its ears. Another bullet smacked near it, and it bolted.

The mystery was solved, and I got up out of my hole, raging, and accosted a sporting lance bombardier of artillery at his evening pig hunt. He met me calmly, and, ignoring my senior rank, said familiarly, as many gunners will: 'What cheer, chum. Any idea of where that bloody pig buggered off to?'

I let him have it: three years' condensed experience of the choicest verbiage of two countries. He was quite unconcerned, regarding me as quite normal. So I changed my tactics, and reminded him in an icy voice that a general routine order recently published forbade indiscriminate sporting activities with firearms behind the lines, and I ordered him back to his battery. That appealed more to his English mind. He looked respectful and obeyed, but not before requesting me to keep my hair on.

With frayed nerves I pursued my quest of the missing sentry. God help him, when I got him. Darkness fell, and aided me in my search. He was sitting over a large coal fire, in the ruins of a bombarded cottage. The household supply of fuel had caught light, and the deserter was roasting a plucked fowl, spitted on a stick, over the red coals. Above his head, a second fowl roosted innocently in the branches of a small tree. A peaceful scene.

I sat down on an upturned bucket near my squatting man.

'Well,' I opened, 'what have you got to say for yourself?'

'What for?' he countered, cheerfully, giving his chicken a twist.

'Look here, my lad. Are you aware that you have committed an action that amounts to deserting your post in the face of the enemy?' And seeing him looking only slightly bored, I added tersely: 'And you're looting!'

I looked as savage as I could.

'Ah, come off it, Corporal. What's an ould hen? And I never ran away from the bloody Germans. I saw nobody's face. There wasn't a man of 'em within miles of me. But they smashed up that wood, and that hole you gave me was worse than nottin'.'

'Well, consider yourself under arrest for desertion, and come along.'

'Here,' he said indignantly, 'what's the bloody joke, anyway?'

He stood up. I caught him by the collar of his greatcoat with both hands, and backed him against the tree.

'This is the bloody joke,' I said, emphasising every few words by banging the back of his head against the tree trunk. 'You are now a soldier on active service. You were given a responsible job on which the safety of the regiment depended. You left that job without being properly relieved, and without reason. Do you know I could have you shot?'

'Ah, for God's sake, Corporal, let's go, and chuck it. Without reason indeed! What bloody man would stay there?'

'Anyway, you're for a court martial.' I released him. He simply did not believe me.

'I came out here to fight,' he said, 'and not to stand for a bloody cockshy.' And attending to immediate affairs, he picked up his cap, slung his rifle, and carefully collecting his roast chicken, stumped after me.

I was really perturbed, and I lied boldly to cover him when we got back.

It was an education for soldiers from urban backgrounds to see how those who were raised in the countryside turned their hand to foraging and making do with whatever came to hand. Hunger opened up a completely new range of delicacies for many men who were aghast at what could pass as food.

L/Cpl Alfred Vivian, 4th Middlesex Regt

One of our number, foraging about, now captured a hedgehog, which he brought to the circle with him. Here, with a very businesslike air, he produced his knife and killed it. I was rather surprised at this brutal and wanton action, and I asked him why he had done it.

'Ter eat o' course,' he replied, smacking his lips and evincing signs of anticipation of gastronomic pleasure.

The body of the little beast was enclosed in a ball of clay. A fire was kindled and the ball placed in it and covered over. The remainder sat around, watching these proceedings with great interest, not unmixed with repulsion at the thought of anybody eating such a thing.

Presently, the ball having cracked open through the effects of the heat, our gourmet removed it, and, breaking it in half, exposed to our view the steaming carcass of the hedgehog, devoid of all its bristles, which had been left imprisoned in the clay. The result was a tasty looking and pleasant smelling morsel.

He handed this product of his culinary prowess around, permitting each of us to take one small pinch by way of a taster, and, as he put it, to teach us to refrain from sneering at the knowledge possessed by our betters.

It proved extremely succulent and delicious, and we sat around him, enviously watching him with watering mouths, like a crowd of expectant hounds, as he consumed the remainder with aggravating noises of profound enjoyment and satisfaction.

With the onset of winter, the fighting died down. The supply of food was a little more regular than it had once been, but anything that could be bought or stolen locally to supplement the diet was always welcome. Pilfering was not reserved for other ranks, either; officers were also not averse to helping themselves. One, a Lieutenant Gallaher, was chased by pitchfork-wielding French peasants after being discovered illegally fishing. Gallaher and his batman had caught two salmon, both of which had been stuffed down their breeches. The fish continued to struggle as both men ran across fields to make good their escape.

Anonymous, 4th (Royal Irish) Dragoon Guards

'Nasty' Carter thought it would be a good idea if the troop had some fish for dinner, so he and some of the lads set some dead lines in the local river. As the water was a bit low, they shut off the sluices and then got down to some serious fishing. About one o'clock in the morning the guards woke me up and told me that the horse lines were under water. We soon opened the gates again and for the next few days the whole troop was feeding off rainbow trout. It takes a war to do these things *and* get away with it.

Driver Charles Keller, RHA

One of our gunners who must have been a fisherman in civil life made himself a small net on a wire loop and put it on a long pole to get eggs out of the hen house which the farmer's wife always kept locked. He was almost caught by the farmer's wife and had to run, leaving his net behind. She took the net as evidence to the Commanding Officer when reporting the incident; also claiming the loss of some of her chickens, which could probably be true, and demanding payment. We didn't hear whether she was paid or not but she probably was.

That winter, both sides settled down to a prolonged period of peace and quiet. The countryside was dormant, very little appeared to be living except for the vermin that had been attracted to the trenches by waste food, and to the dead, both human and animal, that festooned parts of no-man's-land. Attempts to bury the dead were made, but it was a thankless task. The only up side was that, while carcasses smelt, they smelt nothing like as badly as they would in hot weather. Vermin would come to plague men's lives, but, when it came to being pestered, the louse crawling about the body was king of all species.

Pte Cyril Baker, 1/28th London Rgt (Artists Rifles)

Imagine a village absolutely in ruins and smelling badly from old tins, filth, farmyards and the numerous lightly buried men in gardens or what used to be gardens. Imagine snow on the ground and a full moon, deserted houses with holes in both front and back, with part of the roof only remaining and no sound except the constant whizzing of bullets, or the scurry of a deserted cat as you climb through a hole into the room, and you will get an idea of the sort of place I have been in and the weirdness of the walks I have had each night when visiting posts . . . I have found a little bunch of snowdrops in the ruins of what had been a garden, a most cheering sight amidst all this desolation. Our machine-gun officer told me that, in the ruined convent he was occupying, the wind was in the habit of tolling the bell in funereal fashion at night . . . How desolate everything is, with houses knocked to bits and roofs off, although sometimes the china still stands on the mantelpiece. The cats and dogs live on the benevolence of the soldiers, and possibly to some extent on the numerous rats which live on the refuse. Many of these deserted cats have become wild with hunger, and spit if you attempt friendship.

Trp. Benjamin Clouting, 4th (Royal Irish) Dragoon Guards

Where lice originally came from I never knew, some said from straw, but all I know is that for three or four days I had become frantic to get rid of them. I did not think I could tell anyone; I felt embarrassed and ashamed. I dumped my underpants in the hope that that would help, but of course it made no difference at all. Little did I know that everyone else was just as lousy. No one said anything at first, but then in talk the truth came out.

From that time onwards, we all suffered from interminable itching as these creatures roamed around our clothes, leaving blotchy red bite marks whenever they stopped to feast.

L/Cpl Arthur Cook, 1st Somerset Light Infantry

Had a lovely hot bath and change of clothing this morning. On arrival at the brewery where we were going to have our bath, we undressed in a room, taking off everything except our shirt and boots; our khaki coat, trousers and cap less the chinstrap were tied in a bundle and placed in the fumigator, and our vest, pants and socks were carted off (lice and all) for boiling.

We were glad to get inside the bathroom which was nice and warm. Our bath tub consisted of large beer vats and ten men were allotted to each vat, so on discarding shirts and boots we clambered up into the vats like a lot of excited kids. Every now and again we peeped over the side to see if our boots were OK for we had been told to keep our eye on them as they were likely to be pinched. By this time we were a very lousy crowd, the lack of washing facilities had bred lice by the thousand, and the surface of our bath water had a thick scum of these vermin. But we didn't care, we helped scratch each others' backs (which already looked as if a lot of cats had been scratching them) to ease the itching. We were of course given a piece of soap and towel, and after ten minutes we were ordered out and dried ourselves and were given a clean shirt. We were then issued with clean vest, pants and socks, then out came our clothes all steaming hot which we put on. My! What a sight we looked with all our creases and our hats all shapes. Anyway, we felt nice and clean for a while, but it would not be long before our warm bodies became alive again with nits in the seams, which had not been destroyed in the washing process, making themselves active.

The hiatus in fighting left men not serving in the trenches with time on their hands. Football and rugby matches were arranged for the

*men and trophies presented, while some officers made a happy return
to a popular peacetime hobby, hunting. The partridge and pheasant
season, which ran from October to February, was immensely popular,
with officers sending home for their hunting rifles. Shoots were properly organised with safety zones marked out even though enemy shells
burst in the distance. General Hunter-Weston presided over one event
at Ploegsteert (even as the fighting raged at Ypres), with French game-
keepers assisting officers and beaters driving the game from cover; a
telephone cable back to Divisional HQ was manned by an operator
in case of an urgent call. Elsewhere, a pack of dogs was brought out
from England by one popular captain, Romer Williams, and became
known as the 2nd Cavalry Brigade Beagles. Their stay in France was
short-lived. A French law forbidding* la chasse *in time of war was
discovered to be applicable to British officers too, and as a consequence
after just a few runs the pack was sent back to England.*

Capt. Arthur Corbett-Smith, RFA

The officers needed recreation if anyone did, and there was very
little for them outside an occasional game of soccer with the men.
As a matter of fact, officers are never off duty; at least, they never
were during the first winter. But when you have British troops on
active service you may be certain that the officers will find something in the way of sport. Did not the Iron Duke have a pack of
hounds with him out in Spain? An admirable precedent!

Some cheery souls went out partridge-shooting near Hazebrouck.
Birds were fairly plentiful and a good many brace found their way
to officers' messes. But more than one officer complained that it
was rather dull when he couldn't hear the report of his own gun
owing to the heavy firing going on.

1915

The War in 1915

The Territorial Force had largely saved the day in late 1914 when they had been hurriedly sent overseas to plug the ever-growing hole in the ranks of the hard-pressed regular army. These territorials might not match the regulars in terms of battlefield performance, but at least some of the discrepancy in training could be made up by enthusiasm – and the territorials had plenty of that.

In March, the British launched their first large-scale and planned attack of the conflict at Neuve Chapelle. A short but intensive bombardment was followed by an infantry attack that, after some initial success, became bogged down. It set the tone for many offensives in the future. It was one thing to break the enemy line, quite another to know how to exploit the success on a grand scale.

Small-scale operations continued elsewhere for the next few weeks until, in late April, the Germans attacked Allied forces again at Ypres. Using the evil of poison gas for the first time, they breached the British defences and international law. But once again British and Empire troops held firm and another door of opportunity for the German army was slammed shut.

Allied efforts to take the war to the Germans led to other intense but short-lived attacks in May. However, an acute shortage of ammunition severely hindered the chances of any success when brief preliminary bombardments could not sufficiently soften up improved enemy defences. On 9 May, regular and territorial troops attacked German positions at Aubers Ridge and then shortly afterwards at Festubert. Neither was a success.

Politically, it was important that the British were seen actively to support the French, who had suffered by far the largest number of casualties in the war. This imperative led to a joint Allied offensive, the British being invited to attack in the mining district of Loos. Despite senior officers' concerns that the ground chosen for an attack was unsuitable, six British Divisions were sent to attack enemy positions. Once again initial success could not be exploited, with the blame being laid squarely on the shoulders of the Commander-in-Chief, Sir John French, who, it was claimed, had not released the reserves quickly enough to capitalise on the breakthrough. Soon afterwards, he was replaced by a new commanding officer, Sir Douglas Haig.

A scandal over the shortage of ammunition forced the British government to reorganise key elements of industry. By the end of 1915 the supply of munitions to the front was not only far greater in volume, but questions over the quality of artillery shells had also been addressed. The supply of troops was also deemed too pressing to leave recruitment simply to appeals for voluntary enlistment. Conscription would have to be introduced. Such sweeping changes in the government's mindset would bring about a fundamental shift in the balance of power in the West. The Allies would soon have parity of firepower with the Germans.

The Natural World in 1915

The trenches in 1915 wended their way around farms and châteaux, through the edges of woods, across untended cornfields and meadows. Farm implements lay unretrieved in the fields, while corn stooks and haystacks rotted in no-man's-land. In many ways, were a soldier brave or daft enough to look over the top, the scene meeting his eyes would have been one of a countryside largely unblemished by war, where copses and woods remained in full growth, and dykes and ditches were largely unbroken. With the arrival of spring and then summer, this natural environment supported new life, as it always had done.

As the grass grew and the weeds took hold, so the trenches became suffused with midges and butterflies, bees and spiders, much to the delight of the soldiers who basked in warm sunshine. Larger animals such as stoats and weasels visited the trenches, and the birds chirruped for all they were worth in bushes and trees. There were problems with all this activity: a rat, a stray cat or dog proceeding at night through the undergrowth could scare a sentry out of his wits; grass grew so high in front of the trench that it afforded the sniper a perfect hiding place or concealed a raiding party. Working parties were sent out not just to reinforce the protective barbed wire but to scythe the grass and chop down the weeds. Detailed trench maps of the time included not only notations on the impediments seen in no-man's-land, the shell-holes and barbed wire, but in places the specific height of the grass which can have been measured only at close proximity.

Looking through trench periscopes, men marvelled at times that the enemy sat just a hundred yards away and in between was a lush and verdant world that nevertheless hid the occasional body, a dead horse or cow, the stench of which overrode nature's more delicate scents.

For the young officers of Kitchener's new civilian army, many men down from university and some still in their teens, trench life was full of interest and intrigue, and in letters home they fully described the circumstances in which they found themselves, describing in detail the flora and fauna around them, perhaps in a desire to protect loved ones from the horrors that war brought but also, one suspects, because they revelled in their love of nature and the natural sciences.

The battles of 1915 were intense and vicious but they were small in comparison with those to be fought in the years to come. A battlefield could become littered with the dead, shelling could tear up the ground, and when it rained the trenches became an oozing quagmire – but not like the Somme, not like Arras and not like Passchendaele. The barrages of 1915 were of limited intensity, and it would be those that followed a year or two later that created a land more in tune with the popular memory of the Great War, devoid, or so it seemed, of wildlife.

Meanwhile, in January 1915, with the war in abeyance, there was hunting to be done, until, as we have seen, the French government banned the sport, much to the ire of one twenty-year-old officer in particular.

Soldiers' Memories

Edward, Prince of Wales, Lt, 1st Grenadier Guards

31 Jan 1915

Dear Captain [F.W.] Sopper [18th (Queen Mary's Own) Hussars]

It was very nice of you to send me what, alas, proved to be the last card of the meets of the 2nd Cavalry Brigade Beagles, and must thank you very much for writing and for having had an orderly to meet me each day.

To my great regret I never got a 2nd hunt for I was away on a trip in the French lines from Jan. 13–22 and when I returned I found the order that all hunting and shooting had been stopped. I was mad about it, as you all must have been, for that Saturday when by the purest luck I came upon the meet, was the only day I have felt really fit out here. I did enjoy that afternoon's run and it did me worlds of good!! It was very bad luck on poor R[omer] Williams who took all the trouble to bring out that fine pack; and then to get so little fun out of it.

I don't know the real reason for *all* sport being stopped, but I fancy those bloody French objected and I don't think it was popular at [the] War Office either. But they didn't know the facts of the case. I hear you are to go to the trenches again, but leave your horses. It must be a relief and good news for you must be pretty fed up after two months in reserve. Best of luck!!

Yours sincerely Edward

The 'bloody French' might have passed the law prohibiting hunting, but Prince Edward was right: the War Office was not happy about

*hunting either. Too many officers had broken their arms, legs and even
necks in pursuit of foxes and hares, coming a cropper in dykes and
ditches or as they tried to jump hedges, and although the beagle pack
was not destined to stay very long in France, it had been out every other
day for several weeks.*

It is also likely that the War Office were more than 'with au fait *the
facts of the case'. There was always the risk that with men firing hunting rifles in back areas, accidents might occur. The British officer class
had suffered greatly in* 1914 *and with newly commissioned subalterns
being sent to the front as young as seventeen, this was not a time to lose
unnecessarily an officer of any rank.*

Maj. Patrick Butler, 2nd Royal Irish Rgt

In spite of the prohibition which existed in France against the
shooting of game in wartime, I managed to wheedle a 16-bore
gun and cartridges out of the caretaker, and another officer and
I used to go out together of an afternoon on horseback and bag
a few hares and partridges. We used to take it in turns to shoot,
while the one who was not shooting held the ponies. We were
even making arrangements for a pigstick, when our marching
orders came.

*Not all sports had been banned just yet, and cockfighting was one
of the most popular in northern France, especially in the region of
Pas-de-Calais.*

Pte Frank Richards, 2nd Royal Welsh Fusiliers

The general rule around these [mining] places was church in the
morning, and after church the men went to the cafés for a drink
and a game of cards, then in the afternoon cockfights were held in
the back of the cafés. There were still a lot of miners working in
the pits around here and Sunday was the only day when they could
get a bit of pleasure. I saw some wonderful cockfights around this
area and thoroughly enjoyed them. About the middle of 1916

cockfighting was prohibited until the war was over. It went on just the same.

In a café in one of these mining villages was a fine stuffed cockerel. I had never seen a stuffed cockerel before so I asked the landlord the reason for it. He burst out crying! I asked his wife. She burst out crying too, and so did their eldest daughter . . . After they had calmed down a bit the landlord explained in French and bits of English that the bird had been the champion fighting-cock of the whole of the La Bassée district, and undefeated for three years. Every Sunday afternoon, when it was fighting, crowds of people used to visit the café and much champagne and other wines were drunk. He had won thousands of francs on that cock's matches. Then one morning he had found him dead in his cot. At this point they all started crying again. Both he and his wife then told me that they would have parted with one of their children sooner than lose that bird. And knowing the fondness for shekels these people all had, I quite believed them.

Trp. Arthur Brice, 1/1st Essex Yeo.

In the afternoon we heard there was some cockfighting in an inn. We went at 3 o'clock and saw three fights with gloves, and had to come away at 4 for stables. After we had finished we went back but found the fighting all over – two birds having been killed. Six of us gave the promoter 10 francs for the winner of a proper, spurred fight, and this came off, one bird being killed. They are quite peasants who keep the birds, which are mostly cross-breeds. It was 6.30 when we came out and we had to go by headquarters. It was very funny running into other troopers sneaking home, each thinking the other an officer. However, we arrived back safely before roll call.

2/Lt Wilfrid Ewart, 1st Scots Guards

What a desolate country, such squalid people, such squalid straggling towns and tenements! Opposite was a house with a gaping hole in the roof where, a few days before, a German shell had burst. This was our first taste of the war. Henceforth many of the houses by the roadside were similarly damaged, albeit they seemed to be occupied; for besides soldiers, women and children swarmed in the streets . . . Surely this could not be a real war, I thought repeatedly. Surely this must be a dream, or an exhibition, or some kind of excursion, or a moving picture! Yes, no – it was war right enough.

I am writing this now in a farmhouse a mile from the German trenches. An occasional gun goes off, otherwise nothing comes out of the damp mist but the bark of a dog or the sound of our men chopping firewood outside. It is the strangest thing to see life running its normal course within a mile of the fighting line – children playing outside the cottages, peasants ploughing and threshing.

Rifleman Aubrey Smith,
1/5th London Rgt (London Rifle Brigade)

The battalion was billeted in various big farms which were dotted round the neighbouring country, the one with the muddiest field being allotted to the transport section . . . When we had disposed of our horses, we turned to see what billet had been provided for us and were directed to the farmhouse at the entrance to the field, one of those three-sided Flemish farmsteads with an evil-smelling midden and refuse heap in the centre.

Up a rickety ladder we climbed, emerging in a low-roofed loft filled with straw, situated over the pigsties. This was our billet. There was loud abuse of our dear Lance Corporal Hurford, who acted as transport Quarter Master Sergeant, for not having secured a better residence, but he merely grinned and informed us that the NCOs' billet was a glorified dog kennel.

2/Lt Alexander Gillespie,
2nd Argyll and Sutherland Highlanders

The farms here are fortresses in themselves; they are built all round a square courtyard, the middle of which forms a manure heap, the

size of which I never saw equalled, in any part of the world . . .
Three sides of the square are given over to horses, cows, calves, pigs,
sheep and goats; and the fourth side is the house proper, where the
old farmer, his whole family, and all his labourers seem to live. You
can imagine the confusion, when 500 soldiers have to find their way
in, too. They lie down in the stalls beside the cows, climb up hen
ladders to roost in the lofts, and curl up in any corner where they
put a bundle of straw. I found four horses in the place allotted to
my men and had a tremendous argument with the farmer and the
farmer's wife, who refused to put them in beside the cows.

2/Lt Wilfrid Ewart, 1st Scots Guards
The British soldier is lounging about with all his accustomed
insouciance, the stump of a cigarette in his mouth; the cocks and
hens (with crested heads) and one or two fat black pigs are scratching and burrowing in the somewhat pungent and very plentiful
manure of the farmyard. Madame, wizened and old, with two rubi-
cund daughters, is heavily committed in the matter of washing
linen outside the kitchen door. Monsieur le père, who has a short
white pipe which he never ceases to smoke, leans contemplatively
on the door of a cowhouse regarding the unwonted scene. Who
would think that the opposing lines of trenches, locked together
in the grim death struggle, are so near? Yet hardly has the thought
occurred when in the middle distance a gun booms ominously.

*To escape the farmyard animals and their associated smells, even for a
short while, men would leave their billets and head towards any local
estaminet for a change of scenery, the chance to relax in a warm and
convivial atmosphere and the chance to buy eggs and chips.*

Pte Horace Smith, 1/8th Worcestershire Rgt
A little way along the village street was the Café du Nord, to
which we often went in the evenings to play cards or drink wine
and coffee.

I can see every part of the public room of that little café now: the entrance from a narrow passage leading on to the street; the long French stove at the far end of the room on which usually stood a pot containing hot coffee. Most of our party sat round the table playing some card games, while I usually sat by the stove with the cat on my knees. The animal took a fancy to me at once, and I think for this reason Madame always had a soft spot in her heart for me. Her husband was away serving in the French army, and she had three young children.

Occasionally we held impromptu concerts, and although the good woman of the house could understand but a few words of English, she listened with evident interest to the songs or to the recitations by myself and joined heartily in the applause. Occasionally, when we had just returned from the trenches, she would inquire where so-and-so was, and if we had to tell her he had been killed or wounded she was always greatly upset and sometimes wept.

Cpl William Watson, RE, 5th Div.

A dog of no possible breed belonged to the estaminet. Madame called him 'Automobile Anglaise', because he was always rushing about for no conceivable reason.

The war was never far away: you could see it, hear it, and, what was more, smell it too. For men going up the line in the dark, it was possible to find one's way as much by the sensitivity of the nose as by strength of sight. For soldiers new to the line, like Wilfrid Ewart, all the senses were employed to come to terms with this new world.

Lt Denis Barnett, 2nd Prince of Wales' Leinster Rgt

It is a very difficult journey from here to where we are digging, and the sailing directions are like this. Across field to haystack; bear half left to dead pig; cross stream 25 yards below dead horse; up hedge to shell-hole, and then follow the smell of three dead cows across a field, and you'll arrive at exactly the right place!

The best of these landmarks is that you can use them on the darkest night. I brought my lads back by a short cut I devised for myself, including a couple of dead dogs and a certain amount of one German. It is a much better way, and I got the bearing so well that I walked right up to the last cow without even smelling her, so strong was the wind blowing the other way.

2/Lt Wilfrid Ewart, 1st Scots Guards

I see a wide and shadowy country. The moon is rising out of the calm night. A little wind whines and whispers among the sandbags. I see dimly a land of poplars and small trees (dwarf oaks), orchards, and plentiful willows. I see flat fields and ditches and stagnant water, and red farms whose roofs are gone, stark skeletons in the moonlight. I see broad flat spaces and then a ridge – the ridge of Aubers. Only the German lines are hidden from sight.

No sign of life. Silence and desolation reign. But here and there the faint glimmer of a fire indicates the presence of the enemy. Afar off, rockets, red and green and white, shoot up to the sky; star shells bursting above our trenches cast their baleful light around. Strange twisted figures of trees stand out against the horizon. There is no sound but an occasional home-like mating call of partridges in the fields and the peculiar laughing cry of the little speckled owl which here, as in England, dwells among the orchards.

2/Lt Alexander Gillespie,
2nd Argyll and Sutherland Highlanders

This day began for me about midnight, as I lay in my dugout in the breastwork watching the Plough swing slowly round. [It was] still, that is, except for the snipers' rifles, and the rattle of the machine guns, and sometimes the boom of a big gun far away, coming so long after the flash that you had almost forgotten to expect it. The breastwork which we held ran through an orchard and along some hedgerows. There was a sweet smell of wet earth and wet grass after the rain, and since I could not sleep, I wandered about among the ghostly cherry trees all in white, and watched the star shells rising and falling to north and south.

Presently a misty moon came up, and a nightingale began to sing. I have only heard him once before, in the daytime, near Farley Mount at Winchester; but, of course, I knew him at once, and it was strange to stand there and listen, for the song seemed to come all the more sweetly and clearly in the quiet intervals between the bursts of firing. There was something infinitely sweet and sad about it, as if the countryside were singing gently to itself, in the midst of all our noise and confusion and muddy work; so that you felt the nightingale's song was the only real thing which would remain when all the rest was long past and forgotten. It is such an old song too, handed on from nightingale to nightingale through the summer nights of so many innumerable years . . . So I stood there, and thought of all the men and women who had listened to that song who were once so strong and active, and now are so quiet.

Some of the best prose of the war would come from these young highly educated officers, so many of whom, like Second Lieutenant Gillespie, would not survive the war.

Gillespie's gentle flights of fancy were not ones that Private Frank Richards would have ascribed to his Commanding Officer, Buffalo Bill, the bullying major who had, the previous year, threatened to shoot a man for losing the company's milk-giving cow. The cow had now been forgotten and instead a dog had captured his perhaps over-fertile imagination.

Pte Frank Richards, 2nd Royal Welsh Fusiliers

Buffalo Bill bought a large and powerful dog with harness and got the pioneer sergeant to make a little cart. All over Flanders it was a common sight to see dogs in harness working and pulling little carts about, which in England is against the law. Buffalo Bill calculated that the dog would be able to pull as much trench stores to the front-line trench in one journey as six men could carry, thereby saving six men who could work repairing the trenches. He appointed a man to take charge of the dog, whom he afterwards called the Dog-Major on the lines of the Goat-Major, the lance corporal who has charge of the regimental goat. He told this man he would hold him responsible for the dog's safety.

The idea was all right but the dog had other ideas. On the first night that it made the trip, it was deemed advisable to send another man with the Dog-Major. I was detailed off to accompany him. We loaded the cart up with reels of barbed wire and other small trench materials and set off for the trench. The dog strode out resolutely along the road and the Dog-Major remarked that we would put a little heavier load on for the next journey. I replied that we had not completed this one yet, and that it was time to talk when we had safely landed in the trench with the load we had got.

As soon as we left the main road and got on the track our troubles began. We had not proceeded very far when the dog left the track, the cart upset and everything was in the mud. We cursed, got the dog and cart back on the track, loaded up and got going again. We had not proceeded very far when a small shell exploded some distance from us. The dog gave a leap off the track, pulling cart and stores into a shell-hole which was knee-deep in mud and water. It took us about an hour to get the dog and cart back on the track and load up again. This happened a couple more times, and then I carried as much as I could of the load whilst the Dog-Major tried to guide him. But it made no difference. He would have left the track even if the cart had been quite empty. I tried to persuade the Dog-Major to let me shoot the dog or bayonet it, and he could report to Buffalo Bill that a piece of shrapnel did the trick. But he wouldn't agree to it. Just before dawn we landed in the trench thoroughly exhausted. We reported to Buffalo Bill the trouble we had had, but he said that the dog was strange to that work, and after a few nights would be making six or eight trips a night.

The next night another journey was made, with a similar result. The dog was not popular with the men. A sandbagged kennel had been erected close to the officers' billet and in the morning six bayonet thrusts were found through the sandbags into the kennel, no doubt, according to Richards, as the men had passed up the trench. The news was reported to Buffalo Bill.

Pte Frank Richards, 2nd Royal Welsh Fusiliers
The Dog-Major was now struck off all trench duties and ordered to take up his abode in the kennel with the dog. Buffalo Bill warned him, pulling out his revolver, that if anything happened to the dog something just as serious would happen to him.

Then the cart, which used to be left some yards from the kennel, was blown to pieces. I don't know whether the dog knew that his troubles were over for the time being but for the rest of the day he was yelping and barking with delight.

When Buffalo Bill left us, the dog stayed with the company but never did any more work. He got used to shells and rifle grenades when they were coming over, and it was very funny to see him flatten his body against the wall of a trench when he heard the whine of a shell which he knew would be falling somewhere near him. He used to wander around the trench, but he would never attempt to jump on top during the daytime. He seemed to sense that it was not safe. We all got to like the dog, which used to go in and out of the line with us. About a month before we left the Bois Grenier sector, and during one of our little spells out of the line, he got lost. I expect a Frenchman pinched him.

Nine months later when we were in Béthune, two old soldiers of A Company were having a stroll around the town when a large dog came running up to them, barking and wagging his tail with delight. They recognised him at once and took him back with them. He was given a permanent home with the transport. In the autumn of 1917, when we were around the Ypres sector, he was killed by a shell splinter when the transport lines were shelled. He had survived four or five months in a front-line trench but was killed miles behind one.

Lt Denis Barnett, 2nd Prince of Wales' Leinster Rgt
There is a little grave about 2ft by 3ft in the middle of a bust-up farm, and on the cross there is this: 'Here lies Tim, a little brown dog, killed by a shell during the bombardment of this house by the Germans on April 23, 1915. RIP'. That was the end of our mascot. He went out of the trench into the farm to see why the bricks kept jumping about. He did his bit all right. The RBs [Rifle Brigade] had a kitten, but she was shot by a sniper while walking on the parapet with her tail straight up in the air. Hermann the German must have been riled by pussy reminding him of his poor chance of going that way when the RBs lay him out. Hope they have by now.

The adoption of a mascot was widespread among units serving over-seas. Unlike 'Tim', many seemed to have shown remarkable levels of intelligence.

Lt Denis Barnett, 2nd Prince of Wales' Leinster Rgt
I've lately made the acquaintance of a great character here, the machine gunners' goat. She's a most extraordinary beast, and has taken to machine-gun tactics in a wonderful way. She will fall in with the gun teams; you can pull her away by main force, but she comes back at the double. She gets awfully excited at the command 'Action', and helps the gunners by running between their legs, and standing where they want to mount the gun; she's never more than a yard out at most. When the guns are

mounted she stands in front and licks their nose lovingly – an unwise thing to do with a friend of such habits. But we're all very fond of her, and the gunners have adopted her entirely; and she now bears the mystic sign MG on the side of her, in emerald-green paint.

The onset of spring brought the trenches to life. All of a sudden the natural world woke up: flowers and foliage grew with unrestricted vigour. It was a time of wonderment for men, as creatures other than the ubiquitous rat and mouse paid regular visits to the front lines, particularly in those parts of the line where there was little enemy activity, such as Armentières and Ploegsteert, quiet backwaters in comparison to Ypres when the second battle for the town opened in April.

2/Lt Alexander Gillespie,
2nd Argyll and Sutherland Highlanders

We still have April sunshine, so that, in spite of the cold winds and frosty nights, the hawthorn hedges are quite green, and the desolate cabbages in among our barbed wire are sprouting vigorously. We have leeks there too, and every night a party goes out to gather them, so that at all hours of the day and night there is a fragrant smell of frying leek from various corners.

Capt. Lionel Crouch,
1st Oxford and Buckinghamshire Light Infantry

I am pestered here with a plague of midges which bite like the devil. The days are frightfully hot, but very pleasant. The trees and hedges are coming out beautifully. I have got some rather pretty flowers in my dugout. Wheeler picks them for me. Today he got two very nice narcissi which smell ripping. From the gardens of this ruined village we get potatoes, rhubarb and spinach. This is very good for the men, and I encourage them to go at night to get garden stuff.

2/Lt Alexander Gillespie,
2nd Argyll and Sutherland Highlanders

I watered our garden; the pansies and forget-me-nots are growing well; the other plants are not so happy after their transplanting, and the Middlesex, being townsmen, do not seem to understand about gardens, and when they water the plants at all, they do it at midday, under a blazing sun. I found a nest full of young hedge sparrows too beside the stream which runs through our breastwork, and saw the very father of all the water beetles at the bottom. Remembering how hard these large water beetles can bite, I left him severely alone.

2/Lt Cyril Winterbotham, 1/5th Gloucestershire Rgt

It is a perfect night after a lovely May day and my heart has been at home with the dear English countryside and the dear faces in England. The country has changed wonderfully with the spring and now the may is out in the hedges and the beans and corn crops are well up and 'All the land in flowering squares smelt of the coming summer'.

The buttercups are a sight and the trees too. Every year I wonder at the beauty of just a hedgerow elm against the blue spring sky. One amusing feature of the spring here is the frogs. I watched one with great interest the other day. He had his head out of water and was singing fit to burst himself. Each time he did it a large white blister swelled out each side of his head as if he had a hideous attack of mumps. I hope his inamorata appreciated his efforts.

The beauty of the landscape and the vitality of nature affected men differently: some were able at least temporarily to set aside the predicament they were in and enjoy the sights and sounds, while for others the stark contrast between the burgeoning natural world around them and the reality of shellfire and sudden death was sometimes almost too much to bear.

Pte Norman Edwards, 1/6th Gloucestershire Rgt

Sick at heart, bodily and spiritually, I wandered into the wood.
[Friedrich von] Bernhardi [Prussian general and military histo-
rian] wrote of the elevating influence of war, but what I had just
seen made me curse war and the people who had started it. The
sun shone, birds sang joyously, flowers blossomed in profusion,
and nature with amazing prodigality was at work covering the
evil work of man with a garment of green. Death lurked in this
quiet place, for I had to drop flat as a machine gun sent a stream
of lead back and forth, clipping off branches and quelling the
heavenly melody of the birds with its hellish din.

In a jagged hole, rent in the base of an oak by a shell, I found a
thrush quietly and sanely carrying on its life work. I peeped into
the nest and the flawless perfection of those four blue eggs, warm
and pregnant with life, diverted my thoughts as perhaps nothing
else could have done.

This horror which had come down upon the world was, after
all, but a transitory thing and would presently depart. That small
bird stood for the eternal and changeless things that will emerge
again . . .

How can I describe the spell at Ploegsteert Wood, not the
horrors of which I have just written, but the living impalpable
beauty of the place? To the men of the 4th Division who captured
it and held it in the winter it was doubtless a place of evil memory,
but to us who were fortunate enough to occupy it in May when
the earth was warm with spring and the enemy comparatively
quiet, it was a peaceful spot. To turn one's back to the parapet
and watch the edge of the wood take on the pale golden glow of
dawn, later to lie down amid the forget-me-nots in the warm sun
or stand naked and bathe in a shell-hole filled with water, were
experiences that aroused one's aesthetic facilities to a high pitch.
One realised how close one was living to nature, closer perhaps
than ever before, and the thought that possibly each dawn might
be the last accentuated the delight.

The dawns at this time were particularly beautiful. Before any definite light appeared, the larks would soar up and a faint twittering in the wood grew to a buzz of noise as the birds stood-to with us.

Lt Richard Talbot Kelly, 52nd Brigade, RFA

To me, half the war is a memory of trees: fallen and tortured trees; trees untouched in summer moonlight, torn and shattered winter trees, trees green and brown, grey and white, living and dead. They gave names to roads and trenches, strongpoints and areas. Beneath their branches I found the best and the worst of war: heard nightingales and smelt primroses, heard the scream of endless shells and breathed gas; rested in their shade, spied from their branches, cowered in their roots. They carried our telephone lines, hid our horses, guided us to and from battle and formed the memorial to many efforts of our arms.

For most men, interest in nature and wildlife was a passing pleasure, a transitory moment when a tree, a hedgerow, an animal or insect attracted their attention before more pressing concerns took over and the moment was forgotten. Not so Philip Gosse. In contrast, pressing concerns were interruptions to his love of animal life and, although he undertook his work as a medical officer with absolute professionalism, any opportunity to pursue his personal interests was taken. Indeed, it would be his passion for wildlife that would, in the end, lead to promotion and an end to trench life.

In mid-1915 he had only recently arrived in France and was being led up to the front line to meet another medical officer, Charles McKerrow. McKerrow was in the act of skinning a vole when Gosse entered a dugout. Gosse, an amateur taxidermist, felt an immediate affinity with his superior officer, although he was a little taken aback to discover that McKerrow was in fact using the skin to make a muff to send home for his daughter's doll.

Lt Philip Gosse,
RAMC attd. 10th Northumberland Fusiliers

From that morning McKerrow and I became fast friends, and whenever we could we would meet and talk of all sorts of matters not connected with war or medicine, such as birds and flowers . . .

It was the sight of McKerrow skinning a vole that prompted me to write to my old friend Oldfield Thomas, the Keeper of Mammals in the Natural History Museum in Cromwell Road, to ask him if the Museum was well provided with specimens of the small mammals of Flanders, and if not, whether he would like me to procure some. Thomas, who was always ready to encourage amateurs to collect, wrote back to say that they were in great need of specimens from Western Europe, and he sent also some of the museum labels and some arsenical soap for preserving their skins. I then asked my mother to send me a dozen 'break-back' mousetraps, and as soon as they arrived I set about collecting and skinning mice and shrews.

Collecting animals for the Natural History Museum was not an alternative full-time job, but to some it might have looked like one.

Lt Philip Gosse,
RAMC attd. 10th Northumberland Fusiliers

In the evening I would go out with my haversack full of traps and a piece of ration cheese for bait. Creeping about in the wet ditches and hedgerows, I would look out for the tiny beaten tracks of my small jungle game: wood mice, voles or shrews. Setting traps for even such small game as this calls for a certain amount of skill, or at least, hedge-cunning, for a dozen traps placed anyhow and anywhere will catch nothing . . .

On returning to the dugout, each specimen was carefully examined and measured. These measurements had to be written on the labels and recorded in millimetres, the length from point of nose to stump of tail, the length of tail, which must not include any hairs at the tip, and the length of the ears and paws. Then the place where the specimen was caught, the date, and its sex, had to be noted down . . .

This hunting of small mammals was all very well in the back areas, miles away from the line, but in or just behind the trenches the risks were not only on the side of the small mammals. Sometimes the hunter became the hunted. Well-intentioned sentries and other armed patriots, seeing a suspicious person, dressed – more or less – in the uniform of a British officer, skulking in waste places, or creeping about in water-logged ditches, were apt to jump to the conclusion that he was an enemy spy. When challenged, I found that the simple truth that I was only setting traps for field mice failed, in most cases, to allay suspicion, and on one occasion I was hurried, under an armed guard, to explain my suspicious actions to higher authorities.

Trapping and skinning so many small mammals left a surplus of flesh and bones. With so many larger carcasses around, most smelling to high heaven, Gosse's search for a hygienic method of disposal was hardly worth bothering about. In fact he needed to look no further than a friendly cat known to all as Félicité.

Lt Philip Gosse,
RAMC attd. 10th Northumberland Fusiliers
Up here in Flanders I was sorry to find cats were all too few, and those I did see were poor skulking specimens of a noble race. But there was one exception: Félicité. She was a small and rather scrubby white-and-tortoiseshell cat, but very intelligent and affectionate. She was the most confidential cat I ever knew, and was forever whispering something in my ear which I could never quite catch. While I was writing she would come and sit very close beside me and read what I wrote and purr loudly. Every night after I had gone to bed she would stroll in and leap up on to my bed and sleep curled up beside me. This adoration was, I fear,

largely cupboard love, for each day after I had finished skinning
a mouse or a vole I would give her the carcass, for I only wanted
the skin and Félicité would oblige me by disposing of the corpse,
and nobody was more concerned than she over the success of each
night's trapping.

Most animals, at least those not considered edible, were no more than
transient visitors to the trench system. However, one animal that was
neither edible nor transient was the trench cat. Useful for catching
rats and even small mice, she was also a reminder of home, a great
companion and a focus for affection. Some cats had grown wild since
losing their civilian masters, others had, as so many cats are prone to
do, followed the line of least resistance and sought out a provider, then
settled in to become part of the fixtures and fittings.

2/Lt Alexander Gillespie,
2nd Argyll and Sutherland Highlanders

Writing is difficult, for Sonia, the trench cat, is paddling about on
my knees, and making herself into a living sporran. She has come
from the ruined farm behind, I suppose, but she takes the change
very philosophically, and is a sort of permanent housekeeper, who
never leaves company headquarters in this dugout, but is handed
over to each relieving regiment along with other fixtures, appearing in the official indent after the ammunition, spades, fascines,
RE material, etc as 'Cat and box 1'. She has no real affections, but
prefers kilts, because they give more accommodation in the lap
than breeches; on the other hand, she has an unpleasant habit of
using bare knees as a ladder to reach the desired spot.

Cats such as Sonia were frequently valued out of all proportion to their
actual worth, as front-line entertainment and morale boosters. Captain
James Dunn recalled in his book, The War the Infantry Knew, *that there were two 'much-made-of-kittens' in their Company HQ. He*
believed that when the poet Robert Graves managed to tread on one of

the kittens, his eviction from the unit was not far behind. 'Graves had reputedly the largest feet in the army, and a genius for putting both of them in everything. He put one on a kitten: it was enough. Not long afterwards he was transferred to the 1st Battalion.'

Lt Philip Gosse,
RAMC attd. 10th Northumberland Fusiliers

It seemed that ever since the British took over this line of trenches from the French, the medical officer of each battalion had instructed the medical officer of the next to be careful to look after the Landlady, who proved to be a cat, and was the one and only remaining civilian of Givenchy.

The regimental doctor produced a tin of preserved milk and gave me precise instructions as to its proper dilution and the hours of the daily feeds, just as in peacetime he must have done to many a mother over her first baby's bottle. He explained that the Landlady was out, that she went out at dusk every evening, but would return at dawn and expect to find her saucer of milk ready prepared and in its usual place.

As to her other rations, it seemed she supplied herself with these by catching rats and field mice every night. These duties I gladly promised to perform and we said goodbye.

Tired and wet after the long march, I was glad to get out of my damp clothes and curl up in the less damp blankets on the low bunk which had been made up by cutting away the chalk on one side of the dugout. I soon fell asleep and must have been so for some hours, when something heavy fell on me which woke me up with a start. At first I thought a shell had struck the roof and that I was buried in the debris. Then I became aware that the weight on my legs was moving as though alive and I lay quite still, afraid to stir.

Whatever could it be? I dared not put down my hand to feel for fear it was a rat, but if it was it must have been one of those huge monsters an Irish soldier had told me of, 'as big as a dog'.

Meanwhile the movements of the heavy object had become rhythmical, a sort of prodding was going on, accompanied by an odd, deep, throbbing sound. Then all of a sudden, as sleep cleared away, it dawned on me that my waker could be no other than my Landlady; gingerly I reached in the direction of the object and felt the soft fur of a cat, busy at that exercise all cats enjoy, of kneading with alternate paws . . .

During the whole day she slept curled up on my bunk and did not wake up until the evening. Then, a little while before sunset, she arose, tripped up the steps of the dugout and inspected the skies. From where she sat she had a good view of Notre Dame de Lorette behind our lines, and of the broken spire of the church of Ablain-St-Nazaire, beyond the crumpled village of Souchez.

After a while she sauntered up the trench which led towards the front line, and at a respectful distance I followed her. Presently she reached the fire trench and without warning leaped up on the parapet, where she sat gazing across no-man's-land, with all the tranquillity of a peacetime cat seated on the wall of its own backyard. No doubt from her point of vantage she could see the ruined mine shafts of Lens and even German soldiers moving about in their trenches.

But I trembled for her. Only fifty yards separated our front line from that of the enemy. At that very moment, more than one German sniper must have been watching her; perhaps was then drawing a bead on her with his rifle. Down many a periscope her image was being thrown by artfully adjusted mirrors into the retina of bloodthirsty Boches. Each second I expected to hear the crack of a rifle and to see my Landlady leap into the air and then fall dead or mortally wounded into the bottom of the trench.

But nothing of the sort happened, and I was led to suppose that all Germans were not as black as they were painted.

Then, to add to her foolhardiness, the Landlady commenced her evening toilet, in full view of two vast contending armies, each armed to the teeth with every device invented by civilised man to destroy life and limb . . .

It was strange, I thought, that the Landlady could sit up there for twenty minutes in perfect safety while if I, a non-combatant whose profession was to succour the sick and wounded, whether friend or foe, showed my head for but one moment above the same trench, I would receive a bullet through my brain. How incalculable are the ways of man.

The Landlady, unperplexed by such reflections, having rested after her ablutions, rose, stretched herself, and then disappeared over the parapet into no-man's-land – and not a sound, not a shot. What she did there until she came back to bed with me some eight hours later no one knows. Probably she hunted rats and mice in the long grass that grew so rankly amongst the coils of barbed wire out there. Those small mammals were her sport and her supper.

But who can say if she had not friends in the German lines? Who knows but what she was a spy in German pay? But no, it would be treachery even to think such a thing.

Did she, I used to wonder, leap up on the German parapet and make herself at home in the enemy's line as in ours? That I can well believe, but what happened beyond our front line she kept to herself, a profound secret . . .

When the time came for us to leave those trenches I said goodbye to the Landlady with real regret, and was punctilious to inform the relieving medical officer of her requirements and habits.

When cats became part of the trench fabric, it was likely that, in due course, some would have kittens, and a generation of kittens was destined to be born and raised in or close to the front line.

2/Lt Alexander Gillespie,
2nd Argyll and Sutherland Highlanders

We are back again in the old trenches which we used to hold at the end of March, when the weather first began to get fine. There is a great difference since then: the grass has grown so long every-where that we can hardly see the German parapet, and the trees hide a great deal of the front too, now that they are in full leaf . . . These trenches are much deeper than the others I have been in, for somehow or other they never flooded so badly, so they still hold the original line of last October, through the middle of a wheat field which was never harvested. Now the wheat has sown itself, and is growing up everywhere in tall bunches on the parapet; in fact, it is in the ear already. Sonia, the cat, is now the happy mother of three kittens, very pretty little kittens too. Never having known any home except this trench, I suppose they would be most indignant if our line went forward and left them. In the meantime, they and their mother and three servants live in one dugout, when they are not sprawling in the sun.

Capt. Charles McKerrow,
RAMC attd. 10th Northumberland Fusiliers

I have just returned from having tea at the mess. I was suspicious of little pussy, so made a thorough examination of my bed. I found that she had decided to produce her family on my pyjamas and that the event was not far distant. I hastily removed her to a box, but at present she is under my bed. I have just had a look and one has arrived. She seems to understand all about the business herself and I see no reason to help. The ungrateful beast refuses to look at a sandbag I offered in place of the white tiles. I daresay she knows best. My future efforts will be required to prevent her insinuating her infants into my sleeping bag.

2/Lt Alexander Gillespie,
2nd Argyll and Sutherland Highlanders

All is quiet today on the front held by the 93rd, except that fierce engagements go on night and day between the three kittens, and also between Sonia, a proud mother, and a small black terrier pup, called Satan Macpherson, who belongs to the machine-gun officer.

Satan has the best intentions in the world, and is only anxious to do his best for the new army by paying a friendly call; but as soon as he attempts to advance, he is met with high explosive and driven from his position at the point of the bayonet. Fighting still continues.

In late April the Germans introduced a new horror to the fighting in Belgium: chlorine gas. The first soldiers affected had no protection and suffered terribly as a consequence. In the days and weeks that followed, some basic protection was rushed up to the front line and, in time, increasingly effective gas helmets were manufactured and distributed.

Lt Denis Barnett, 2nd Prince of Wales' Leinster Rgt
Young had to go off this morning to a village a few miles back to be gassed. He (and a lot of staff men) were put in a trench and given a dose, with respirators on, of course. They found the respirators worked admirably, though there were two unhappy frogs in the bottom of the trench who curled up and died at the first whiff.

2/Lt John Gamble, 14th Durham Light Infantry
One thing I must tell you, before I stop, and that is about a little bit of diversion during the gas attack.

I had just been bandaging up a couple of wounded, when one of them called my attention to a couple of big rats which were staggering about on their hind legs as if drunk. It really was one of the funniest sights imaginable. One usually only gets glimpses of rats as they scuttle rapidly by (during the day), but these two were right out in the open, and their antics were too quaint. They were half-gassed of course, but strangely enough it was one of the things I remembered best after the show was over. One good thing the gas did was to kill a lot of the little beasts.

Capt. James Dunn, RAMC attd. 2nd Royal Welsh Fusiliers
Gas drifted through the village at five and again at 7.30 this morning. The Germans put it over at Hulloch, a couple of miles to our

right, and entered 300 yards of front and support trenches. Here, the gas crept along the ground in thin dilution, at a fair pace, well below the height of a man standing . . . Horses and tethered cattle were startled, and tugged at their head ropes. A little dog on a heavy chain, unable to scramble on to his kennel, ran about frantically; hens flew on to walls and outhouses clucking loudly; little chickens stood on tiptoe, craning to raise their gaping beaks above the vapour; mice came out of their holes; one climbed the gable of a barn only to fall back when near the top. Seedling peas and other vegetables were bleached and wilted.

The first pad-like respirators were manufactured and handed out within two days of the first gas attack, while gas hoods or helmets were supplied to all front-line troops just weeks later.

Pte Arthur Empey, Royal Fusiliers (City of London Rgt)

German gas is heavier than air and soon fills the trenches and dugouts, where it has been known to lurk for two or three days, until the air is purified by means of large chemical sprayers.

We had to work quickly, as Fritz generally follows the gas with an infantry attack. A company man on our right was too slow in getting on his helmet; he sank to the ground, clutching at his throat, and after a few spasmodic twistings, went West [died]. It was horrible to see him die, but we were powerless to help him.

In the corner of a traverse, a little, muddy cur dog, one of the company's pets, was lying dead, with his two paws over his nose. It's the animals that suffer the most, the horses, mules, cattle, dogs, cats, and rats, they having no helmets to save them. Tommy does not sympathise with rats in a gas attack.

At times, gas has been known to travel, with dire results, fifteen miles behind the lines. A gas, or smoke helmet, as it is called, at the best is a vile-smelling thing, and it is not long before one gets a violent headache from wearing it.

With the improving weather and the warm, balmy evenings, life in the trenches could be not only tolerable but almost enjoyable. The sound of artillery fire could be just a distant and sporadic rumble, rifle and machine-gun fire infrequent, and so a sense of peace and tranquillity pervaded the trenches.

Anonymous cpl, 9th Highland Light Infantry

There are good times in the trenches, especially in the summer. Plenty of grub, ripping weather, a decent dugout for two, and sentry duty for only one hour in seventeen. We loafed about visiting our friends in other dugouts, reading or writing our letters with nothing to worry us, and when the afternoon sun became too hot we got into the shady dugout and lay there watching the moles and lizards crawling about the empty trench. Yes, that was a fine spell.

And then there were our bivouacs, little lodgings rigged up by branches tied together with the waterproof sheets, which every soldier carries, stretched over and pegged down at the sides. We spread straw and grass to keep the damp from rising. Outside the bivouacs was our camp fire with the dixie on for tea, and we ourselves, stretched out on the grass near the fire, yarning [and] smoking to keep mosquitoes from getting busy. There *is* romance in our life out here. Don't believe anyone who tells you otherwise.

Pte Norman Edwards, 1/6th Gloucestershire Rgt

I remember one afternoon lying down on the grass feeling the earth's firmness, breathing the pure air, inhaling the exquisite colour and sweetness of the blue heaven and forgetting the petty circumstances and annoyances of existence. In the mellow sunlight, the bronze, yellow and flaming reds of nature blended into a sort of beauty infinitely soothing to the spirit. Great restful clouds warmed with colour from the dying sun, breasted the rim of the hills in fleecy manes like celestial Alps. A long way off, a band was playing, so far that only occasionally a strain of music drifted across the quiet air, but the boom of the drum outcarried the music rising and falling in rhythmic throbs like a tom-tom – conveying news across the jungle. Other faraway sounds, the barking of a dog, faint bursts of cheering from a football match, and desultory rumbles of gunfire, stole gently on my hearing, but none were of sufficient sharpness to obtrude on the quietness that enveloped me. Myriads of insects were busy, frantically busy knowing that the vital warmth would soon depart from the sunbeams and that earth would no longer respond to their touch. From an ivy that flowered on an old wall nearby, a hum of activity arose as countless flies flitted from flower to flower, and the drone of a passing bee seemed loud in comparison with the countless small sounds that in the aggregate made up an exquisite undertone of nature so faint that it trembled on the edge of hearing. Yet my senses were acutely aware of them, and I was thankful that no aeroplane came over to break the contact. As the light faded, the woods took on a purple hue, and a column of gnats danced unceasingly over the gun. Then twilight, mist in the valley and the plod back to the little barn with a companion, yawning after a good afternoon's sleep. I did not envy him for I too had been resting. Not only my body but my mind and spirit felt strangely cleaned and refreshed.

2/Lt Alexander Gillespie,
2nd Argyll and Sutherland Highlanders

The weather is still perfect; our trenches and breastworks are brown and bare and dusty, and the sandbags are getting bleached in the sun, but everything else is green. The meadow behind is yellow with buttercups and dandelions; there's a large patch of yellow mustard out between the lines, and a forest of leeks and cabbages. Even the walnut trees, which seem to be the last of all, are beginning to give a little shade, and the broken stumps of poplars are doing their best to repair the damage of the shells.

I spent part of the morning skittling in the stream for where an old trench crossed it; some hopeful idiot last autumn had built a dam of bricks, as if that were likely to keep the water out. The remains were still blocking the current and making a stagnant pool, so I cleared them out, to the great disgust of the water beetles and other tenants who had been living there so long. There was a pleasant smell of warm mint and waterweeds . . . Swallows and house martins are very busy, but it will puzzle them this year to find a house left with eaves within a mile of the trenches on either side. Certainly there are none about here, and few walls as high as a second storey. My hedge sparrows are nearly ready to fly, but I found another nest with young birds, in a pollard willow, a common sparrow's, I think; but there were three bullet holes scored on the bark within a foot of it, so that I did not care to climb up and look inside. The birds don't care, and I often see them crossing between the lines; in fact, there are just too many pigeons crossing, and I wish I had a shotgun to stop some of them. There was a tit's nest too, as usual in a hole too small for my hand, and too deep for my fingers, so that I must watch for the bird to see what kind it is . . . The war must have come upon these farms very quickly, for almost all the cattle have been killed, and they still trouble us. But a gunner who was here then described to me how he had seen men dash out from their trenches, in spite of the snipers, and run along to cut a steak from the buttocks, and back again. For in those days rations were not so plentiful as they are now, and fresh meat even scarcer.

Lt Denis Barnett, 2nd Prince of Wales' Leinster Rgt

There is a cow here that walks about in the day, and by night is put away carefully in a dugout, in the hope that one day she'll give some milk. So far there's nothing doing, and I'm afraid she'll be hit before she gets a sufficiently peaceful day to begin to think of what she can do for other people.

We spend a lot of time here strafing flies. There's rather a lot about, though our trench is as clean as a new sewer, really very nice. We seem to have made a difference to them already, and the

majority seem to belong to Ersatz and Landwehr formations, the
bluebottles of the first line having all been accounted for . . . By
Jove, I picked up a shrapnel bullet and threw it at a bluebottle
sitting on the parapet about five yards off and got him pop! He
never smiled again. That's one of the best shots I've ever done.

Pte Norman Edwards, 1/6th Gloucestershire Rgt

It became unbearably hot and steamy. The trenches stank, the
old French latrine nearby sent forth a pestilential odour, and our
dugout added its quota to the general foulness until I unearthed
and buried a lump of stinking meat that had been left under the
straw. I made a trip to the pioneers' dugout, lifted a can of creo-
sote, and by a generous distribution of this over the main sources
of contamination, made the air a little purer. Flies swarmed everywhere, including those horrible brown horseflies that drew blood
when they bit, and very fittingly, on this reeking sweaty day,
amidst the horrible filth, we found ourselves lousy for the first
time.

2/Lt Alexander Gillespie,
2nd Argyll and Sutherland Highlanders

I never saw a billet like this for flies; they hang in great black clusters on the walls like swarming bees; flypapers get covered two or
three deep in half an hour; we are trying poison too, but however
many we strafe there are just as many left.

*Flies were not only bothersome but also spread disease and so the work
of sanitary officers was critical in staving off illness in the line. They
were nicknamed 'OC Stinks', and they were not always listened to and
their advice was often ignored. When Lieutenant McQueen discovered
that a number of the lidded toilet seats he had seen incorporated in a
trench were cut up and used for firewood, he had a right to be annoyed.
Sadly, he never really stopped feeling that he was considered as just as
much a nuisance as a help.*

Lt James McQueen, Sanitary Officer, 51st Div.

At the end of ten to twelve hours of bright sunshine, you lift up one of the latrine lids which have served some hundreds of men, and you find that one fly escapes. 'Now,' I said, 'first of all, how many contacts would you have had in this latrine had it been a shallow one, dependent upon some careful soldier to cover with earth? In the course of ten hours you might have thousands of contacts of flies with the excreta, and just as many contacts of excreta-contaminated flies with jam, sugar, butter and other articles of a soldier's diet that are not subjected to sterilisation by heat. At the end of ten or twelve hours you see one fly emerge, and it is a very doubtful proposition as to whether that fly has ever been near the excreta at the bottom of the 9ft pit.' Whereupon the major demanded abruptly, 'How do you know that, McQueen?' I said, 'Because a fly does not fly into the dark; it buzzes round in the light. The bottom of a deep latrine is too dark for a fly.'

McQueen had disagreements with a number of officers who could see only extra, and to their minds unnecessary, work for their men to do to maintain hygiene. Yet McQueen's advice was not only practical but sound. Flies had been estimated to cover between 300 yards and one mile in any direction in a twenty-four-hour period, laying their eggs in anything from rotten meat to rotting straw, from decaying vegetables to horse manure. A single fly could deposit 500–800 eggs in a summer, and the development of the egg to the perfect fly could take as little as ten days. The new generation of flies could lay eggs within a further ten days and, although the fly's life cycle was short, the damage they could do to men's health was serious. Unfortunately for the men in the front line, they were not the only pest.

2/Lt Alexander Gillespie,
2nd Argyll and Sutherland Highlanders

This has been a very hot sultry day, as I know to my cost, for I spent the morning with my platoon digging a new trench about half a mile behind the firing line. We were well screened from view, even from the captive balloon which was hanging in the air over the German lines as usual, like a great caterpillar; so that we could work by daylight which is always more satisfactory. The men were working practically naked, and the only disadvantage was a very poisonous wasps' nest close beside the trench. I got stung twice on the knee, but either it is a very long time since I was stung, or these French wasps are not so venomous, for their stings don't bother you after five minutes. Some of the men were stung too, and were much more alarmed by the wasps in pursuit than by some shrapnel which the Germans put over just in front of us.

Occasionally the ubiquitous presence of trench insects and vermin could, with a little ingenuity, be turned to the soldier's advantage.

Lt Graham Reid, 59th Field Coy, RE
The French were marvellous in the art of camouflage. In one place there was a body hanging on the wire just in front of the French lines. Observation just here was difficult. The French made a papier mâché model of the body, tunnelled out to the wire, replaced the body with the imitation. By standing up at the end of the tunnel, an observer could get a good view by looking through a hole in the 'dead man's' stomach. This was in July or August. To give a realistic touch, the man responsible for this chef d'oeuvre spread honey over the papier mâché dummy to attract the flies.

Lt Bernard Adams, 1st Royal Welsh Fusiliers
Some tea was on the table, and bully and bread and butter; there was no sugar, however. Richards [an officer's servant] smiled and said the rats had eaten it all. Whenever anything was missing, these rats had eaten it, just as they were responsible for men's equipment and packs getting torn, and their emergency rations lost. In many cases the excuse was quite a just one; but when it came to rats running off with canteen lids, our sympathy for the rat-ridden Tommy was not always very strong.

Today, a new reason was found for the loss of three teaspoons.

'Lost in the scuffle, sir, the night of the raid,' was the answer given to the demand for an explanation . . .

I remembered there had been some confusion and noise behind when the Germans raided on the left; apparently all the knives and forks had fallen to the ground and several had snapped under the martial trampling of feet when our retainers stood to arms. For many days afterwards when anything was lost, one's anger was appeased by 'Lost in the scuffle, sir'. At last it got too much of a good thing.

'Why this new teapot, Davies?' I said a few days later.

'The old one was lost in the scuffle, sir.'

'Look here,' I said, 'we had the old one yesterday, and this morning I saw it broken on Madame's manure heap. Here endeth "Lost in the scuffle". See? Go back to the rats.'

'Very good, sir.'

As most work was carried out at night, daytime was used for rest and a chance to write a letter home to a loved one. In writing to a young son or daughter, or to a favourite niece, there was a limit to the number of things a man could sensibly write about. He could talk about home, but then he might not have seen home for months; he could talk about war in a gung-ho, Boy's Own *fashion, but such talk would last only for so long. Easier, perhaps, to resort to descriptions of life in the line, the nice, reassuring stories that a child would understand. Second Lieutenants Foulis, writing to his daughter Nancy, and Andrew Buxton, to his niece Rachael, epitomised the letters of many when they talked about nature.*

2/Lt James Foulis,
5th Queen's Own Cameron Highlanders
My dear little Nancy . . .

The 'Germs' are about 100 yards away, and we often throw shells and bombs and things at each other, but our trench is a jolly strong one so they cannot do us any harm.

We have got a lot of enormous rats and tiny mice. They scuttle and scamper about everywhere and do not bother about the war at all. This morning one of our soldiers killed a large rat with a spade. Now we have a bomb-throwing machine, so we put this rat on to the machine and threw it all the way into the German trench. I wonder if they had it for breakfast?

2/Lt Andrew Buxton, 3rd Rifle Brigade
My dear old Rachael . . .

You can't think how I loved getting your letter telling me of your animals and the carrier pigeon. It is such a different world that you are in to what I am with war going on, but some day I shall come back and see all your things, and keep some perhaps myself like I used to do. I am writing this in the middle of culti-vated fields where we are practising. In the hedges here are lots of caterpillars; some in bunches in thick webs which they have made, and some lovely coloured ones with yellow ones, and red and black lines down their sides.

I am wearing shorts, so my knees are getting sunburnt and quite sore. At present I am in a farm with lots of white pigs about, which the farm people try to sort out and put in different sties, etc, calling out all sorts of funny noises to make them come. The same way, they shut up ducks at night and calves. They had a great hunt after two calves yesterday, which got out into the corn. My men helped get them in.

2/Lt James Foulis,
5th Queen's Own Cameron Highlanders
My dear Nancy . . .

Do you remember me telling you about the little white dog we had at Aldershot? Well, we still have it. It has gone with the regi-ment everywhere they went. It is a mascot. There are a dreadful lot of big rats here so the dog is getting very fat. You see, it eats so many rats. Soon it will get so fat it will not be able to catch any more rats. Then it will not get enough to eat so it will get thin again. And then it will be able to start catching more rats and get fat again . . .

We are living in a lovely big green wood and you would be surprised at the number of birds there are in it. They don't seem to care a button for all the shells that are flying about and keep on singing merrily all the time. There are cuckoos and turtle doves, blackbirds, thrushes, linnets and all sorts of others, and even one or two pheasants. There are also lots of great big frogs in the pools and they go croaking and chattering to themselves all day long.

Heaps of love from Uncle Jim

With time on their hands and the summer in full bloom, there was ample opportunity for men to wax lyrical about insects in their letters home, eschewing any idea that trench life was anything but prolonged periods of boredom in which the search was keen for anything to stimulate the intellect.

2/Lt Alexander Gillespie,
2nd Argyll and Sutherland Highlanders

I woke up with the sound of ducks quacking in the farmyard just outside; they seemed to have an intolerable lot to say, and as I lay I noticed the most gigantic Daddy-long-legs I have ever seen on the ceiling above me. It suddenly occurred to me, what on earth can he use his legs for? They are far too long, and the joints all go the wrong way; he has wings, so he needn't use them for wading; perhaps they act like the tail of a kite to keep him steady on the wing, but in that case it would have been better to give him a better pair of wings. Or perhaps he thinks his long slim legs are irresistible to Granny-long-legs. If Darwin's right, there must be some purpose in his legs to fit him to survive, but I can't see it; they are like the appendix.

2/Lt Andrew Buxton, 3rd Rifle Brigade

I forgot to tell you, in the bombardment we had in the last trenches on 10 September, it was interesting to see how the shock of the exploding shells made the spiders drop down from the hedges and trees and hang by their threads, then work up, only again to fall. We had the joy up there of a dead cow just beyond one of the sap heads from which our patrol usually got out, and then did their listening work, often sitting just by it, or even on it, I think. When I went out there, I preferred a few yards more to the right to listen, though I must say it's a marvellous cow, not smelling at all in spite of having been there a very long time. You see I give you all the details of this wonderful life as they occur to me . . .

In the summer, the British Army took over part of the French-held line to the north of the River Somme. The area had been something of a backwater and would remain that way for another ten months. In 1915, there was clear but nevertheless patchy evidence of Franco-German fighting, but by and large it remained a beautiful part of France. To the naked eye it had more than a passing resemblance to the chalky countryside of the English South Downs, a fact the British Tommy appreciated. To many units of Kitchener's new civilian army, it would be at the autumnal Somme that they would receive their first introduction to war.

Pte Thomas Williams, 19th King's Liverpool Rgt

It is hard to believe that after months of hard training we are at last in France. The surrounding countryside might well be taken for a typical English scene. It is a rather flat, undulating landscape covered with a patchwork pattern of fields. Where the plough has been at work, the patches are dark in colour from the newly turned soil furrows, but many acres of yellow stubble remain unploughed from the late harvest.

The villages nestle down in the hollows where the tall elm trees and the hedgerows are still covered with dead leaves which gives them a beautiful russet tint when viewed from a distance. There are, however, a few points to remind us that we are not back on the open chalkland country of Salisbury Plain. The long avenues of trees by the roadsides, the sunken grass-grown lanes which wind through the fields, the wayside crucifix or shrine, and finally the distant rumble of the guns, all help to impress upon us that we are no longer on English soil.

Pte Horace Smith, 1/8th Worcestershire Rgt

There was a strange, though false, air of peacefulness about these trenches in the valley of the Ancre. Their deep sides were lined with wild flowers, and every morning at 'stand-to' the larks rose from 'no-man's-land' and sang hymns of praise. Mingled with the long grass, which was as high as our barbed wire entanglements, were millions of vivid red poppies. But in that narrow valley which separated the opposing forces lay many bodies, both French and German, for there had been bitter fighting here earlier in the year, and had we but known it, this ground was to be the grave of many of our own men in the bloodbath of the Somme.

Pte Thomas Williams, 19th King's Liverpool Rgt

One morning a tabby cat wandered in through the doorway of the old cowshed. She mewed plaintively. The poor creature was nothing but a walking bag of bones. How on earth she got any food in this deserted place it was difficult to imagine. When I endeavoured to stroke her she drew back, spitting savagely. However, a drop of milk in an old tin worked wonders and soon she became quite tame and confiding . . .

At night-time I discovered that the farmyard was by no means deserted. Standing there in the bright moonlight, the scene was a grim one with black ruins silhouetted against a starlit sky. In the centre of the yard the midden was alive with small, moving forms. Twin pairs of flittering eyes were watching in the shadows and high-pitched squeaky calls came from every corner.

Rats! They were everywhere! They gambolled over the midden, fought with each other on the cobblestones and went scavenging in parties through the gloom of the tumble-down buildings. It was not difficult to guess how the lean tabby cat had kept alive all these months: Here was food enough and to spare. But puss was not the only one to levy a toll on the over-abundant rat population.

As I stood watching this strange spectacle, a dark shadow passed over the moonlit ruins. This was followed by a sudden and shrill scream of pain from the far side of the yard. Descending on silent wings, a great white barn owl had snatched up a victim. A wild scurry for cover and the yard was deserted. But not for long. In a very few minutes the hordes of rats were back once more at their nightly revels . . .

**Capt. Charles McKerrow,
RAMC attd. 10th Northumberland Fusiliers**
I am back with the mice in my dugout, but this time I am armed with two traps bought for a few centimes. They are most efficient and quite instantaneous. In six hours I have got seven, ranging from Pa and Ma who were large and fat, to the smallest baby who was quite otherwise. I shall continue like Nero till not a mouse remains . . . I go rat-hunting with my automatic pistol in the evenings, but with little success, as much practice has made the rats of the neighbourhood very wily. There are crowds of them but they won't sit still. I have, however, fourteen mice and caught a lovely fawn one last night. I have cured the skin and shall send it home.

Not everyone was as intent on ridding a dugout of all vermin. Rats were rarely put up with, but mice, on the other hand, had at least a chance of turning a situation to their advantage. John Mackie's delightful description of one small mouse is interesting. It is not only indicative of his deft powers of observation but also a good example of the time officers had to pass in inconsequential pursuits when little or nothing was going on outside.

Capt. John Mackie,
1/5th Argyll and Sutherland Highlanders

We called him Adolphus because he looked such an old rake. He lived in a reserve trench where he spent his time in consuming other people's rations. A pale-faced little fellow, dapper and urbane, he welcomed each successive set of visitors with an easy tolerance, making them free of his quarters all day, and only asserting himself by night. Then indeed he strolled jauntily out to look his guests over and sample their food. Adolphus was only a mouse, but he was much admired, as well for his high spirit and fine carriage as because he undoubtedly represented the original inhabitants of the land. Even the trench rats I tolerated, recognising that they had a better right to the place than I; so you will easily understand that Adolphus made me feel very ephemeral indeed. He possessed that air of indefinable superiority otherwise found only in head waiters, who albeit they accept your tip, yet do it condescendingly as receiving the just tribute of evanescence to perpetuity – 'You cannot afford to dine here every night, but I, I am always here' . . .

[Lt] Grey filled his pipe with a sigh of relief and complimented me on my cunning in teaching the subs [new officers] a new card game.

'They're good lads,' he said, 'none better, especially in the front line. But I get most infernally tired of their eternal prattle when we're in reserve. I'm too old for it . . . Yes they're fine young fellows, but one does feel the need of something more intellectual than their conversation.'

To us, as we smoked in silence, came Adolphus. The candles had been lit and we lay on the two wire frames which answered as beds, or if one chose to sit upright, as chairs. Between us was the rough table which was the only other article of furniture in the dugout. Adolphus, after collecting the crumbs under the table, took post on my toes, whence he regarded me with the appraising, condescending look of which I have spoken. I stirred uneasily and Adolphus vanished.

Grey, eager for intellectual pursuits, placed a piece of biscuit on the floor, and covered it with his tin hat. Then he propped up one side of the helmet with a match to which he had attached a piece of string. Five minutes later Adolphus was not greatly dismayed or apprehensive – 'The young gen'lmen will have their little jokes.'

It was time we varied the performance so I put a drop of whisky (it wasn't so dear then) into a 'Gold Flake' tin lid, and mixed in a few crumbs of biscuit. Next time Adolphus was released, he reappeared with a little friend (suspected feminine) and both were entrapped as usual. When the helmet was lifted they seemed reluctant to run away, and although – in deference to custom no doubt – they eventually retreated, it was only to emerge at once with all the lads of the village in their train.

The little roués gathered round the cigarette tin lid in a warm brown bunch, and their tails protruded all round till the whole thing looked like an enormous spider wriggling on the floor. Every now and again some slight noise sent them scuttling to their holes, but as the 'binge' proceeded, Adolphus got less able to scuttle. His pale face made him easily recognisable in the gay throng, but his jaunty manner had altogether vanished. Long after the rest of the band had been dispersed, Adolphus remained at the tin lid, sometimes inserting a tentative paw, sometimes sitting on his hind legs with a thoughtful expression. It took much more than a casual noise to disturb him now.

If you put out your hand towards him he made no movement at all until the last moment, when he would take an electric leap into the air. It seemed to us that he landed with a rather heavy flop and it is certain that he had not the least idea where he was when he came to earth again. His bosom companions had left him; even the first little friend, with true feminine caution, had forsaken him. There were no kindly tramlines to direct his steps, no helpful police to advise him, but perhaps, in some dark recess of the dugout, Mrs Adolphus was awaiting his return.

Lt Andrew McCormick, 182nd Labour Coy

There was a very cheeky little mouse which used to scamper along just under the iron roof and rumble chalk down on to the head of Drake, who was my stablemate at that particular time. I dubbed that mouse 'Robert the Bruce' because he seemed to have such an antipathy to Mr Englishman. One day Drake was sitting near my bed and he said, 'Gracious me, look at that.' I looked up and there was the little mousie scampering along the ledge whilst a lump of tissue paper hung from its mouth. Drake said, 'Is it building a nest or what's it after?' I said, 'The explanation is quite simple. Hitherto the rats have kept to this side and the mice to that and now "King Robert" is waving a flag of truce to the rats to unite against the common enemy – Mr Englishman.' One night I heard a continuous stampede of rats above my head. I rose on my elbow and turned my flashlight on to the usual spot where I could see them streaking past. There, to my greater alarm, I saw the little red eyes of a weasel. Drake saw them too and we both said, 'That's done it.' Next day we gave orders to have the dugout lined with Boche timber.

In or out of the line, the army was never keen to allow men to have too much time on their hands as light work was an encouragement to mischief. As in civilian life, a lake, pond or river immediately attracted those who enjoyed fishing, and if the opportunity arose men would fashion rods and bait and try their luck. However, the British soldier had also become a seasoned scrounger and was therefore unwilling to leave anywhere empty-handed. A fishing rod might bring success, but if not there was an alternative.

Pte Frank Richards, 2nd Royal Welsh Fusiliers

Paddy and I had bought some cheap rods and lines and went for a day's fishing, also taking a couple of Mills bombs in case we met with no success. After three hours' fishing not one of us had caught a tadpole. An elderly Frenchman then commenced fishing by us and in no time he had caught half a dozen lovely fish. We stuck it another hour but with no results. We then gave it up and walked a couple of hundred yards down the canal, and after a careful look round pulled the pins out of our bombs and dropped them in. Ten seconds later we had more fish than what we could carry back. This was a favourite method of fishing with some of us although strictly prohibited: if a man was caught the least punishment he could expect was twenty-eight days Number Ones [daily humiliation of being tied to a wheel of a gun carriage].

As throwing grenades into any lake or river to stun fish was illegal, the assumption made by officers and Frenchmen alike was that if any stretch of water was bereft of life then 'other ranks' were to blame. Not so.

Capt. Charles McKerrow,
RAMC attd. 10th Northumberland Fusiliers

In the afternoon, Scott of 12th DLI (Durham Light Infantry) came in and suggested a fishing expedition in the evening. I was keen on it so he collected some pills from the store. At 6.30 we set off with shovels and gumboots. The boat was on the south side of the reservoir, well hidden in rushes. We baled her out and started with some vigorous shoving. We tried some casts in the middle with no success. We were rather noisy I'm afraid, and it was fairly light. We tried closer in shore on the north side. One cast gave us about 30 or 40 nice dace and roach, and another nearly as many. We practically filled a sandbag and then paddled home. We hid the boat as far as possible in the rushes. Scott came in and supped with me on fried trout etc. The fish were not all bad, though a trifle bony.

In his diary, Charles McKerrow had barely bothered to conceal that 'pills' meant grenades. He was more candid when recounting the same episode in a letter home to his family.

Capt. Charles McKerrow,
RAMC attd. 10th Northumberland Fusiliers

I had a great evening fishing last night. I brought in about a sandbag full of roach and dace, which were nearly as good as trout when fried by Mat [the cook] in ration butter. The method of fishing was, perhaps, not entirely sporting, being not unconnected with high explosives. It was really rather fun, however, and no one fishes in the place as it is exposed to view by day.

2/Lt Andrew Buxton, 3rd Rifle Brigade

I have been in about half an hour from a long walk round certain front-line trenches, which I had not seen before . . . We have a small, shallow pond just by our dugouts, with low rushes by the side, in which I saw a ripping pike of about 5lb muddling about. I had a shot with my revolver, and apparently stunned him for about a minute, as after that he began to move off again, but difficult to see whereabouts his head or tail was. I thought I got him with another shot, which was about right as it seemed, but he only went off with a big rush. I was very sorry not to get him, as it would have given the men great joy to have had him for breakfast.

A couple of days later he had another go.

2/Lt Andrew Buxton, 3rd Rifle Brigade

I told you I missed a pike in a pond, but yesterday I shot a fish, probably a 1lb roach, or something of the sort. Quite fun trying to recover it in the rushes; the mud was too deep for gumboots, so got a tub, in which one of the servants made a perilous journey through rushes, but, instead of retrieving it, stupidly drove it into the mud!

It was a well-known military mantra not to volunteer for anything in the army. No one would freely volunteer for a miserable job so it was normally misdescribed by the sergeant in order to get a taker. It was fortunate for Driver Pugh, then, that when the sergeant major sought a man who could trap moles, he really did mean a man who could trap moles.

Lt Philip Gosse,
RAMC attd. 10th Northumberland Fusiliers

I had already learned in the army that whenever at a loss the regimental sergeant major was the right man to appeal to for help. So I sent for him and explained that I wanted some moles, that I had some traps, and asked if he thought he could find a man in the ambulance who knew how to use them. Off went the regimental sergeant major, and half an hour later, while I was still sitting at the desk in the orderly room, I heard sounds of approaching steps and the regimental sergeant major marched in, followed by a depressed and rather scared looking Army Service Corps driver.

'Driver Pugh, sir,' bawled the RSM, 'admits to being a mole-catcher in civil life.'

Then stepped forward Driver Pugh, who in reply to my questions said that before the war he had worked on a farm in Wales near a village with an unpronounceable name, and that his principal duty at this farm had been to catch moles. The very man I wanted. So it was arranged that Driver Pugh should be excused all duties that afternoon, and he was sent off with my traps. This piece of news, coupled with the sight of the traps, brought about an instant and miraculous change in the Welshman's demeanour.

For in place of a sad, browbeaten man, he instantly became alert, smiling, and self-confident.

How he did it I do not know, but next morning, chaperoned by the RSM, Driver Pugh entered the presence bearing in his hands two handsome Flemish moles.

Pte Thomas Williams, 19th King's Liverpool Rgt

We were to journey up to the trenches under cover of darkness on the following night. The orderly sergeant broke the news when he came to our billet with battalion orders. Nobody seemed to care. We were too leg-weary and footsore to take much notice.

'Can anyone here milk a cow?' It was the sergeant speaking, but no reply to this strange question was forthcoming. If he had asked for a volunteer to kill a pig the request could not have been more unexpected. The next moment, however, my elbow was nudged. 'Go on, chum. Speak up. There's a soft job for you!'

'Can you milk a cow?' said the sergeant, eyeing me suspiciously. I nodded my head. 'Then in future you will be attached to Headquarters' Company. Tomorrow you will parade at 3.30 a.m. to march with the advance party for the trenches.' Without any further word of explanation, the sergeant turned and walked through the doorway, out into the darkness of the deserted village street . . .

There is little need to dwell upon the discomforts of the following morning. The early rise in the dark and the parade of Headquarters' Company in the keen, frosty air. 'Is the cowman there? – Right.' Off we trudged along the road to the trenches . . .

Carnoy was Battalion Headquarters for the troops holding the line. On one side of the road was the colonel's dugout. Opposite were the remains of a farmstead and nearby a communication trench labelled Montauban Alley. Here amid the tumbledown debris of bricks and mortar I was to find a home.

'Is the cowman there?' asked a sleepy voice. 'Come on, chum. Follow me. I'll show you what kind of a job you've been let in for!' The speaker had evidently just emerged from beneath his blanket. I followed him between two buildings where once there had been a gateway. The gateway had belonged to the farmyard which had been square in shape, a large midden in the centre and outbuildings all round. The midden was still there. No cows, no horses, no pigs were to be seen. Not even a barn-door fowl. The buildings were in ruins and a death-like silence seemed to brood over the whole place.

'Here we are,' said my sleepy companion as we clattered over the cobblestones and halted in front of the only building with any semblance of a roof. Somewhere in the darkness beyond the open doorway there was a movement which produced a faint rustling noise. There was no mistaking that familiar sound. It was the swish of a cow's tail.

There were two cows. One dry and the other giving a bare quart of milk, I was told. The milk was to be taken to the colonel's dugout . . . Undoing the tethering ropes, we led the cows out of the farmyard and along the roadway to a piece of wasteland behind the colonel's dugout. Here we fastened them to two long ropes which were pegged into the ground. 'That's all they get to eat,' said my companion, and he pointed to the withered, brown grass which grew between the shell-holes. 'If it doesn't fatten it'll fill,' he remarked, and with that we left the poor beasts grazing peacefully.

Back once more in the farmyard, we made our way across to the far side of the ruins where a layer of ice glistened on the surface of a waterlogged shell-hole. Here lay the main source of our water supply for the cows. But one had to be careful, for the spot was overlooked from the enemy's trenches. 'Keep your head down. That bloomin' sniper ain't a bad shot.' With these words I received final instructions for my newly acquired job as the colonel's cowman . . .

Lt Philip Gosse,
RAMC attd. 10th Northumberland Fusiliers

It was sometimes quite pathetic to see how much men liked following again their old peacetime callings. Once while I was acting as temporary medical officer to a battalion, an order arrived from Divisional Headquarters instructing the commanding officer to make inquiries whether there were in his battalion any men with first-hand knowledge of the care of carrier pigeons, because several experts were required to take charge of some mobile pigeon lofts which were being sent out. This news soon spread and caused much excitement. The battalion had been recruited in a Yorkshire town where pigeon fancying and pigeon racing were popular hobbies and sports. Here, it seemed, was a chance to get a 'cushy' job well away from the line, near some comfortable estaminet, with no officer, still more no RSM and no parades. Indeed, it seemed to hold out the realisation of the golden dreams of almost every infantry soldier. At noon the battalion paraded, the order was read out and any man who knew about the care of carrier pigeons and how to fly them was instructed at the word 'Advance' to take two steps forward. When the order rang out . . . 'Advance' . . . the whole battalion moved two paces forward and halted.

The adjutant had a difficult task before him, to select the two or three required, when confronted by some four hundred carrier-pigeon experts from which to choose.

Pte Thomas Williams, 19th King's Liverpool Rgt

My job as the colonel's cowman was a pleasant occupation compared to life in the front line. Once, when we attempted to increase the milk yield, the CO demanded that hay should be sent up the line. I got into the transport officer's bad books for stealing his clover! Otherwise there were few happenings of note. A shell or two now and then and that damned sniper forever trying to knock the last remaining scrap of plaster off the farm buildings. That was about all.

For nearly two months the battalion journeyed backwards and forwards between Bray and the Carnoy sector. But at length there came rumours of a move. We were going to take over another lot of trenches on the right. This meant, of course, that our headquarters would no longer be at Carnoy. It also meant that our colonel would no longer have fresh milk for his breakfast.

We are told that all good things come to an end sooner or later. I myself could not grumble, for the cowman's job had saved me many hours of tedious fire step duty in the front line. We were resting at Bray when news of the move came through and with it came orders for the colonel's cowman to be returned to his old company.

I saw no more of the Carnoy cows and can't even say what happened to them. It may be that the German sniper put an end to their precarious existence, or perhaps they were killed in that tornado of shellfire which heralded the Somme attack. On the other hand it is quite possible that they may have lived on to greet the astonished eyes of the old farmer when he returned to his ruined village.

One thing, however, I certainly do know and it is this. During the rest of my stay in France, when we were experiencing all the hardships and horrors of the fighting on the Somme, at Arras and in the Ypres Salient, my thoughts were constantly returning to the snug little dugout at Carnoy and the happy days spent with Headquarters' Company as the colonel's cowman.

In early autumn, as the British settled on the Somme, another Allied offensive was launched at Loos. The battle began well but the wider objectives were not met and so after several weeks the campaign was allowed to peter out as the troops settled in for the winter. For men looking after horses, it would be another testing time.

Pte Aubrey Smith, 1/5th London Rgt (London Rifle Brigade)
The authorities had been so convinced that our September 'Push' was going to alter the whole position of the firing line that they

had not taken the first step towards building stables in this quarter. The transports and artillery of some twenty to thirty British Divisions were left, for the most part, without overhead cover or standing for their horses until the second winter of the war had well set in; and then, under pressure, the authorities thought about it and sanctioned building stables.

Lt Reginald Hancock, Veterinary Officer,
61st Howitzer Brigade, RFA

The weather had by now broken. To keep the horses from bogging down on their lines in the open, many batteries started to tie their horses round the bases of the numerous slag heaps round the mines. The clinker-like material made a good solid standing. Unfortunately, due to what we should call mineral deficiency, the majority of the animals started to eat large quantities of this slag. The result was the large bowel became completely occluded by a cement-like mass of clinker, and substantial numbers died from an incurable obstructive colic. Authority decreed that the horses must go back into the boggy fields and live in a foot of liquid, evil-smelling mud, compounded of the rich alluvial soil in the district, dung and urine. The result was enormous festering sores round the heels and fetlocks, and our horses were being evacuated as fast as they could be taken to base hospitals with ulcerated extremities beyond the powers of us poor mudlarks to heal.

The chain of medical treatment given to animals broadly replicated that afforded to soldiers. Initial treatment was given by veterinary officers such as Hancock, serving with a mounted unit or infantry brigade, before further more intensive treatment was offered by the Mobile Veterinary Sections. If required, the horse could then be transferred via the Veterinary Evacuation Hospitals, of which several dozen existed in France and Belgium, to large Stationary Veterinary Hospitals, similar to base hospitals for men. Here as many as two thousand wounded horses or mules could be dealt with at a time. The front-line conditions were such that there was no shortage of patients. If the horses had a difficult time, for those looking after them it was unremitting hell.

Pte Aubrey Smith, 1/5th London Rgt (London Rifle Brigade)

You turn out and wade through this sea [of mud] with rain coming down, and visit your poor horses, who are stuck fast. You undo their head ropes, all soaked with the sloppy mud: the ends are frayed and they flick a stream of mud into your face. After an effort you get the horses out and take them for a short walk, ending up at a stream, where you water them. Then you enter the morass again, where their hoofs splash your mackintosh right up to the neck. You tie them up and get a spray of mud again, put on the nosebags – which are more like wet mud swabs – and receive biffs in the face with them, leaving you with a face and neck of Flanders soil.

After breakfast you do your best to remove some of the mud on your face, but without proper washing arrangements this is a somewhat difficult matter. At nine o'clock it has probably left off raining for the moment and we set forth again to saddle up the horses for exercise. To do this, we first remove the horse rugs, great heavy things which are quite a respectable weight to lift when walking on hard ground, let alone in such a field as this when the rugs themselves are sodden. The tabs and cords trail in the mud: you tread on them and probably drop your load. In stooping to pick it up, your mac and coat have a new mud bath, both inside and out, just to keep them wet and heavy. You get the saddle blanket which, needless to say, is dripping wet from the day before, and the saddle, which is caked with mud, and a pair of nice red rusty bits, and put these on your animals, finally filing out on to the road for a two hours' walk and trot. This is the best part of the day's routine.

Midday 'stables' mean, of course, a continual standing in and trudging through mud and it is such a difficult matter to extri-cate your feet that nearly everybody is suffering from sore heels, for the mud seems to drag the leather off the boots so that a ridge forms about an inch up the heel. You come in at dinnertime in an even bigger mess than before. Some of you have to leave for the trenches with rations and fuel limbers in the afternoon, which will return about ten o'clock at night. If you are luckier you possibly have to go with a limber to a coal dump or the brigade post office: in either case you turn out soon, after a plateful of skilly, to put your harness on. Squelch, squelch, squelch go your socks. It may be raining, but off the horse rugs have to come again; you put them on some turnips – the driest spot. Then you lead your horses up to the limber, tie them up with their sopping head ropes and carry your harness across to them piece by piece. To hook in, you back one horse each side of the limber pole and then, plunging your hands into the deep morass where you think the end of the pole may be, retrieve both pole and pole bar from their submerged resting place, lifting them up with the greatest difficulty. Harnessing up, hooking in, getting the horses' feeds ready to take with you, putting on your leg iron etc, taking anything up to three-quarters of an hour under these conditions. Then you start off and, although the knees of your breeches feel wet and your hands are in a nice old state, you are glad at last to have your feet out of the mire. You probably get back after teatime, in the dark, unharness, water the horses, search for the blankets, tie the horses on the line, give them their nosebags and finally flop into the tent again.

Lt Reginald Hancock, Veterinary Officer, 61st Howitzer Brigade, RFA

The number of units a veterinary officer had to visit varied, but rarely less than fifteen hundred horses came under my care at any given moment. The chief duty was to teach sound stable management. The way a line of horses was tied up could, if the natural habits of horses were not appreciated, lead to a crippling number of wounds or even fractures from kicks. The obvious way to tie up horses in a long line stretched between two wagons or trees seemed to be, on a windy wet night, to put them facing the direction of the wind. But the student of animal behaviour knows that a horse always turns his rump to the wind, for his nasal region cannot bear more than the gentlest breeze, so sensitive it is. It took all my time to inculcate this elementary point into the minds of officers and men. All too often I arrived at a wagon line after a wet night to find a number of casualties, some of which could only be shot forthwith, all because the animals had reversed or attempted to reverse their positions, become entangled in their ropes and with each other, and started kicking matches.

Then there were the horses that went thin and became too weak to work. In nine cases out of ten, observation during feeding hours showed that these were negative characters tied alongside a bully. The dominant animal lay back his ears, showed the whites of his eyes, and so terrorised his nervous companion that he dared not take a mouthful of hay after the hay nets were hung up . . . These things were not taught or to be found in military manuals; few veterinary officers, even, knew them; thousands of unnecessary debility cases were sent down to base hospitals every month from front-line units.

Pte Aubrey Smith, 1/5th London Rgt (London Rifle Brigade)
The wants of man are of secondary importance to those of beast. A driver's primary consideration was his horses, for on those poor dumb brutes fell the heavy burden of the day's work, and they relied faithfully upon their masters giving them drink and oats as soon as possible at the end of their journey. Never in my experience did a transport man – however weary or hungry he might be – defer his horse's meal in order to satisfy his own wants and these were pressing enough at times.

1916

The War in 1916

The introduction of conscription in January 1916 supplied the British Army with guaranteed reinforcements at a level required to prosecute the war with an intensity unimaginable just months before. But as the regular army and Territorial Force had had to await the arrival of Kitchener's Army, so it would be many months before conscripts would arrive in enough numbers to make a difference.

In February, the Germans launched a massive offensive against the French at Verdun. It quickly dissolved into a war of attrition on a hitherto undreamed of scale in which both sides fought themselves to a standstill.

The arrival of British forces on the Somme demonstrated to the French that Britain's commitment to the war was unquestionable. To further cement relations, an agreement had been made to launch a joint Anglo-French offensive in the region in 1916. Preparations were well under way when the Germans attacked at Verdun. The French compulsion to defend the city that was so much a symbol of national pride meant that not only were they forced to reduce their involvement in the proposed battle on the Somme but they appealed to the British to bring forward the start date so as to force the Germans to draw off their reserves from Verdun.

Once again the British complied with French wishes and on 1 July they attacked. The disaster of the first day and the casualties inflicted on the New Army battalions were heinous but it was one

day, and one day only. The British, after drawing breath, resumed
the offensive two days later. The Germans were forced to with-
draw artillery from Verdun and although fighting continued at
Verdun until December, the Germans could not maintain such an
enormous effort on two fronts and so scaled back their campaign
against the French.

On the Somme, the Germans were once again forced to contest
each wood, each village, each sunken lane. Losses on both sides
mounted remorselessly, but it was the Germans who could no
longer afford the cost in both human life and munitions. Britain's
military strength on the Western Front continued to grow while
the enemy's waned. In September 1916 the British Army introduced a new weapon of war, the tank, but while the machine had
the desired effect of shocking the enemy, it was not a weapon that,
on its own, would change the course of the conflict. The British
learnt much from the offensive, but the ability to utilise all available facets of the army and air force in a combined operation was
still some way off.

The Natural World in 1916

The Allied offensives of 1915 had been relatively brief affairs, lasting as little as a day at Aubers Ridge in May to nearly three weeks during the heaviest assault that year, at Loos. They had little in common with the rolling battle that would so besmirch the once picturesque farmland of the Somme, a 138-day battle of almost ceaseless attrition. Shellfire was becoming not only more accurate but far heavier in concentration, and while the land was not obliterated overnight, each new objective was given a thorough pounding by Allied guns. Then, if the position fell after heavy fighting, an almost equally heavy counter-barrage by the enemy churned up the land once again.

The horses and mules on which the war effort depended were driven to the extremes of hardship. In the summer, shellfire and poison gas were but two of their afflictions; broiling heat and raging thirst afflicted horses and mules in a land in which access to fresh water was limited. Both man and beast were reliant on army-constructed pumping stations, pipes, water butts and troughs, for no horse would ever drink water from a shell-hole. Watering the horses and mules could mean a long trek along rutted roads, festooned with shards of metal and discarded nails, any of which could put paid to a horse's life with one false step. And then there was the winter, one of the harshest in living memory, the cloying mud that was typical of the region, the weeks of snow and ice and the shortage of winter stabling and food. The suffering was immense.

In the natural world, many species were seemingly eradicated from the fighting zone as natural habitats were lost. Nevertheless, some animals stayed and adapted to the conditions, and it was with a different sense of awe that men looked upon them, no longer entranced by their simple beauty but rather lost in an admiration for their perseverance in adverse conditions. Diaries and letters from this time seem to agree that some species, particularly birds, appeared more accommodating than normal, living in very close proximity to soldiers, even becoming tactile when hunger and cold drove them to find food and warmth among the men. In response, men came to look upon wildlife as proof that the natural order would one day re-emerge, that the carnage was but a moment in time. For some, the presence of these creatures was more than a help to get through the day; it could help save a man's sanity.

Soldiers' Memories

Only in the spring did the opposing armies, like nature, emerge from an enforced hibernation. The soldiers and their animals had shivered throughout the long, dark days, all desperate for warmer weather. Even though the intensity of the war had increased dramatically towards the end of 1915, soldiers continued to see civilians working close to the opposing trenches, ekeing out a living, unwilling and perhaps unable to leave. Their admiration for those who struggled on was at times as obvious as it was heartfelt.

Lt Harold Hemming, 84th Brigade, RFA

I remember one gallant and very tough old lady who lived in a tiny cottage in a little depression about half a mile behind our front line, halfway up the Vimy Ridge. She used to waddle up and down the long communicating trench that wound its way back almost to Mont-St-Eloi to buy her food. The speciality of this old lady was bee-keeping and the sale of honey.

'You see,' she explained to me, 'no-man's-land is a mass of wild flowers and it is really beautiful. It's so wonderful for my bees, and I am so near no-man's-land that they don't have to fly very far. That is why I have so much honey to sell.' So we all used to buy her honey. Then one day when I went up to buy some more, she was gone and so was her cottage which had been hit by a crump (a German 5.9 shell). But the bees were still there and as busy as ever. I tried to find out what happened to her and whether she was still alive, but nobody knew.

2/Lt Wilfrid Ewart, 1st Scots Guards

Two fields away a peasant is ploughing stolidly, heedless of the shells which now and again scream over his head. The greatest battle in the world's history may be raging a mile and a half away, but that is no reason why he should not finish his spring ploughing. Nearby, a little stream eddies through reeds and water plants, making tinkling music, and its sunny banks are agreeably warm. Skylarks rise and sing not less vigorously, not less merrily than on any quiet morning of an English springtime, though their outpourings are drowned at times in the whirr and buzz of circling aeroplanes.

Signaller Cyril Newman, 1/9th London Rgt (Queen Victoria Rifles)

I have just returned to billets – a barn – from a lonely but enjoyable stroll across fields in the stillness of the evening to the hills above the town from which there spreads a beautiful view of the long valley lined with trees threaded by a large river [the Somme]. Directly below where I was, there were the stone walls of an old windmill and further on, the white-washed houses and barns of the town nestling round its church. I stayed long enough to see all but the spire vanished in a white mist rising from the river. On my way back I came across an old French peasant pulling up turnips and carrots from a field. Women in France do much outdoor work on the farms. Yesterday I saw one ploughing. This peasant was shrunken and wrinkled like most peasant women I have seen. We talked – more than once I had to gasp 'Ne compries' – and I carried her large bundle of vegetables to a house for her. I felt glad at doing a 'good turn'.

2/Lt Robert Vernede, 12th Rifle Brigade

It's a beautiful day, and I'm sitting in the remains of a huge cellar of a farm not far from the front lines. We got here yesterday after being shelled for about half an hour when at the farm. The old farmer's wife and a girl hand spent the time trying to drive their cows into a shed – mostly under shrapnel fire.

I never saw such coolness and stupidity. Of course whenever a shell fell near, the cows scattered, and the women, after a shriek, chased them and got a shell on the other side. Meanwhile the British Army crouched under a wall, sensibly enough. Two cows and a calf were hit, and I expected to see both the women laid out, and shouted in vain to them to leave the cows. They simply would not.

Capt. John Marshall, 468th Field Coy, RE
The Frenchman who farmed the land was either a lunatic or a spy. Two of my men found him pulling up my marking tapes, which were not even on his land. I had him brought to me and told him that if any more tapes were touched, I would shoot him off-hand. The man's actions were strange in many ways. He always ploughed with three horses, a black, a bay and a white. At times he would leave them tethered to a fence but always at the top of a certain field, in full view. I often wondered whether any special arrangements of the three distinctive coloured horses conveyed any information to the enemy.

Capt. D.P. Hirsch VC (post.),
4th Yorkshire Rgt (Green Howards)
I've learnt quite a lot of French. I've also billeted the battalion twice, each time without an interpreter and once with a population that could only be mildly described as hostile, as they had suffered rather heavily from close billeting and slack supervision of hungry and cold troops, a fact that resulted in the disappearance of eggs and chickens, vegetables and bee hives, butter and milk and in the burning of anything wooden up to window frames.

Capt. Charles McKerrow,
RAMC attd. 10th Northumberland Fusiliers
I have just been asked by the mess cook to pass judgement on a fowl for which the price demanded is five francs. It was hard and

old so I told him to tell the farmer it was 'no bong' [no good].
This evidently has enraged the farmer as I can hear him expostu-
lating from afar.

Despite these frictions and suspicions, British troops on the whole
rubbed along well with French civilians. There were grouses on both
sides, of course. Spy mania had swept the army in 1915 with farmers
working near the line coming under suspicion, especially if their prop-
erty remained curiously unscathed by war. On more everyday matters,
Tommies occasionally accused French farmers of removing handles
from water pumps, and most felt the estaminets charged too much for
food. Likewise, there was the feeling among the French that, while the
British liked the idea of 'scrounging', they, the French, preferred to call
it 'stealing'.

Stealing or legitimate scrounging was, perhaps, a matter of opinion.
Yet, when it came to the treatment of animals, the British soldier was
in no doubt. The Frenchman's behaviour was at best odd and at worst
utterly reprehensible, with farm dogs in particular suffering at the
hands of their masters.

Trp. Benjamin Clouting, 4th (Royal Irish) Dragoon Guards

In France, the dog was an integral part of village and farm life
and was not a luxury. Animals earned their keep, those that did
not, or were surplus to requirements, had harsh and usually
short lives. On the Mont des Cats, as with many villages we
came to during the war, it was common to see the local milk-
man going round not with a pony but with a large dog as his
main mode of transport. This dog would plod along, harnessed
into a cart, on the back of which stood the village's milk churn.
When not pulling the milk, the dog worked the butter churn.
To the encouragement of *'vite, vite!'* the dog ran on a wheel like a
treadmill, the motion of which turned the churn over and over,
forming the butter.

2/Lt Andrew Buxton, 3rd Rifle Brigade

I suppose there is no licence fee for keeping dogs, hence every one keeps them, and in many cases two or three, and they are most abominably thoughtless. For the most part dogs are continuously tied up, sometimes in a little kennel, sometimes just to a wall, sometimes to a little round brick place; one such place where we were two nights ago had an entrance at the bottom of a slope in the yard, so that the water ran down into it, and a poor little shivering dog lying in the sodden bottom of it.

It is interesting to note in different parts how the same habits prevail among the people over different things. Here everyone feeds their dogs on diluted-looking milk, with just the suspicion of bread in it, and a few beans.

I found one tied to a wall, a most charming looking fox terrier, but so painfully starved, and with claws quite worn down. I gave it an old box as some shelter, and let it out this afternoon, such terrific joy at getting a run round.

A brute of an old woman in a little house just by has also a nice little fox terrier, tied short to a fairly decent kennel, but so that it has three bits of heavy chain to its collar, and so that it can only just get its head into the entrance of the kennel, and cannot curl itself up, or get to the back. A real terror of a woman, who says she never gives it 'promenade', and feeds it on milk and bread. The poor little dog is frightfully starved.

Yesterday I gave a little terrier here some dry bread, and a tiny bit of meat – all I had – and really too awful to see its intense hunger . . . I may be wrong in thinking they suffer as I do, but it is very wretched to see this treatment on every hand. It puts me off *my* good meals badly!

When Andrew Buxton was killed, in 1917, a fellow officer wrote to Buxton's parents describing how their son was forever arguing with civilians over their treatment of animals. One lady had threatened to throw Buxton out of her home after he objected to the way her dog

was tied up with barely room to turn around. That night Buxton
returned, climbing over a fence and lengthening the dog's chain. He
only narrowly escaped detection.

Sapper Guy Buckeridge, 37th Div., Signal Coy, RE

The farm people had two Great Dane dogs and for two hours each
day they ran round a big wheel which was used for churning. The
dogs were hard and fit and in good condition but surly in temper
like all dogs used for work in Belgium. It used to irritate me to
see ordinary companionable animals used as beasts of burden and
spoiled in temper. The shell dogs were the only friendly ones.
They were always glad of a snack and a game. Their breed was a
mystery to me. Generally they resembled Irish terriers but were
black in colour. They were uncannily efficient and intelligent, very
pally with me, but with their owners always appeared cowered
and browbeaten.

On the whole the French and Belgians were not friendly with
their animals, as we are, and their lives seemed pretty miserable
in consequence. Their cows were always on a rope and tied up to
feed and I never saw a horse out to grass. In consequence they too
seemed miserable in temper and flabby.

2/Lt Stephen Hewitt, Royal Warwickshire Rgt

It is possible to be very miserable in a great city, and it is possible
to be very happy in a single field, literally, for I have only once
been out of a single field this week, except on duty and for meals,
and that once was to a neighbouring town for 'some fun', where I
spent a thoroughly dull evening. You see, we live in little canvas
huts, rather like bathing boxes, two officers to each hut, pitched
along a flowering hedge in a field carpeted with daisies and
already sprinkled with buttercups. On every side of the field are
the tall thin trees with shapes of perfect gracefulness, for which I
believe France is famous; five days ago they were lightly feathered
with a transparent foliage which softened their outlines without

hiding them, today they are already becoming dense and losing their individual shapes under the unfolding green. The huts have many little windows as well as their doors, and can be opened out at the sides: so they are always fresh even in this burning weather, and every morning I wake up after a deep slumber unbroken by watches or orders to turn out at 3.30, with a breeze on my cheek, sunshine in my eyes and the sight of the green trees shimmering, and in my ears the hum of a yellow bee, or the cropping of the old mare who shares the field with us. Never have I felt the spring more: and this is the perfection of the year.

There was 'rest' and then there was 'rest' in the British Army. Out on rest but still close to the lines meant nights of heavy work carrying trench materials and food up to the men in the line or perhaps supplying a party to mend roads. Rest, perhaps twenty miles back from the trenches, meant a complete rest from the dangers of war, although normal duties, route marches and the cleaning of equipment still went on. Consequently it was always a difficult time to leave a camp or village in the back areas and make the slow, winding journey back up to the trenches.

Lt Bernard Adams, 1st Royal Welsh Fusiliers

Farewell to Montagne. All the fellows were dull. Even Sawyer the smiling, who had been prominent with his cheery face in the loading-up, was silent and dull. No life. No spirit. A mournful lot, save for the plum-pudding dog that galloped ahead and on either flank, smelling and pouncing and tossing his mongrel ears in delight. He belonged to one of the men, a gift from a warm-hearted daughter of France . . . It was a fifteen-mile march. At the third halt I gave half an hour for the eating of bread and cheese. Then was the hour of the plum-pudding hound; also appeared a sort of Newfoundland collie, very big in the hindquarters, and very dirty as well as ill-bred. Between them they made rich harvest of crusts and cheese . . .

We marched, two deep now, and I felt most strongly that strange glamour of unreality . . . The rain beads on the red-brown birch trees; the ivy, the oaks; the strange stillness in the thick wood after the gusts of wind and slashes of rain; especially the sounds – chattering jays, invisible peeping birds, the squelching of boots on a wet grass track – everything reminded me of a past world that seemed immeasurably distant, of past winters that had been completely forgotten. Then we emerged into a wide clearing along the edge of the wood, full of stunted gorse and junipers. Long coarse grass grew in tussocks that matted underfoot and now I could see the whole company straggling along in front of me, slipping and sliding about on the wet grass in their curious kilt-like costumes. Everyone was pleased with life. A halt was called at length, and while officers discussed buying shotguns at Amiens, or stalking the wily hare with a revolver, Tommy, I have reason to believe, was planning more effective means of snaring Brer Rabbit. Next day appeared an extract from corps orders re prohibition of poaching and destruction of game. It was all part of the dream that we were surprised, almost shocked, at this unwarranted exhibition of property rights! Not that there was much game about, anyhow.

Capt. Charles McKerrow, RAMC attd.
10th Northumberland Fusiliers

I wish I could describe how the sun rose this morning as I walked the half mile to my Aid Post. Facing me, and some two miles away, were the German lines. Over them brooded, dark and heavy with rain, a mass of cloud. Its upper edge, torn and ragged with the wind, took on a warmer glow. Fanwise across the sky the radiance spread. The eastward face of every little cloudlet warmed to life. The great spaces of windswept void softened from green to blue. Lost in the growing day, the moon and stars faded and were gone. Each twig, each furrow, every half-frozen pool softened in expectancy. Then, like a giant refreshed, the sun leapt into the sky, and in one wild rush of gold and crimson the day arrived. Far overhead three carrion crows flap in deliberate, noiseless flight towards the firing line. Even they, members of the grey tribes who feast on decay, gleam with borrowed glory.

Capt. Lionel Crouch,
1/1st Oxfordshire and Buckinghamshire Light Infantry
The men have made a garden on the side of a communication trench. It is labelled 'Kew Gardens – Do not pinch the flowers'. All our spirits are reviving under the influence of the better weather. The trenches are beautiful and quite like old times. The apple trees and hedges are budding; some of the hedges are quite green . . .

I have started a garden at my company headquarters. Will you please send as soon as possible two packets of candytuft and two packets of nasturtium seeds? My daffodils and hyacinths are topping. I told you about 'Kew Gardens'. The men have now put on the grass two bones labelled, 'Here lieth all that remains of the last man who walked on the L'hawn'.

Such peace was only ever temporary and 'reality' would come back with not so much a bump as a single well-targeted shot, a belt or pannier worth of machine-gun fire or a shattering series of explosions. It was to be expected. This said, a callous, unnecessary act of violence by one's own side was never appreciated.

Pte Albert Conn, 8th Devonshire Rgt
A small bird sang on a stunted tree in Mansell Copse. At the break of dawn we used to listen to it and wonder that amongst so much misery and death a bird could sing. One morning a corporal visiting the fire posts heard the bird singing, and muttering 'What the hell have you got to sing about?' fired and killed it. A couple of the lads told him to fuck off out of it. We missed the bird.

2/Lt Wilfrid Ewart, 1st Scots Guards

Occasionally through the night a terrific explosion causes the
atmosphere to reverberate and everyone to start. It is a Minenwerfer
bomb bursting somewhere away on the right, and it is followed
by a succession of sharp reports and heavy explosions from one
of our own trench guns retaliating. In the silent pauses between
these sounds may be heard the harsh cry of some bird – I know not
its name – which haunts the coarse grass and secret places of the
Salient. Occasionally a distant rattle and a harsh grating sound
becomes audible – the German transport on the roads beyond the
ridge . . . Every now and again, too, in silent pauses, the barking
of dogs may be distinguished – these are the German pets which
they keep in their trenches.

Pte F.J. Field, 15th Warwickshire Rgt

Sunday began in brilliant sunshine. A bright blue sky, visible
from the depths of our trenches, and a lack of gunfire lulled us
into a momentary peace of mind. Our heightened awareness of
spring compelled us to a new appreciation of the yellow charlock
and red poppies that peeped downwards at us where a trench had
been undisturbed. And how we envied the soaring skylarks their
airspace!

Then the enemy bombardment broke loose with the sudden
violence of an earthquake. A tornado of shells of all calibres struck
at us with mad intensity from four till seven in the evening. Those
of us who survived felt like chaff in the wind. We were choked
by dust and acrid fumes and deafened by the inferno of noise. B
Company, in the centre, apart from sentry groups, was shelter-
ing in a deep dugout ready to rush out and man the defences as
soon as the barrage lifted. But all were killed when a heavy shell
penetrated the depths.

*Trench warfare remained the physical manifestation of a static war
and the ground between opposing forces had been named no-man's-land*

goat becomes a unit mascot: this particular animal was born during the desperate fighting in he Ypres Salient when the Germans launched a surprise chlorine gas attack, the first of the war. etween the goat's ears is the cap badge of the Army Veterinary Corps.

S.E & C.R

10.

Stévenard, edit., Boulogne-sur-Mer

A horse is unloaded at Boulogne harbour, August 1914. Many horses suffered severe attacks of fear and anxiety when stowed away in fetid conditions on board ship and a number had to be put down while at sea.

Stévenard edit., Boulogne-sur-Mer

Campagne 1914

24.   *Arrivée de Cavalerie Anglaise à Boulogne-sur-Mer*

English Cavalry arriving in Boulogne-sur-Mer

An unknown cavalry regiment leaves the port and makes its way through the town of Boulogne. Only three weeks after the outbreak of war, the cavalry would be involved in the first skirmishes with the enemy close to the Belgian town of Mons.

The Kitten and the fighting Devils who never war on the defenceless

Le petit chat et les diables batailleurs qui me font jamais la guerre aux êtres sans défence

stray kitten is given a drink by men of an unknown transport unit. The rapid movement of the ar overtook not only farm animals and domestic pets, but also collections of exotic creatures eld privately or in zoos. Many animals simply starved to death, although a small number ended p as unit mascots.

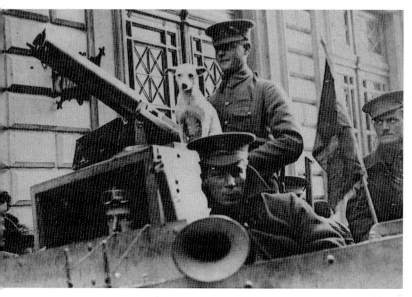

escued from a burnt-out village near Antwerp, this abandoned terrier is taken into care by the oyal Naval Division.

The 9th Lancers attack the enemy: such depictions of battle were largely fanciful. The charge by three regiments of cavalry on 24 August 1914 did not get within several hundred yards of the enemy batteries before being driven off by the weight of enemy shell and machine-gun fire.

Belgian civilians take to the roads with their possessions hurriedly stacked on top of a wagon pulled by a farm bullock. To the amazement of British soldiers, almost any strong animal could be pressed into service: even farmyard dogs pulled small carts or prams.

'Buster', one of the larger battalion mascots. This animal belonged to the 48th battalion (Canadian Scottish).

November 1917: an old campaigner, this baboon had been in continual service as a mascot with his unit since 1914. Note the pipe in its mouth.

The adoption of a unit mascot became almost de rigueur during the war. The vast majority were abandoned animals such as dogs and goats. Nevertheless, a number of units had more exotic creatures, such as these two brought to the front by men of the South African Infantry.

Lost in translation, perhaps: this French postcard refers to mascots as a 'Fétiche britannique', translated crudely as 'A British Fetich' [sic].

915: Jacko, the pet monkey of a signals officer serving with the 6th Sherwood Foresters. This
onkey was taken to France in early 1915 and is seen here serving with the battalion at Kemmel.
1 January 1916 the unit moved to Marseille ahead of an anticipated move to Egypt. While
aying in the city, Jacko suffered frostbite and died.

Two soldiers of the 1/4th Royal Berkshire Regiment help load hay on to a cart near the Somme village of Hebuterne, 1915.

The horse and the mule: the two animals on which the British Army heavily depended for transport.

Men of B Company, 1/2nd London Regiment, billeted at the Mayor farm in Sericourt. In the background they can be seen clearing away the ubiquitous midden. These stinking dung heaps were breeding grounds for thousands of flies and were described in soldiers' letters as utterly nauseating.

'Bees swarming', according to the caption. The picture, taken by Sergeant Bisgood of the 1/2nd London Regiment, shows a soldier collecting bees in what appears to be a large net. When out on rest, many soldiers happily volunteered to help local farmers with tilling the ground or harvesting crops.

In stark contrast to the popular idea of trenches being barren and mucky, this trench on the Somme had flowers and wildlife in abundance in the summer months, and working parties were often sent to cut down grass and weeds to give a clear field of fire.

How to get tastey bits
by means of a shapnel proof
Helmet.

Catching food the hard way: a cartoon drawn by Acting Sergeant Herbert Gibson, RAMC, and sent to his girlfriend in Newcastle upon Tyne. Soldiers were almost always hungry and many were willing to eat even the smallest birds once they were cooked.

The second use of the shrapnel-proof helmet, according to Gibson, was as a suitable container for the laying of eggs. He did not record where the hen came from – purchased, found or scrounged.

Obtaining a variety of food by bombing fish at POTIJZE!

Fishing by hand grenade at Potijze, near Ypres. This possibly unique photograph was taken by an officer of the Rifle Brigade. The explosion stunned the fish, making them easy to collect as they floated to the surface. Bombing a lake quickly deprived it of its fish and the activity was banned, though not stopped, by the army.

Royal Engineers with a shotgun and gun dog pose for the camera in France. Hunting was banned by the French for the duration of the war but the law was often ignored by British troops. Nevertheless, it is highly unusual to see an ordinary rank with a private gun.

Geese being bought at Bailleul market to be fattened up for Christmas, 1916. The strange case of Jimmy and Jane revealed that not every goose purchased ended up on the dinner table.

Dissecting a cow to supply food for troops at the front. Soldiers who were butchers in civilian life were often chosen specifically for their skills.

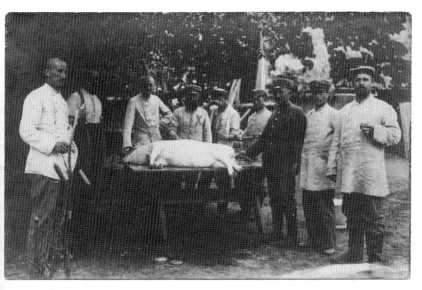

German soldiers pose with a dead pig. At Christmas 1914 a pig was roasted on the Messines Ridge in no-man's-land and shared between men of the 1st Cheshire Regiment and the Württemberg Regiment.

16th June, 1917. No. 148. Vol. 6.

Illustrated

A PICTURE-RECORD *of Events by Land, Sea and Air.* *Edited by* J. A. HAMMERTON

AT THE SIGN OF THE CAT AND WHISTLE.—Many British soldiers take back to the trenches canine and feline friends they have found in village rest billets behind the lines. Mr. Stanley L. Wood here depicts a pleasant "off hour" scene at a dug-out entrance, where the men enjoy a comrade's solo on a tin whistle and the company of their pets.

A depiction of a soldier with cats and a dog in the trenches, as it appeared on the front cover of weekly newspaper *The War Illustrated*. Unlike other over-imaginative depictions of battle, this peaceful scene was closer to reality.

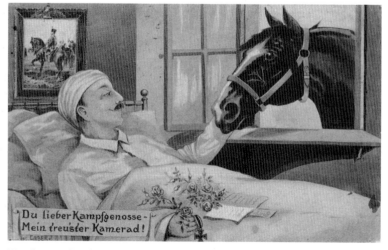

'You dear war friend – my truest comrade!' A somewhat romanticised depiction of a wounded German and his beloved horse. Nevertheless, the bond between a soldier and his horse was frequently intense.

puppy mascot belonging to a tank crew stationed at Rollencourt, June 1917.

lion cub as a pet was highly unusual but not
nique. Brigadier General GTM 'Tom' Bridges
so kept a cub he named 'Poilu' with him at the
ont until finally persuaded to return the animal to
ngland and a private zoo.

A Royal Engineer signaller poses with his
pet fox.

'Somewhere in France' with a pet rabbit.

for a very good reason. Other than going over the top or simply lobbing shells at one another, there was only one route by which to wage war: underground. Highly experienced miners drawn almost straight from the pits at home were brought to the Western Front. Here they conducted an increasingly sophisticated campaign underground, tunnelling their way towards the enemy trenches to lay explosives that were subsequently detonated. It was a highly dangerous occupation, with mining and counter-mining as each side sought to gain an advantage. Fighting could break out underground if two opposing tunnels met, and, as if that were not bad enough, there was always the risk of a natural build-up of lethal levels of poison gas. As at home, men took both mice and birds underground to act as an early warning system.

2/Lt George Eager, Second Army Mines Rescue School

A mouse used in a cage generally crouches motionless in a corner, and apart from the fact that it passes a very small volume of air into and out of its lungs, it is very difficult to say when it is affected by small percentages of gas . . .

The best method of using mice is to have them thoroughly tamed and accustomed to handling. They can be carried in a button-up pocket or little pouch and pulled out in the air to be tested. If a mouse is made to exercise by making it crawl from hand to hand, it takes a great deal more of the tainted air into its lungs, and it will usually collapse more rapidly than a bird sitting on a perch will show symptoms of distress. A mouse used in this way rapidly loses the use of its legs and lies helpless on the palm of the hand.

Lt Frederick Mulqueen, 172nd Tunnelling Coy, RE

Early in mine warfare, it became important to find a means to quickly identify its [carbon monoxide] presence and white mice were used for this purpose. Colonies of them were kept at tunnelling headquarters in the front line and many amusing tales were told of them. The British miner is an inveterate gambler and it was common practice to run pools on the different colonies, i.e. which could produce the greatest progeny within a given time. You have no idea of the amount of interest and discussion this created among the different shifts.

On occasions some of the mice would escape and, while their life expectancy under such circumstances was low due to the large rat population, nevertheless they did find their way into extraordinary places such as the dugout occupied by the colonel commanding the battalion in the line. Whether that officer thought he had had too much war or that the Scotch was more potent than advertised, the record does not say. In any event it was a relatively short time before the mining officer was seized upon as culprit.

If mice were not used, the alternative was to take a cage down with one or more canaries inside. Tunnels were narrow and inspecting officers were often forced to crawl, wearing such protective items as kneepads and gardening gloves. In one hand they carried a torch or candle while between their teeth they suspended a small cage containing a canary. It was not good to be claustrophobic.

Men had been taught to watch out for the first signs of poisoning: typically the bird rubbed its beak on the cage wire or perch followed by a vigorous shake of the head and a bringing up of seed. The second stage saw the bird panting, its body crouching, before the final stage when, after swaying backwards and forwards in an effort to keep its balance, the bird would collapse to the bottom of the cage. By this time the men should have already evacuated the tunnel. That was the theory.

Lt Frederick Mulqueen, 172nd Tunnelling Coy, RE

I remember on one occasion I was making a tour during the night shift and in one heading I found the men working although the canary was flat on its back with its feet in the air. I wanted to know what they meant by continuing to work under such conditions and the sapper in charge expressed the view of the shift when

he said 'That bloody bird ain't got no guts, sir.' Needless to say
the shift was quickly chased out.

Lt Geoffrey Cassels, 175th Tunnelling Coy, RE

One night when I was in Mademoiselle's bar in Armentières,
a signaller arrived with an urgent message for me to return to
Erquinghem. I was drinking gin and Italian and had had a convivial evening. I mounted my motorbike and returned. There I was
told that the Germans had blown in one of our galleries near
Armentières and as I understood rescue apparatus I was to go and
get the men out.

Near the front line I met the men who had attempted rescue
but were overcome by the fumes from the explosion. The MO was
one of them and he whispered to me, being practically speechless,
'carbon monoxide'.

The gallery was about 3 feet high and 2 feet wide. It had duckboards covered by mud and water, leaving only 1 foot 6 inches to
2 feet of headroom and air space. There was a blacksmith's bellows
and tubing available. This was manned and my batman and I
descended, taking turns with the air supply from the tube and
holding our breath in between.

After crawling some considerable distance we came to a junc-
tion and turned right, and there we saw a face of a man almost
completely buried by sand and obviously dead. The second man
lying nearer to us was also dead, by carbon monoxide as he was
rigid and had the telltale pink marks under the armpits and in
soft spots. Before attempting the hard effort of extricating them,
I decided to obtain canaries from Armentières to test the fumes.
Two in a cage were purchased from a barber's shop. He was shaving a customer when a shell fell nearby. Without stopping his
shaving, he waved his razor in the air and exclaimed, 'Ecoutez,
monsieur, encore une bombe.'

We floated the canaries on a board before us. One died and the
other survived. We ourselves still shared the air tube. On reaching

the first man, we found it impossible to move him with one hand; the other was needed to hold the air tube. Rigor mortis had set in and his left foot was stuck fast in the duckboard. Only one of us could work as there was no room to pass each other. For the same reason we could not reach the face man until the first was out of the way. We reluctantly decided that it was no use risking further lives, so we tied the end of the air tube to some casing and left it there to clear the air until the next day when it would be safe and two hands could be used.

On my way out without an air supply I took a breath of foul atmosphere and nearly succumbed. The second canary died. I was assisted out of the shaft but bemused by gas. I had a splitting headache and was nearly deaf but got to the road and mounted my motorbike to drive home. On the way I heard a faint cry of 'Halt' bang in front of me, and then louder and louder, so pulled up sharply, but not before I had run on to a sentry's bayonet levelled at me. Luckily it only cut the skin over my Adam's apple, but had I gone another few inches I would have had it.

I must have presented a sorry sight – dripping wet, covered in mud, no cap, no tunic, unrecognisable as an officer. The sentry would hear none of my tale of woe and I was detained in a guard-room while contact was made with the tunnelling company's CO, Major Danford.

Underground or overground, man's abundant industry entrapped any number of animals and insects by both accident and design. Sumps dug to release water or pits excavated for latrines captured any number of unwary creatures, and even trenches themselves were the recipients of animals that had failed to negotiate a jump across and subsequently had neither the strength nor intelligence to find a way out.

Lt Bernard Adams, 1st Royal Welsh Fusiliers

I take a long mazy journey down the communication trench, which is six feet deep at least, and mostly paved with bricks from a neighbouring brick field. There are an amazing lot of mice about the trenches, and they fall in and can't get out. Most of them get squashed. Frogs too, which make a green and worse mess than the mice. Our CO always stops and throws a frog out if he meets one. Tommy, needless to say, is not so sentimental. These trenches have been built a long time, and grass stalks, dried scabious and plantain stalks grow over the edges, which must make them very invisible from above.

Capt. Archibald McGilchrist, 1/10th King's Liverpool Regt
One curious thing about the Epéhy trenches was that they appeared to have attracted to them all the frogs in France. The battalion had long looked on rats as a necessary evil but frogs were a new experience and nearly as unwelcome. By day they remained hidden in the trench drains and in out-of-the-way corners but at night they swarmed into the fire-bays and communication trenches and became a general nuisance to all who had to walk the duckboards after dark . . . it is as slippery as a banana skin and makes an unpleasant plopping sound if solidly stepped on which is distinctly unmanning. One hypersensitive subaltern when on trench duty always insisted on his runner preceding him at night to clear the frogs from his path. When, one day, he found a frog in his newly completed dugout he gave orders for the floorboards to be lifted and the frog removed . . . When his batman shortly afterwards produced the result of his labours, one hundred and fifty frogs in a sandbag, the subaltern was noticeably shaken and his friend declare that he has never been the same since.

Capt. Alexander Shaw, 1st King's Own Scottish Borderers
On fatigue from 8 a.m. to 2 p.m. digging sumps at side of big communication trench . . . Hundreds of mice, field voles, moles and small deer fall into these trenches and finally get to the sumps where the soil is too wet and slippery, so engineering operations fail. They have no discipline and the galleries get

crowded; the tail of the queue push forward and the workers at the head get forced over and fall 6 or 7 feet to the bottom. If one gets injured in this fall, his fellows immediately set on him and tear him to pieces and fight over the cannibalistic feast in a dreadful orgy of hunger and despair. The moles do better, and where there is a mole he digs a tunnel whereby all escape and are saved. I found a bewildered mole lying at the bottom of a sump in hard chalk. Here all his ingenuity and perseverance failed. I carried him to a pit full of mice and he set to work at once and soon disappeared, followed by all the mice. This mole had wonderful black velvety skin. Mice do not understand the law of gravitation; they dig galleries mostly vertically where an incline would save them.

Signaller Cyril Newman,
1/9th London Rgt (Queen Victoria Rifles)
'Tis a beautiful morning and the air is full of the restless buzzing of aeroplanes. Not only has the sunshine brought out aeroplanes, but also the small inhabitants of the lower world – ants, huge beetles, things with 'umptun' legs and other creepy-crawly insects found in freshly dug earth. I have just been watching a large greenish beetle trying to scale the walls of the trench. On his hind legs he has a pair of spurs, like climbing irons, which he digs into the soil to get a hold. However, either he hasn't learnt how to use them properly or has lived too well and grown fat, for four attempts have failed. He would doubtless have made many more had I not had compassion, spread one of *your* envelopes before him, enticed him on it and thrown him overboard. Now, was not that kind? The ants are too industrious; not content with the trench, they must crawl over me – as if I had notions to spare them! There is a nasty, black, jumping tribe of spiders – I kill any who come near me. I don't like them.

Lt Arthur Terry,
23rd Northumberland Fusiliers (4th Tyneside Scottish)

Being out in the open is a perfect delight – one hears the hum of insect life, the song of birds, and one sees the swallows darting past nearly under your horse's nose and butterflies of all colours and sizes, and now and again a flying beetle comes smack against one's face as it sails along without any steerage way.

These beetles look very funny as they drift along perpendicularly and industriously fluttering their wings as much as to say 'Don't you dare to imagine I'm not as good as any bird at flying for I am' – and all the time they haven't the faintest idea where they are going and blunder on until somebody's face or something else brings them up with a sound turn!

Pte Hugh Quigley, 12th Royal Scots

I have taken a new interest in beetles, especially when wakened at midnight by an inquisitive gentleman exploring my chest. They crawl up and down the walls of the dugout, strange jet-black monsters, shaped to inspire terror in a child's soul. Caterpillars are very constant with their attentions, dear little playfellows escorted by earwigs and huge spiders. Ladybirds preen themselves on your knees and go to sleep in boots; ants delight to scamper up one leg and down the other, get lost sometimes and emerge at your neck in a great state of bewilderment. Greenflies and bluebottles utter dulcet melody all day long, strange buzzers hover on the face and tickle the ears and nostrils. There is a constant interchange of courtesies between grasshoppers on the banks, and crickets rattle lugubriously by the roadside at night . . .

There is something wonderfully picturesque in the life. Two nights ago, while heaving up earth, I saw what resembled a piece of phosphorus lying at my feet. I stooped down and picked it up. When it began to squirm and wriggle over my hand I knew it was a glow-worm, and digging took on interest. Henceforth my concern was to uncover glow-worms not to pile up a parapet.

Apart from their beauty, association makes them precious. I remembered Shelley's lines on the skylark:

'Like a glow-worm golden in a dell of dew.'

The antiquarian imagination raised that humble creature lying quiescent on the ground into the scope of fine imagery and broad-winged thought, touching it to the angel and posing it above the sordid. For the moment I forgot I was in the war, and not in the grasp of romance centred in narrative, alive in fiction.

It has been said that glow-worms, when collected in enough numbers, could produce a low luminous light, just enough to read a trench map, or perhaps to write a letter by. Whether there is any truth in this story is uncertain as no quote from a veteran has, so far, been discovered to substantiate it.

Part of the obvious interest in observing insects or animals was the parallels that could be drawn between their lives and those of human beings. There was the aggressive fight for life described by Captain Shaw, the 'orgy of hunger and despair', but more often the descriptions were either of 'fun' in which creatures appeared to mimic human traits, or a human-like desire to 'pull a fast one'.

2/Lt Charles Douie, 1st Dorsetshire Rgt

I was sitting one morning in my dugout overlooking the orchard when I witnessed a strange little comedy. I was growing drowsy; we had been through a time of great strain. Our trenches had been destroyed by a barrage of great intensity; the Germans had attacked, and there had been heavy fighting with bomb and bayonet in our lines. Now there was a lull. The sun was warm, and a breeze whispered in the shell-riven trees. There was no sound of war but the intermittent thud of a sniper's bullet from the ruins of the château as it struck the earth. I was nearly asleep when my eye was caught by a most unwarlike scene in the entrance to the dugout. A dud shell lay partly embedded in the dry mud. A mouse with his head on one side peered at me, then took refuge behind the shell, reappearing a moment later on the far side. This was repeated several times. Then, emboldened, the mouse departed and brought back a friend. A game ensued, and whenever I blinked the two fell over each other in a ludicrously human way as they sought the security of their strange haven.

Capt. Charles Rose, RFA, 2nd Army

The war horse is an extraordinarily intelligent animal and appreciates anything done for him in the way of comfort. He also becomes very cute and cunning, and always knows the routine of the day, and can tell his time of feeding almost to the minute, and, if allowed, would go by himself automatically to the water troughs and return to his own particular standing in the stable.

One horse familiarly known by the name of 'Shrapnel', owing to several wounds of that kind which refused to close up and completely heal, knew at once when he was 'warned' for the line. Now he disliked going out at nights, and consequently was in the habit of 'scrimp-shanking', and proceeded forthwith to go lame. At first he managed to fool everybody, but on close investigation it was discovered that nothing at all was the matter with him.

Capt. James Dunn, RAMC attd. 2nd Royal Welsh Fusiliers

A draught dog of the village, wounded in both forelegs, hobbled only a step or two at a time. He submitted trustfully to be handled, and looked grateful. Several medical officers and orderlies must have dressed him since he was hit and given him food . . . At 4 o'clock gas shells wakened me, none were near enough to worry about. The dog had gone. Dogs are like a lot of the wounded, think themselves unfit as long as they are made, or allowed, to wear a bandage.

Lt Andrew McCormick, 182nd Labour Coy

One dog, named 'Towser', was most faithful – always accompanying the company when they set out to work in the morning. One day Towser's leg got gashed by barbed wire. The wounded leg was bandaged up by an NCO and to the amazement of all next day he did not go out with the company, but instead accompanied the sick to the hospital!

The human-like understanding that Shrapnel and Towser appeared to have was observed in a number of animals. Dogs and other creatures were often held in the trenches to warn of an imminent raid. Whether it was simply a case of relying on a dog's acute hearing or there was something more prescient about any warning is not entirely clear.

Capt. James Dunn, RAMC attd. 2nd Royal Welsh Fusiliers

A bomb dropped quite near our billets, killed three RFC officers; they had gone out of their cottage and lain down in the garden to look up at the raiders. Those of us who slept near poultry had timely warning of aircraft we could not hear or see; the restlessness of the roosting hens and the loud quacking of the ducks was a sure sign of their coming.

Sapper Albert Martin, 122nd Signal Coy, 41st Div., RE

A black-and-white kitten, about three-quarters grown, lives in our dugout, and forms a centre of common interest. While things are quiet it will run about outside but it will not go far away. It recognises the sound of travelling shells but what is really remarkable is its ability to differentiate between ours and the enemy's. Shells coming from guns behind us make a noise similar to that of Jerry's coming towards us. But this cat can appreciate the difference in direction and also understands that danger comes from one direction only. Batteries of all sizes are around us at distances of two or three hundred yards and they are tolerably active. But puss takes no notice of our guns firing nor of the sing and whistle of our own shells coming towards us from the rear and passing over us towards the enemy; but directly Fritz starts to send any over to us she makes a beeline for the dugout. She doesn't wait for the shell to burst; as soon as she hears its whistle she is off, no matter what she is doing;

she will even leave her dinner and won't come out of the dugout until the shelling is finished although none of the shells may fall dangerously near us. There is something more than instinct in that.

Incidents such as these were benign moments that served only to arouse men's curiosity. Much rarer were those that appeared to be malevolent in nature and far harder to explain. Private Frank Richards, the down-to-earth pre-war regular, saw such an example, the only one of its kind that he witnessed in his entire war.

Pte Frank Richards, 2nd Royal Welsh Fusiliers

During one spell in the line at Hulloch, Dann and I came out of our little dugout, which was about fifteen yards behind the front-line trench, to clean our rifles and bayonets. We were just about to begin when there appeared, on the back of the trench we were in, the largest rat that I ever saw in my life. It was jet-black and was looking intently at Dann, who threw a clod of earth at it but missed, and it didn't even attempt to dodge it. I threw a clod at it, then it sprung out of the way, but not far and began staring at Dann again. This got on Dann's nerves; he threw another clod but missed again, and it never even flinched.

I had my bayonet fixed and made a lunge at it; it sprung out of the way for me all right, but had another intent look at Dann before it disappeared over the top. I would have shot it, for I had a round in the breach, but we were not allowed to fire over the top to the rear of us for fear of hitting men in the support trench; one or two men had been hit in this way by men shooting at rats, and orders were very strict regarding it.

Dann had gone very pale; I asked him if he was ill. He said that he wasn't but the rat had made him feel queer. I burst out laughing. He said: 'It's all right you laughing, but I know my number is up. You saw how that rat never even flinched when I threw at it, and I saw something besides that you didn't see or you wouldn't be laughing at me. Mark my words, when I go West

that rat will be close by.' I told him not to talk so wet and that
we may be a hundred miles from this part of the front in a week's
time. He said: 'That don't matter; if it's two hundred miles off
or a thousand, that rat will still be knocking around when I go
West.' Dann was a very brave and cheery fellow, the same as the
rest of us, and never shirked a dangerous job, but all his former
cheeriness had left him. Old soldiers who knew him well often
asked me what was wrong with him. But I never told them; they
might have chaffed him about it. Neither I nor Dann ever made
any reference about the rat from that day on, and though we two
had passed many hours together shooting rats for sport in those
trenches, especially along at Givenchy by the canal bank, he never
went shooting them again.

*That summer, the preparations for the long-anticipated joint Allied
offensive were well under way. New Divisions fresh out from England, as
well as seasoned men who had seen action, all converged on the Somme. It
was a region suitable not just for a battle but with two rivers, the Somme
and the smaller Ancre, it was perfect for a spot of fishing, too.*

**Lt Philip Gosse,
RAMC attd. 10th Northumberland Fusiliers**
The Division moved steadily south until we reached the chalky
downlands of the Somme, where we camped in an orchard above
the winding river and within sight of the spires of Amiens
Cathedral. It was now high summer, and I had my bivouac placed
beneath a pear tree in a far corner of the orchard. But I was not
lonely there, for a fat black dog appeared from nowhere, and
would sit close beside me, panting heavily and gazing rapturously
up into my face. A flock of geese, not so friendly but not seriously
hostile, cropped the short grass round my bed, and two motherly
cows completed my family.

While we were here I managed to get a day's fishing in the
River Somme. I caught not a fish, but what did that matter? How

better could a long summer's day be spent than alone among tall reeds, watching a red-tipped float, even if it never bobbed?

There were birds in the reed beds; noisy, suspicious reed warblers and chuckling sedge warblers. Dabchicks dived close by, kingfishers hurried up and down the river on urgent business. One, evidently thinking my rod a convenient resting place, perched on it for a while until, unable to keep still any longer, I moved, and the gorgeous bird went off like a flash of blue.

This was one of those rare days of ecstasy whose memory remains but whose charm and mystery are difficult to convey to others.

A/Bombardier Alfred Richardson, 116th Siege Batt., RGA

Captain Walker sent for me, and asked me to take a horse, and Stead as orderly, and go for a long ride up the river to the source, and then come down slowly and notice all the good places for fly and minnow fishing. We set off towards 10 a.m. and travelled about ten miles upstream right to the very source and had lunch in a village near by. On going again down to the river, I saw a lovely heron. I watched the huge bird fly away until it was only a mere speck. I also noticed a beautiful jay, quite a number of stock doves, linnets and finches; of course, there were crows and magpies in abundance. I ventured to get up to a crow's nest and also a stock dove's, but no luck! After spending half an hour after the birds, I commenced my task.

The source of the river was quite a peculiar spot – a small lake with about half a dozen deep holes round the sides through which the water issued out of the ground. In the centre of the pond, I saw at least forty or fifty fine trout lying in the bottom. I made about a dozen sketches of the whole length of the river in sections, marking all the nice trout 'streams', weirs, gravel and stony bottoms etc and all the essentials appertaining to fly fishing. We arrived back at 3 p.m. after a grand day. Captain Walker was delighted with the sketches and greatly complimented me on them.

This morning I got up at 5 a.m. and went in the trap with Mr Walker up the stream and we spent a lovely three hours' fishing with the minnow on a stretch of three miles. We had two good 'runs' just below a small sluice; Captain Walker has up to now caught 47 fine trout – oh! and we are on 'active service'!!

On 24 June a five-day, later to be extended to a seven-day, bombardment of the German trenches began. It was hoped that the enemy's defensive positions, constructed over the previous eighteen months, would be smashed and the Allies could begin to roll up the German line in France. This would be the first great attritional battle that the British Army had been involved in and the fighting would have a profound effect on the battlefield and all the creatures that lived or worked there.

2/Lt Montague Cleeve, 36th Siege Batt., RGA

The guns were dug into an enormously deep bank about 10 feet deep by the side of a field. The digging we had to do to get into that gun position – 10 feet deep and about 40 feet in length – was simply gigantic. We'd camouflaged it extremely well by putting wire netting over it threaded with real grass. We had an awful job to manoeuvre the guns into it, because the caterpillar tracks were useless, they could get them into the neighbourhood of the guns, but then we had to manhandle these enormous monsters – they weighed several tons. We had to push them into their positions. When they were there they were very well concealed, so much so that a French farmer with his cow walked straight into the net and both fell in. We had the most appalling job getting this beastly cow out of the gun position. The man came out all right, but the cow!

Lt Bernard Adams, 1st Royal Welsh Fusiliers

I stood in the open, completely hidden from the enemy, on the reverse slope of the hill . . . Already I could see smoke curling up from the cookers. There was a faint mist still hanging about over the road there, that the strong light would soon dispel. Close to my feet the meadow was full of buttercups and blue veronica, with occasional daisies starring the grass. And below, above, everywhere, it seemed, was the tremulous song of countless larks, rising, growing, swelling, till the air seemed full to breaking point.

Who could desecrate such a perfect June morning? I felt a mad impulse to run up and across into no-man's-land and cry out that such a day was made for lovers; that we were all enmeshed in a mad nightmare, that needed but a bold man's laugh to free us from its clutches! Surely this most exquisite morning could not be the birth of another day of pain? Yet I felt how vain and hopeless was the longing, as I turned at last and saw the first slanting rays of sunlight touch the white sandbags into life.

On 1 July the British bombardment reached its peak and then, just prior to the men going over the top, several mines were blown under the front line.

Pte Harry Baumber, 10th Lincolnshire Rgt (Grimsby)

The mine went up and the trenches simply rocked like a boat; we seemed to be very close to it and looked in awe as great pieces of earth as big as coal wagons were blasted skywards to hurtle and roll and then start to scream back all around us. A great geyser of mud, chalk and flame had risen and subsided before our gaze and man had created it. I vividly recall as the barrage lifted temporarily and there was just the slightest pause in this torment, several skylarks were singing – incredible!

The following episode took place on the Somme, not on 1 July but a number of weeks later. However, this particular description of an attack has, in almost every way, captured the feeling of that first day, and how officers and men passed those last few hours before going over the top.

Lt G.P.A. Fildes, 2nd Coldstream Guards

Growing brighter minute by minute, the day of ordeal stole upon us. Watched from the new trench in which we had already sought refuge, it approached with unparalleled dignity. Before its stealthy advance, the green and amber hues of twilight faded imperceptibly, and over the face of the country brooded a death-like silence, stirred only from time to time by the wakening notes of a lark. Against the glow the village trees turned from black to purple, countless tints of colour tinged the landscape, while over all hung a motionless haze. From one moment to another, the scene unfolded all the colours of Creation. Before our eyes the flush of the eastern sky gave place to an iridescent glow, purple and crimson lit to red and orange. Then, amid the mists, arose a chant of birds: the world was stirring in its sleep. Soon the heavens glowed with reflected light, each fleeting phase surpassing the former in wondrous beauty, and against this background floated a blotch of clouds, diaphanous and burnished on their lower edges by the first rays of the rising sun. The spectacle seemed to contain an omen.

Now slashing the sky with lurid streaks of fire, the sun proclaims its imminent approach. At the sight, a glorious record of such a dawn steals back to one's memory. Here, lighting the way for History, a soldier's sunrise comes to greet us. Each moment intensifies the impression.

At last the skyline merges into a sheet of fire, the horizon grows dim to dazzled eyes. There! riding upon a flood of glory and mantled in majesty, looms a blazing blood-red orb. Hour after hour this fateful vigil dragged on and on. The daylight, climbing aloft in the cloudless heavens, must have drawn the thoughts of many in its wake. Already our ears were assailed by a furious cannonade.

Hour after hour the air shrieked in torment. We who watched and waited in the narrow trench found distraction in the wanderings of beetles and other insects that crawled along the walls and floor of our refuge. Against the side most of us had cut a seat, but even that did not serve entirely to relieve us in our cramped confinement. These hours seemed an eternity.

How can one describe the emotions with which we watched the last five minutes go? For the hundredth time I looked to see – and as I looked, the hour was struck by an uproar of artillery! The moment of 'Zero' had arrived, bringing with it a spontaneous tempest of gunfire. Overhead, the sounds swelled to an unparalleled volume, and the earth around commenced to throb and tremble. Merging into the din, a new note grew audible – the note one remembered so well at Festubert – the death dirge of machine guns.

Before very long, the surrounding turmoil developed into a frenzy. Heavy earthquakes shook us from head to foot; terrible concussions smote the air. Huddling on to our heels and straining our necks upward to watch the grass beside the trench, we realised that the German barrage had opened; and as it poured on to our line, its crashes followed every second, until they blended into a continuous roar. You could only speak to a neighbour by shouting. Gradually, the shocks approaching, and the trench drumming deafeningly to the storm, fear crept into one's heart. Our minds became dazed, dazed like those of the insignificant insects which, shaken down by the vibrations and alarmed at the inexplicable convulsion that had suddenly engulfed their world, now scurried frantically upon the floor.

Amid this inferno, an order reached us to advance.

Chaplain Thomas Tiplady, Army Chaplains' Dept

I cannot get it out of my mind – that kitten in the crater. I had just come up with my men who had been in another part of the line and we entered the communication trench from the village street. After a time we reached a support trench, and looking over the parapet we could see our own front line, no-man's-land, the German trenches, and the village beyond, with the church pointing with unheeded finger to heaven. Then we came to some forsaken dugouts. They had been rendered untenable by the violence of shellfire. The roofs were battered in, and the debris lay scattered about. 'Look,' said my comrade, and I looked. There, in a crater made by a large shell, was a pretty little kitten. If anything speaks of home, it is a kitten. It carries our memory back to the blazing fire and the cat sleeping within the fender. Yet here are thousands of lads who have not been home for months, and here are poor dugouts – the crudest possible imitations of homes – that have been battered in. Day and night these soldiers dream of home. In a trench a man is as much out of place as a kitten in a crater, and as surely will he leave the trench for the fireside. The home will triumph over the trench. The crater belongs to war; the kitten to peace. The one speaks of death; the other of life.

Cpl Hector Munro, 22nd Royal Fusiliers

At the corner of a stricken wood, at a moment when lyddite and shrapnel and machine-gun fire swept and raked and bespattered that devoted spot as though the artillery of an entire Division had suddenly concentrated on it, a wee hen chaffinch flitted wistfully to and fro, amid splintered and falling branches that had never a green bough left on them. The wounded lying there, if any of them noticed the small bird, may well have wondered why anything having wings and no pressing reason for remaining should have chosen to stay in such a place.

There was a battered orchard alongside the stricken wood, and the probable explanation of the bird's presence was that it had a nest of young ones whom it was too scared to feed, too loyal to desert. Later on, a small flock of chaffinches blundered into the wood, which they were doubtless in the habit of using as a highway to their feeding grounds; unlike the solitary hen bird, they made no secret of their desire to get away as fast as their dazed wits would let them. The only other bird I ever saw there was a magpie, flying low over the wreckage of fallen tree limbs; 'one for sorrow', says the old superstition. There was sorrow enough in that wood.

Lt Philip Gosse,
RAMC attd. 10th Northumberland Fusiliers
Those days on the Somme were not in favour of bird-watching. For one thing there were practically no birds in the battle area, and for the other there were more urgent matters to occupy one's time and attention.

But even at shattered Fricourt there was something pleasing. In the vault of what had once been a house a pair of swallows had their nest, and all day long kept flying in and out through a dark opening in the ground. They must have built their nest, laid their eggs and hatched their young during an almost continual hail of shot and shell.

I wondered if in happier pre-war summers this same pair of swallows nested under the eaves of the house which once stood there and if, when it was destroyed, the homing instinct had been so strong that in spite of every inducement to go elsewhere they had nested in the cellar of their old dwelling.

Cpl Hector Munro,
22nd Royal Fusiliers (City of London Rgt)
Unlike the barn owls, the magpies have had their choice of building sites considerably restricted by the ravages of war; the whole avenues of poplars, where they were accustomed to construct their nests, have been blown to bits, leaving nothing but dreary looking rows of shattered and splintered trunks to show where once they stood. Affection for a particular tree has in one case induced a pair of magpies to build their bulky, domed nest in the battered remnants of a poplar of which so little remained standing that the nest looked almost bigger than the tree; the effect rather suggested an archiepiscopal enthronement taking place in the ruined remains of Melrose Abbey . . .

Cpl G.W. Durham, 7th Canadian Infantry Brigade

Recently I saw one of the most extraordinary things I have seen out here. One of our planes went over and spotted a new trench packed with Germans, and the two [French] batteries started in to destroy the trench and its garrison, with the plane doing the observation work. They got on to the target quickly and were blazing away, getting direct hits. The French were firing salvoes under the direction of the Battery Commander, who stood on a barrel. I never saw a man so pleased. They were getting a sweet revenge for a 75 Battery's crew, still lying dead nearby, when over came a huge covey of partridges, about 30, and dazed by the firing, settled about 50 feet in front of the guns. The French officer, who was directing his battery like a cheerleader with shouts and arm waving, held up his hands, *'Tenez. Tenez'* ['Hold it. Hold it'], and sent a sergeant to drive the birds to the left, lest the concussion of the guns should destroy them. I shall never forget his rolling tongue as he shouted what seemed to me like *'le bruit des canons les écraserait'* (literally, 'the noise of the guns would crush them'). They then continued the slaughter of mere men.

Lt Philip Gosse,
RAMC attd. 10th Northumberland Fusiliers

Starlings were always the first civilians to reoccupy shattered strips of Picardy won back by our advancing troops. Whatever they found to attract them I do not know. Had they been carrion feeders it would have been explained, for there were feasts spread out for vultures. But starlings prefer a diet of fruit and insects. Of the first there was of course none; of insects there were flies in plenty as well as other crawling ones, which thrived and multiplied on the clothing of living men. As for animals, these seemed to have all disappeared, even if trapping had been practicable. Nothing could live in that horrible poison-drenched shell-ploughed waste but man, and his chances of survival were but slender. Even the obsequious trench rat had disappeared. But I did get one addition

to my collection in the battle area, which turned out to be a specimen of the very rare subterranean vole, *Pitymys subterraneus*, which
burrows to a depth of four or five feet in the earth. It was picked
up dead in a trench at Contalmaison by a soldier who gave it to
me.

*There were animals, of course. There were the pets and mascots of
German units. As the line progressed yard by yard, these were liberated
from dugouts and bunkers.*

Lt Carrol Whiteside, 7th Border Rgt

On relief, we went back to deep and very fuggy saps in Fricourt
Wood – deep dugouts made by the Hun. When the battle was to
all intents and purposes over, we had a look through the German
brigadier's apartment down below. The place was 60 feet beneath
the surface, down a steep flight of steps all boarded on the walls
and roof and moreover distempered white. There were about eight
fair-sized rooms, including an orderly room and servants' rooms.
The whole place had been left in a terrible hurry and the only live
things left were a cat and a puppy which positively quivered with
terror and started looking round apprehensively on each shell
burst or gunfire. The puppy finally followed us out to billets and
went the unknown way of all other dogs.

*The dead, human or animal, mounted on both sides in such numbers
that during the summer heat the smell of decay became as natural as it
was intolerable. Bluebottles proliferated and over parts of the battlefield a blue hue would descend and rise in an apparently uniform mass.
In dark, fetid dugouts, it was often the maggot that held sway in
nature's job of reducing everything that had lived to mere bone.*

Lt Edward Allfree, 11th Siege Batt., RGA

Just the other side of the sandbags, about two yards from the
entrance to the pillbox, was a dead Boche, lying with his face in

a shell-hole; a few yards down the trench behind us was another, and just in front of us was a dead British Tommy. They never got buried – it was not worth exposing oneself to the enemy to perform the task. Each time I went to the Observation Post I saw them rotting away – getting thinner and thinner – till at last they were actually skeletons in discoloured uniforms. In the meantime great green-bodied bluebottles swarmed over them, and it was only with difficulty that one kept them off one's bully beef or sandwiches, when partaking of lunch. I suppose they rather fancied a change of diet. At night, I think they went to roost in our pillbox.

Lt Lawrence Gameson, 45th Field Ambulance, RAMC

This evening I killed fourteen flies with one swipe with a rolled-up copy of an ancient *Times*. They are infinitely numerous, leisurely and deliberate in movement, and have large sticky feet. The neighbourhood is an incubator for them. Eggs are laid in corpses of Germans and horses, hatching in the rotting semi-liquid flesh. The rest of their lives, for the most part, is an ephemeral gluttonish revel amongst all that is most revolting in this revolting region of putrefaction and decay. They swarm upon food, they buzz. Night and day this room resounds with their buzzing. The drone becomes a background, it even steals into one's sleep.

Driver James Reynolds, 55th Field Coy, RE

We had to go up to the top of a little rise, and strewn up the hill, in rows like corn that had been mown, lay hundreds of our chaps that looked as though they had run into a machine-gun nest. It was a warm muggy day and the poor chaps' faces and exposed flesh were smothered in flies. The smell was awful. They lay so thick we simply could not avoid running over some of them. The horses, of course, stepped over, as a horse, unless absolutely forced to, will not tread on a prone body. But one could not help the wheels going over a few.

Lt James McQueen, Sanitary Officer, 51st Div.

There was a strenuous campaign in the summer time against flies, by the use of wires with an eye at one end which were dipped in a sugary solution and then taken out and deposited at the various cookhouses in the camps. There was a constant circulation of thousands of these wires going on. They were covered with flies when they were brought back, while fresh ones were deposited in their places. The fly-covered wires were burnt clean, and were then ready for redipping. It was a form of fly-paper without the paper.

In this campaign against flies and fly-borne disease, meat safes played a part, because they were given to each camp with instructions that while troops might move on, meat safes might not. Yet so popular were they that it would be more correct to say that in modern warfare battalions marched out of camp not with banners flying but with meat safes concealed, for there was a constant loss of these safes, which had to be replaced as they were stolen by units on the move.

Lt G.P.A. Fildes, 2nd Coldstream Guards

As the myriads of flies had gone to rest, abandoning for the time being the human wreckage in the vicinity, the night was now still. From the fire step of this front-line trench one could see many a grisly tenant of no-man's-land. Yonder, the body of a corporal had lost its feet, eaten away by rats, and beside an upturned pack the moon shone luridly on a skull.

Broken and mangled, dauntless men of the New Army had vainly crossed this intervening stretch of no-man's-land, and also the ground beyond. Rifles, bombs, helmets and packs were still scattered in wild confusion among the dark silent bodies. Clutched in a mortifying hand was a canvas bucket containing Lewis gun magazines: the carrier had been shot in the act of clearing the parapet and lay sprawling in a heap where he had fallen.

The place was a Golgotha, a charnel-house, amidst which, even at this moment, one could hear the sounds of trench rats as they revelled at their ghastly work. Then a step in the trench behind diverted attention. It was Sergeant Gill, of the Lewis guns.

'Good evening, sir. I'm thinking things look pretty quiet tonight.'

'Let's hope they will continue so, sergeant.'

The vast swarthy figure stepped up beside me on the fire step and sniffed the air.

'Strewth!' The involuntary remark was cut short by the sound of a hearty expectoration. 'Them stiffs are horrible, sir!'

A silence fell between us, broken at last by his hoarse whisper.

'There's a deal of harm comes from them poor chaps, sir; one can 'ardly figure the amount. It's a wonder to me we don't all catch a fever. These trenches must be swarming with microbes and bacilluses. A bullet's all right – I've no objection, scientifically speaking, to that sort of thing – but swallowing dead men's germs is 'orrid. Lice are all right, too; but microbes are different.'

'Where have you found out all this, sergeant?'

'Oh, I'm a reading man, see, in a way of speaking.'

Lt James McQueen, Sanitary Officer, 51st Div.

I got a wire to send up four men to assist the Sanitary Section in the spraying of dead bodies over the top of the line . . . It is a brutal business, is war. To spray dead bodies with disinfectants is no assistance in wartime. After lying in positions that it is not safe to go out and bury them, the best that can be hoped for is that nature should not be retarded in its process of bacterial dissolution, and nothing should ever be placed on a dead body to prevent a rat eating it. If it cannot be buried, get it down to the state of bleached bones as soon as possible.

Lt G.P.A. Fildes, 2nd Coldstream Guards

A glance in any direction revealed merely a fresh vista of devastation. Here and there, patches of colour claimed attention by reason of their rarity. On all sides undulated a monotonous expanse, in places relieved only by yellow patches of high explosive.

But it is not by its awful sordidness alone that a visitor remembers Bernafay [Wood]. The mind was assailed to an equal degree by what the wood hid but did not obliterate. Our burial parties had already done their work, but it called for no effort of imagination for one to realise what the tumbled ground contained. Death encumbered the grisly spot: Nature above, slaughtered Man beneath.

Stumbling onward, I presently came to a halt. Nearby, a skinny hand and arm protruding from a mound of mud seemed outstretched in silent pleading, as if dumbly beseeching the prayers of the passer-by. Gazing in meditation on this relic, one beheld an answer given. There, hovering on the grave, lustrous in the golden sunlight, flitted a fellow pilgrim to this shrine of Valour – a snow-white butterfly.

Capt. Charles McKerrow,
RAMC attd. 10th Northumberland Fusiliers

The battle rages, but I have found another Hun Aid Post and dwell undisturbed beneath many tons of chalk. I regard this Aid Post as my very own as I was there first and had to clean it out. The chief amusement was the removal of a very dead Hun in a waterproof sheet. He was of a piebald hue and dropped maggots wherever he was carried. He would insist in sliding out of the sheet, and the scooping of him back was not only difficult but at times impossible. It was not the whole of him at all when we got him outside.

Lt Lawrence Gameson, 45th Field Ambulance, RAMC

On a preliminary investigation in the dim light I could see only his field boots. I had come without my torch. Subsequently, on looking closer, I found that his flesh was moving with maggots. More precisely, I noticed that portions of his uniform were heaving up and down at points where they touched the seething mass below. The smell was pretty awful. None of the men would touch him, although troops as a rule are not noticeably fastidious. The job was unanimously voted to me, because it's supposed, quite wrongly, that doctors don't mind.

I went down the stairway with a length of telephone wire and lashed it round the poor fellow's feet. We hauled him up and dragged him away for some distance. The corpse left behind it a trail of wriggling sightless maggots, which recalled the trail in a paper chase. Having moulded a shell-hole as a grave, we erected a board at the man's head, 'An unknown German Soldier', with date of burial.

Lt G.P.A. Fildes, 2nd Coldstream Guards

The day of our relief had dawned in auspicious fashion, a common knowledge of our impending rest calling forth a general light-heartedness. A company from a battalion of the South Staffordshire Regiment was expected to make its appearance about 2 p.m., so it was arranged that the work of cleaning up should be completed by the men's dinner hour. This was done accordingly, and by 12.30 all was reported correct in the front line.

Scattered in gossiping groups about the fire bays, the men abandoned themselves to their own devices, some arguing over a venerable newspaper, others, pipe in mouth, basking lazily in the sunshine. The air hummed to the sound of flies, and, emerging from their myriad nooks, beetles and other insect life paid homage to the summer's day. To and fro, winging their course around the parapet, flitted elusive butterflies, whose satin wings contrasted brilliantly with the background of sky. Blending with the voices of nature, countless chirrups arose from invisible grasshoppers, who, from their forest glades, now raised their hymn to heaven, thereby humbly endeavouring to rival the melody of a lark high overhead. Rising and falling in an endless torrent of sound, this seemed to pour forth the utterance of a fairy world.

2/Lt Wilfrid Ewart, 1st Scots Guards

For the first time in many months one seems to leave the war behind, and as we march out into the country – a merry, chaffing, laughing column of schoolboys – no stench of motor lorries and petrol or swarms of troops greet us, but only the heavy silence of the woods and fields and villages, dreaming away their midday rest. A yellow cat strolls across the village streets, dogs lie basking outside the unsubstantial looking inns – peculiar looking dogs and very sleepy. Barely can they raise the energy to wag a tail at the flies which everywhere buzz and hum, creating with the drowsy heat an indescribable languor and murmur of summer. We halt in a shady oak wood, and the men, recklessly happy, throw themselves down amid the long grass, the convolvuli, the straying honeysuckle. Yes, we are happy now, we who have suffered much!

Large tracts of the Somme battlefield resembled a moonscape, for without any great elevation it was hard for the ordinary soldiers to glimpse the distant villages and woods that were yet to be targeted in the battle. For those who could remember them, the battles of 1915 were a distant memory, when farm implements, semi-derelict farmhouses and abandoned crops still gave the battlefield an earthly feel. No more. Villages and woods were likely to be identified by a wooden signpost stuck in the ground. Such sights threw the world behind the lines into the starkest relief imaginable.

2/Lt Wilfrid Ewart, 1st Scots Guards

It was almost pitch-dark, and when after a mile or two we emerged, twilight had descended upon the world, and one could barely distinguish the hillside opposite. Here a halt was made, and it was pleasant to rest upon the bank in the cool dusk,

watching the last embers of a gorgeous sunset die out of the
sky. Close at hand, on the edge of the forest, no sound could be
heard but the ceaseless chirruping of grasshoppers and crickets,
the occasional croaking of a bullfrog in some distant pool, and
the whoo-twhoo-whoo-whoo of an owl coming from the depths
of the woods. Not far off was a railway, and the one lone lamp
which stared out of the middle distance and the occasional whistle of an engine only served to emphasise the remoteness and
solitude of the place.

Now it was completely dark, a thousand summery scents rose
from the earth, the sky was bejewelled with stars, low down on
the horizon a golden-coppery harvest moon, not yet at the full,
sailed in the heavens. The night was indescribably contemplative;
many and strange thoughts came to the mind. It is from this, this
pageant of peace and plenty and beauty, that one goes into the
bloody nightmare of battlefields . . . What do the stars say, those
stars so wise, so inscrutable? What do they say to each man who
in such quiet moments asks himself whether, after all, this is not
the end – of a life? Of how many lives? For many must travel the
same road before the trees have lost their leaves . . .

Lt Philip Gosse,
RAMC attd. 10th Northumberland Fusiliers
It was a hot sunny day and on the top of one of the haycocks
I spied a little owl fast asleep. I approached slowly and quietly,
until I stood within a few yards of it, and still the owl slept with
eyes tightly closed, oblivious of its mortal enemy.

For a good ten minutes I stood there watching the slumbering
owl, when at last he woke up, frowned angrily at me for disturb-
ing him, and flew away. Within an hour he was back again on the
same haycock.

It might be wondered how a grown-up man could sit down in
a hayfield and do nothing for a whole hour, but the truth is that
after being in or about the line for several months, one was content

to sit in the sunshine and do nothing at all, beyond admire the flowers and listen to the song of the birds and enjoy the quiet. It was medicine for the mind and solace for the soul.

On such rare occasions and at such a place, it was blessed, after the noise and the alarms, to sit in the sunshine, forget the past and the future, and revel in the present.

Lt James McQueen, Sanitary Officer, 51st Div.

My men lived in tents and bivvies in the field. The life was excellent and living in tents in the summer time is very pleasant, provided you are not billeted next to an ammunition park with restive mules. Mules appeared to me to have a wonderful faculty for breaking loose in the middle of the night and when one is wakened by them charging between your tents, it is not the danger of a mule crashing with your tent that worries one; it is the danger of a mule being tripped by the guy ropes of the tents that gives the sense of insecurity.

2/Lt Wilfrid Ewart, 1st Scots Guards

Already the birds were awaking, and there was that deliciously fresh feeling in the air which comes just before dawn in summer. Already the cool grey light had begun to peep in through the open doors and windows of the barn.

That barn! It was a place of unknown horrors which in due course the glaring midday sunshine revealed. Black beetles were crawling everywhere – black beetles that fell from the wooden partition; black beetles that crawled into and out of and under one's sleeping bag and – yes, over one's prostrate body; black beetles that did company or battalion drill upon the floor under one's very nose.

Rats: for some men the reaction to their presence could be extreme and bordering on the phobic. For others, they were a nuisance that could be disregarded, annoyance at their company reduced by careful protection of uneaten food and by prudent sleeping arrangements. What could not be eliminated was their noise, their scurrying feet and their incessant squealings.

Driver James Reynolds, 55th Field Coy, RE

We were billeted in a dilapidated old farm just outside the village. That first night Jock Frazer woke us all up by throwing his blankets off him and hollering like blazes. When we asked him what was the matter, he told us he was wakened by a rat running over his face and though, as I found out subsequently, he was a brave chap, he could not stick rats at any price. He packed up his kit there and then, right in the middle of the night, and went over to the house where most of the other drivers were and of course his pal went too. That dugout was rather infested with rats though. I've laid down sometimes of a night with just a candle burning to have a read, and on looking up seen as many as ten or a dozen pairs of bright eyes watching me, no doubt waiting for me to put the light out before going on the scavenge.

Lt Leonard Pratt, 1/4th Duke of Wellington's Rgt

I found out last night where a rat starts eating when he finds a corpse. I was just dozing off in my hammock when I felt a sharp pain in the knuckle of my middle finger, right hand. Evidently a rat had mistaken me for a dead man. Two nights ago I found a similar cut on the knuckle of the same finger of the other hand. It is badly swollen now. Why the rats should start there I cannot imagine.

L/Cpl Arthur Cook, 1st Somerset Light Infantry

Where we are is the worst we have struck for rats, there are thousands of 'em. You cannot put a mouthful down but what they won't pinch it. We have to suspend our food in sandbags from the roofs of our dugouts, and wake up in the night, to find them having a swing on the bags, cheeky rascals. We have to cover our faces at night as several men have been bitten, and we only have our greatcoats for cover, we keep our boots and putties on to protect our legs. They crawl over you at night, and we give the thing a biff from under the coat and send him squealing in the air, there is a short silence, then a thump as he reaches the ground, a scuffle, and he is gone. If you walk along the track near the reserve trenches with a torch at night you can kick a rat every two paces.

Lt Richard Talbot Kelly, 52nd Brigade, RFA

One morning, up at the Observation Post, a very large rat came and sat right in the middle of my loophole, completely blocking my view of the enemy lines and obstructing the observation I was supposed to be carrying out. It sat just out of arm's reach and washed. I shouted at it, flicked mud at it, threw pebbles at it and not the slightest heed was taken. Eventually in desperation I fetched my stick and, measuring the distance carefully, was able to give it a very violent jab in the middle. It then moved to one side and continued to wash. But I was determined that next time I went up to the OP I would bring my revolver and deal with it more thoroughly. This I did, shooting it through the throat.

Rifleman Alfred Read,
1/18th London Rgt (London Irish Rifles)

Another night while walking along the duckboard track, another orderly and myself saw two rats just in front. Being only room enough to walk in single file we could not pass, so made a noise to frighten them. They were both about a foot long and too fat to run. This is because they used to feed on our dead, excuse enough for us to detest them. Well, one flopped into the water, but the other became bold, turning round and making a hissing noise. I, being the nearest, had visions of having my throat clawed, so bringing my rifle down, I took aim from about five feet and fired. I hit him fair and square, but the noise brought plenty of chaps (in reserve) running from dugouts wondering what had happened and I was lucky not to get into trouble. After this we always carried a stout stick (cosh) to protect ourselves.

The rat population was barely controlled. Poisons such as Rodine could be sent by friends at home, but there were simply too many rats to kill, and the effectiveness of the poisons was, at times, dubious.

Capt. Charles McKerrow, RAMC attd. 10th Northumberland Fusiliers

The rat poison merely stimulated our domestic rodents till they flew up and down the walls of our dugout like flying squirrels. I found a corpse shortly after the poison was put down and hailed it as my first victim, till one of our servants explained that 'a bash t' b-b-b-wi' a brick'. The exact rendering would pain the censor.

Frank Richards was many miles away from where he had seen an enormous rat staring fixedly at Dann. Since then, the battalion had moved to the Somme and Richards and his close friend were to be found sitting in a wood which had only recently been taken in bitter fighting.

Pte Frank Richards, 2nd Royal Welsh Fusiliers

Just inside [Mametz] Wood, which was a great tangle of broken trees and branches, was a German trench, and all around it our dead and their dead were lying. I was in luck's way: I got two tins of Maconochie's and half a loaf of bread, also two topcoats. The bread was very stale and it was a wonder that rats hadn't got at it. Although gas destroyed large numbers of them, there were always plenty of them left skipping about. I returned to Dann, telling him how lucky I had been, and that we would have a feed. 'Righto,' he replied, 'but I think I'll write out a couple of quick-firers [brief letters] first.'

Enemy shells were now coming over and a lot of spent machine-gun bullets were zipping about. He sat on the back of the trench writing his quick-firers when – zip – and he rolled over, clutching his neck. Then a terrified look came in his face as he pointed one hand behind me. I turned and just behind me on the back of the trench saw the huge black rat that we had seen in Hulloch. It was looking straight past me at Dann. I was paralysed myself for a moment, and without looking at me it turned and disappeared in a shell-hole behind. I turned around and instantly flattened myself on the bottom of the trench, a fraction of a second before a shell burst behind me. I picked myself up amid a shower of dirt and clods and looked at Dann, but he was dead. The spent bullet had sufficient force to penetrate his neck and touch the spinal column. And there by his side, also dead, was the large rat: the explosion of the shell had blown it up and it had dropped by the side of him. I seized hold of its tail and swung it back in the shell-hole it had been blown from. I was getting the creeps. Although Mametz Wood was, I daresay, over fifty miles as the crow flies from Hulloch, I had no doubt in my own mind that it was the same rat that we had seen in the latter place. It was the only weird experience I had during the whole of the war. There was no one near us at the time and men on the right and left of us did not know Dann was killed until I told them. If I hadn't handled that rat and flung it away I should have thought that I had been seeing things.

It was not quite the only 'weird experience' that Frank Richards had. His survival was just as odd. A pre-war regular soldier, he went to France in August 1914 and remained with the battalion for the whole conflict and was never once injured.

Richards had had the dubious privilege of serving under the explosive Commanding Officer Buffalo Bill (Major Clifton Stockwell). There were a number of such officers known for their aggressive personalities, men who could be just as affectionate, even dotty, about a dog or cat, as any other rank. How that affection manifested itself varied immensely from officer to officer.

Pte John Lucy, 2nd Royal Irish Rgt

The major fished his pet from the pocket of his coat – a tiny, mewing kitten. This kitten accompanied him everywhere and was always in a blown-up condition from drinking too much milk. The little animal was a minor nuisance to all except its master, who held up the war in his vicinity whenever the kitten wanted to feed or relieve itself.

He [the major] was transferred from us to another battalion and in a very short time he was shot dead leading an attack. His death was an occasion of outstanding sadness and loss to us all, and those of us who believed in a heavenly host hoped that he had joined the bright company of the angels. We got no news about his little kitten.

Sapper Albert Martin, 122nd Signal Coy, 41st Div., RE

There is no doubt Col. Carey-Barnard is an efficient soldier although he must be a strange sort of man if the tales we hear are true, although these merely give evidence of the military mind. His dog absented itself without leave for a couple of days and on its return he awarded it Field Punishment No 1. It was tied to a tree and fed only on biscuits and water for a prescribed period.

Maj. H.M. Dillon, 1st West Yorkshire Rgt

Our last general has got the push and we now have a hunting, racing, thrusting sort of cove who I rather like – (Bridgeford). If he doesn't get killed, which he probably will as he walks about quite regardless of trifles like shells, he is going to take on a pack of foxhounds as soon as the war is over. He spends most of his time with two terriers going round the trenches catching rats, quite exciting work as you may go down a 40-foot hole on to a dump of bombs, or a trench mortar or something. He has only broken two ribs at this pastime so far.

Maj. Gen. G.T.M. 'Tom' Bridges, CO, 19th (Western) Div.

In the spring of 1916 I got a recruit for the Division. During a short leave, while lunching with Arthur Capel in Paris, I saw something strange in his garden which proved to be a lion cub, won in a Red Cross raffle a few days before. He offered me the beast and I took it away in a champagne hamper in the car to its new home. We called him Poilu . . .

Poilu soon made himself at home, for he was an amiable beast, and never showed temper and he stayed with us, running loose, until September 1917 when I was wounded . . . He was not *persona grata* with the adjutant general, and I had intimations from him that the Commander-in-Chief disapproved and that Poilu should be sent away. But the answer was 'Come and take him' or words to that effect. He helped to amuse the men and the legend grew that he was being trained to go over the top as soon as he was big enough. He was not difficult to feed and it was an aide-de-camp's job to see that he did not go hungry and this officer could be heard sometimes telephoning, 'Anybody got a dead horse this morning? All right, I'll send a car down for a haunch.' . . .

My headquarters were then in dugouts in the Scherpenberg Hill, a prominent point where distinguished visitors could come and actually see shells bursting. Such callers were frequent, and they often dropped in for refreshments. Mr Asquith came one day but his climb to the hill-top was interrupted by meeting Poilu face to face. 'I may be wrong,' he said, 'but did I see a lion in the path?'

Eventually sent home by boat in a crate, Poilu managed to break free and briefly terrified passengers until coaxed into a first-class cabin and locked in. At this time, Tom Bridges was convalescing in hospital after a shell burst seriously damaged his leg. The limb was subsequently amputated and, when informed of the medical necessity, Bridges is reputed to have said, 'Well, I hope they gave it to the lion.' Poilu retired to a private zoo in Maidstone where he died in June 1935, aged nineteen.

A lion was perhaps one of the more unusual pets-turned-mascots during

the war. However, the scarcity or otherwise of an animal was of no signifi-
cance to the esteem with which it was held. Almost no self-respecting unit
would be without one and they ranged from tortoises to goats, from common-
or-garden mules to monkeys. They were all loved and fêted.

Pte William Peto, 2nd Cavalry Supply Column, ASC

Some of the mascots amuse us very much. Some colonial troops
had a large goat with his name 'Buller' and regiment stamped on
a piece of shell case which was fixed between his horns. One of
the infantry regiments had a goat and its kid which was almost
full grown. Some of our chaps secretly used to catch mamma goat
and milk her, keeping her very much out of the way of the farmer
to whom they judged she belonged. Imagine our surprise when,
a few days ago, an infantry regiment came down and claimed her
and gave her kid to our Mechanical Transport Workshop nearby.

Last night I saw a field company coming back from the trenches
with a blue-grey chimpanzee walking under a limber.

Maj. Graham Seton, 33rd Bttn, MGC

Dunny had completed two years in the line. These were years
which had entailed long night drives across wasted fields and
dangerous roads, in bitter wind and driving rain, with no other
light to brighten the journey into the unknown than that of fog-
veiled star shell or the quick-cut flash of bursting cordite: years of
endless toil, with short, so-called rests, when he was picketed in
a long line among his kicking friends, up to the hocks in freezing
mud, or facing a dust storm. What a life! His hide bore traces of
shrapnel and his knees were swollen with stumbling beyond his
fault. But Dunny never grumbled. He just smiled. Every driver
knew his smile, and as he passed carefully down the mule lines,
when he came to Dunny, he twisted his tail affectionately . . . The
whole brigade knew Dunny, and loved him for his smile. He was
indeed our mascot. At times of rest from battle, we made fun of
him and dressed him up in trousers, pulled him along backwards

by his leathery tail, perched an old hat on his head and led him out as the clown of a horse show, or to be mocked by peasant children in the towns behind the battle zone. And Dunny just smiled.

To everyone's utter dejection, Dunny was eventually killed bringing up ammunition during the fighting at Arras the following year. Dunny had survived two years 'in action'. The longer and more exotic the service, the greater the prestige an animal could attain within the unit. Special honours were bestowed upon hiem, to the extent that a mascot became almost the titular head or embodiment of the unit. It sometimes got out of hand.

Rifleman Aubrey Smith,
1/5th London Rgt (London Rifle Brigade)

The companies were going by train or bus the following day, when the horses would make their way down as best as they could. The programme was upset, so far as the LRB were concerned, by the horse Julia breaking loose the next night and eating up practically all the oats that had been left for the other horses. Julia was a decrepit old horse that had served in the regiment in the Boer War as the colonel's mount, and had been brought over to France in 1914 as a mascot: she rarely had a stroke of work to do, but on certain occasions reverted to the position of officer's mount. The sudden disappearance of all the rations meant that the grooms would have to get back to the transport as soon as possible, and as we had already started our second day's trek, there was nothing for it but to trot the chargers for about thirty miles. The hungry one did not experience much difficulty, but Julia, completely blown out and never, in the ordinary way, trotted even for a few yards, had the worst day of her life and almost succumbed at the end of it.

Capt. J.R. Tibbles, RAMC attd. 1st East Kent Rgt

I was told the medical officer's servant wasn't coming up but was staying at the transport to look after Joe, the battalion mascot, Joe being the most important person in the battalion after the Quarter

Master. He had some retriever in him but beyond that he was unplaceable. He was black with a rough coat but his most distinctive feature was his tail which was always erect. He had a tail like a scimitar with the concavity forward. He was a great ratter and a great fighter but he wouldn't tackle a dog much bigger than himself. He had his battle honours on brass plates fixed around his collar – Ypres, Somme, Loos, Givenchy. Oh, he was a great dog. As the brigadier once said, 'If he was any breed at all that you could put a name to, everyone would want a dog like Joe.'

In mid-September, the British launched their new wonder weapon, the tank. A slow, cumbersome vehicle, liable to break down, it nevertheless terrified the enemy when it was first used. To those far-sighted enough to see, the tank would inevitably eclipse the horse in warfare, for, while the horse remained the fastest means by which to exploit a breach in the line, it was terribly vulnerable to machine-gun fire and high explosive. As far as horses were concerned, the tank was yet another new, noisy object at which to get spooked.

Rifleman Aubrey Smith,
1/5th London Rgt (London Rifle Brigade)
On the evening of the 14th [September] it was obvious that we meant business, for on my way back from a water-cart job, coming along the Maricourt road, I heard a clanking, snorting sound and the next instant recognised a tank worming its way slowly along with the upcoming traffic. Every pair of horses that saw it had varying degrees of fright. The road seemed to be a kind of circus. My own pair made a dive for the side of the road and ran among some tents. A little way behind me, Butt – one of our water-cart drivers – somehow or other got thrown from his horse, kicked by a mule and squashed flat by an empty limber which passed over him. He had to be taken to hospital, much to our regret, but fortunately rejoined us a few weeks later.

It was not untypical of horses to become fixated on an object to which their response was out of all proportion to its threat.

Rifleman Aubrey Smith,
1/5th London Rgt (London Rifle Brigade)

I found the grey horse was exceedingly nervous and shied almost at his own shadow. His pet aversion was an ordinary pushbike. He scented these half a mile off in the daytime, then pricked up his ears, dilated his eyes, snorted, and did his best to edge away from them; motorcycles did not seem to trouble him so much. Lorries and motor cars he disliked, broken trees he regarded with suspicion, limbers he accepted with equanimity. But let him catch sight of a milestone and watch the result! I tried to make a mental note of where the milestones were placed, in order to be prepared for any antics that might ensue. Then again: wheelbarrows! If I induced him to proceed past one, it was only done with his head twisting round, regarding it, and then a short trot to put distance between himself and the object when once he had passed. These fads of his kept me on the *qui vive* the whole time, for he would think nothing of shying to either side and attempting to scale the bank, limber and all, if he caught sight of anything unusual.

As the autumn rains set in and the ground became a quagmire, the horses required for transporting supplies to the front line began to break down. The larger the horse, the larger the hoof, and the Somme's alluvial mud had a glutinous pull that made it difficult for horses to lift their feet, let alone pull a wagon. Mules were swapped for horses in the traces but even these became mired in the swamp and so ammunition was taken off wagons and placed across the backs of mules.

Horses and mules suffered sores, galls and infections. For those horses that did not become sick or hopelessly stuck in the mud, there was a multitude of dangers from flying shards of metal, dropped nails and shrapnel balls. One risk that was rare but for which it was impossible to prepare was the effect of artillery shells fitted with time-delayed fuses. These shells burrowed into the earth and destroyed dugouts; they also created a thin crust on the ground and a crater beneath, through which a number of horses fell, dragging them almost certainly to their deaths.

Maj. Neil Fraser-Tytler, D Batt., 149th Brigade, RFA

The rain started a few hours after we had reached the new position, and continued without a break for three days and nights. For twenty-four hours the road was absolutely impassable, being completely blocked with about 80 vehicles stuck in the mud, many with their teams and drivers lying dead beside them, the Hun having shelled the road practically without cessation. In fact, the state of the track after the rain necessitated putting ten horses in a limber carrying only 20 rounds, which a battery can fire off in 60 seconds. Very soon it became impossible to get limbers up at all, and all ammunition had to be carried up on horseback, four rounds on each horse.

Lt Reginald Hancock,
Veterinary Officer, 61st Howitzer Brigade, RFA

Tales got around of men slipping from the duckboard paths in darkness and sinking inch by inch, in some cases to drown in the liquid sea of mud around them. Some of my battery horses suffered thus and either drowned slowly by inches or had to be shot before they did so. Once, when a unit was trying to get out of its wagon lines to get back to refit in rest billets, I was summoned to half a dozen horses just visible above the ground. There was nothing to do but shoot them.

Driver Percival Glock, 1st Div., RFA

Can you imagine being pinned under a horse in thick sticky mud; of course you can't even imagine the mud. I had one of my legs pinned down by a horse and a few shells dropping round about to make it more pleasant. The other fellows tied a rope round me and another round the horse's neck and legs, previously they shot the horse so that it should not kick. There were between thirty and forty men pulling on the ropes and it took them over two hours to get me out of it.

Men went to extraordinary lengths to save the lives of horses and mules, and not just for sentimental reasons. Every horse or mule was expensive to replace, many being imported from North America. The horse under Percival Glock may have been shot, but on another occasion Glock recalled trying for twelve hours to extricate a horse from the mud.

In the effort to save equine lives, the Army Veterinary Corps (AVC) was greatly expanded from a strength of just 519 men in 1914 to around 18,000 on the Western Front by the end of the war. The best indication of the value of a horse or mule is given in prices paid by farmers to purchase them at the end of the war. Horses fetched on average £37, mules £36, equal to the basic wage paid to a private for two years' service at the front.

Lt Reginald Hancock,
Veterinary Officer, 61st Howitzer Brigade, RFA

Foot injuries, due for the most part to nails penetrating the sole of the foot, became a serious cause of loss. Only in the finest weather could one attempt to treat such cases under front-line conditions. If the unit was on the move or the ground muddy and wet, then base hospital was the only hope for the patient. Where did all the nails come from? One day, riding along a road past an infantry field kitchen – a contraption on wheels, rather like a gun limber, with an oven in full blast cooking the rations – I realised at least one major source. The usual fuel consisted of the cases, chopped up, in which the tinned foods reached us. Complete with nails, the wood was fed into the kitchen fires as they went along, the nails dropped out through the grates, and lying on the road, were a constant menace to every passing horse.

Trp. Benjamin Clouting, 4th (Royal Irish) Dragoon Guards

Any wounds or cuts suffered by the horses had to be cleaned with petrol, as water froze on the hair. Injuries were usually leg sores, or wounds to the horse's heel. These injuries were common when the rope which held the horses in the lines became entangled in the animals' fetlocks. The friction of the rope created a gall which was very difficult to heal. Only petrol could be used because it dried quickly and kept the dirt and mud out, although later that winter the veterinary officer gave us petroleum jelly to use instead.

We tried as hard as possible to give the horses shelter, often behind the walls of partially destroyed houses, but they suffered very badly.

Driver R.M. Luther, C Batt., 92nd Brigade, RFA

In this cold and hunger, the horses now developed a new habit – they all started chewing – ropes, leather, or even our tunics. While you were attending to one horse, the other would be chewing at you. So we reverted to chains, a big steel chain for pinioning down, another from the horse's nose band, just like a heavy dog chain. The bags from which they were fed oats and corn had become sodden with rain, and when a harness man was placing this on its head, the horse would swing it up and sideways. Many a driver was hit senseless with such a blow. No man could feed two horses like this, so it was again a case of one man per horse, otherwise the horse not being fed would rear up and plunge in all directions. The horses then turned to chewing at one another, and they soon became hairless, and a pitiful sight. This was war, however, and no Inspector from the Society for the Prevention of Cruelty to Animals came that way.

Chaplain David Railton, 1/19th London Rgt (St Pancras)

I was coming back from a dressing station and I came through the transport lines. I had a flashlight and I turned it on some of the dear horses and patted them. I went on to the next. The light showed a great hole all stopped up with wadding. I thought, 'This is one of the wounded horses.' I went on and the next one had a hole in the head, the next in the legs and body, and so it went on. The flashlight showed up enough to tell me how terribly they had been wounded in taking food up to our men. Indeed, so bad were they that the transport officer said he might lose the lot. But all was silent. Only one was breathing a little heavily, that was all.

Horses and mules always presented artillery with a substantial target out in the open. As crossroads, roads and tracks were targeted by the enemy, it was usually the guile of the transport drivers which gave the limber team a better than even chance of surviving a trip up the line. Even so, when the shells were bursting there was often no choice but to drive the horses on through the shower of steel. Too often the teams were killed and their carcasses dragged to the ditch.

Maj. Neil Fraser-Tytler, D Batt., 149th Brigade, RFA

The first wagon successfully negotiated the 250-yard stretch of mud to our lines. But the second, also empty, despite all the efforts of its team of twelve mules, managed to stick after the first thirty yards, and when anything halts, it begins to sink at once. Much advice from onlookers was wafted across to our lines. At that moment a Hun plane loafed up . . . The area round is littered with observation balloons, and when they are sitting on the ground the Hun loves throwing things at them. The third bomb came near us by mistake and killed the cook and three of the above-mentioned team of mules, or rather two were actually killed and the third lay down and died out of sheer cussedness. The poor cook we laid to rest not far from the scene of his labours, and the mules were decently interred by the simple process of standing on them until they had sunk out of sight in the roadway.

Rifleman Aubrey Smith,
1/5th London Rgt (London Rifle Brigade)

The only incident worthy of record was the death of my late steed, Jack, owing to some internal trouble . . . It took several men a day or so to dig a pit for him and the dragging of his corpse to the burial spot by a blindfolded horse was a ticklish job. Over his grave we erected a wooden board bearing the following epitaph:

> *Here lies a steed, a gallant steed, whose Christian name was Jack.*
> *How oft he lugged our limbers to the firing line and back.*
> *Although he's loath to leave us, he is happy on this score –*
> *He won't be in this — rotten Army any more.*

The next day Colonel Bates and some other officers happened to pass this way and we saw them laughing loud and long over the inscription. I wonder how long it remained there – firewood was at a premium!

Pte David Polley, 189th Machine Gun Coy, MGC

To me, one of the beastliest things of the whole war was the way animals had to suffer. It mattered not to them if the Kaiser ruled the whole world; and yet the poor beasts were dragged into hell to haul rations and gear over shell-swept roads and field paths full of holes to satisfy the needs of their lords and masters. Bah! many a gallant horse or mule who had his entrails torn out by a lump of shell was finer in every way than some of the human creatures he was serving. I believe I might normally be described as a peaceful, easy-going sort of chap, but the sight of a team of horses, hitched to a limber, on a road in the forward areas, screaming with fright at a shell burst in the ditch beside them, turned my mind in such a direction, and instilled a desire to wipe out those responsible for the poor brutes' presence.

The offensive ground to a halt in November, to everyone's relief,
although the sub-zero temperatures made simply holding the front line
that Christmas as uncomfortable as it could possibly be. It was vital to
wrap up in as many layers of clothing as possible, yet at the same time
there was an inescapable itching below that was impossible to reach.
Lice were giving men hell. You could laugh or cry, or both.

Pte Frank Harris, 6th King's Own Yorkshire Light Infantry
Despite the Arctic weather, we discover we are lousy! We crawl,
in fact, head to foot with lice. Bert, I recall, wrote home for
pomade some little time ago but did not suspect I was breeding
too – maybe their variety are more voracious feeders. All we have
had to date has been an odd bath and an odd change of clothes.
We start purging them forthwith – a process we call chatting, but killing each louse is a slow and tedious task. Finger-
and thumbnails very messy too! We resort to candle ends, the
flame of which we run up and down the seams . . . It is said or
rumoured that lice fight amongst themselves, which is rot! They
fraternise in the course of which they breed and once you have
admitted to yourself that you've really got these blood-sucking
pests you get no peace of mind, off comes the tunic, trousers,
pants. Believe me, it's a problem, yet in some ways I consider it
a case of willpower and control. You can have them and endure it
– see how long you can tough it out – once you give up, throw in
the towel, so to speak, admit you're not immune, henceforth you
will know no peace. You succumb; you emulate flea-bitten dogs,
subconsciously scratching until drawing blood. They always get
their man.

> *And so you learnt to hunt for lice*
> *In the lining of your shirt*
> *To crack 'em with your fingers*
> *And watch the bastards spurt.*

Pte Charles Heare, 1/2nd Monmouthshire Rgt

Although the mud is bad and the rain, we get as lousy as ever. One fellow suggests we all take our shirts and trousers off, rub fat salt bacon on them, put them by some water and when the chats go off our clothes for a drink, run away with our clothes. That's one way of getting rid of them but we don't try it.

Lt James McQueen, Sanitary Officer, 51st Div.

In the depth of the winter it would appear that the activity of lice was in no way inhibited, and I can remember seeing soldiers in a battalion in the front line stripped naked to the waists with their kilts laid across their knees hunting for lice in the folds of their kilts. It had become generally accepted that trench fever was propagated by lice; consequently, renewed efforts were made to tackle the problem by the diminishing of that pest.

I went to a conference of Sanitary Section OCs in Péronne . . . [where I] listened for about an hour and a quarter to a whole host of fantastic schemes which seemed to resolve themselves into a great intensive sterilisation of soldiers' clothing by the using of home-made apparatus that would never be worth a tinker's cuss . . . I said that the only thing that could be done was to appoint official ironers, five men per battalion, with a proper allowance of charcoal for the heating of the irons, and that it would be the duty of these ironers to systematically iron the folds of the soldiers' uniforms, and that a dugout be set apart for the purpose and that there could be going on day by day, even in the line itself, a steady killing off of the lice and of the eggs by the application of the hot irons . . . [A] major said that the army would never agree to the withdrawal of five bayonets from the line, and I said, 'Very well then, the army had better make up its mind to the loss of fifty to sixty men per day per battalion with trench fever from lice.' It was purely a matter for the military, and involved nothing more or less than elementary arithmetic.

If nothing else, there was Christmas to look forward to. There was a
strict order, after the widely publicised meetings in 1914, that frater-
nisation with the enemy was forbidden. Nevertheless, Christmas Day
would see a curtailment of offensive action by both sides and a chance
to enjoy a better than normal meal. Vast numbers of parcels were sent
from home with presents of clothing and food. For officers, there was a
chance to stock up on some spirits, with perhaps the odd bottle of vintage
whisky.

Capt. Charles Rose, RFA, 2nd Army

As Christmas approached, active preparations were made to exceed
anything we had ever had before in the way of festivities, and
this was possible now that we were out of action. Quarter Master
Sergeants, puffed out with importance, were to be seen strutting
hither and thither, returning with mysterious sacks and parcels,
presumably filled with good cheer.

Plucked geese and turkeys appeared in large numbers,
suspended from the ceilings of billets, and several large barrels
arrived on the scene and were duly placed under lock and key in
the canteen, awaiting the auspicious day. Much competition took
place between batteries for the possession of the only two live
pigs in the village, which eventually went to the highest bidders,
while the remainder procured their joints in the form of pork from
Doullens. One of the batteries meanwhile grew so attached to its
prospective Christmas fare that it was almost decided to spare his
life and adopt him as a mascot. His fate was sealed, however, when
one day it was discovered that he had disposed of several parcels
of food which had, inadvertently, been placed within his reach by
some of the men.

Capt. Charles McKerrow,
RAMC attd. 10th Northumberland Fusiliers

A very funny thing happened yesterday. One of our transport
mules turned up in the transport lines of another battalion,

covered with mud. It appears that this mule was affected with colic, right up near the line, three days ago. Llewelyn went out from our HQ and gave it a bottle of whisky. With tears in his eyes he returned to the others and said that the mule had drunk the whisky, given a groan (presumably of satisfaction) and died. He described very graphically how its eyes glazed and it shuddered. A burial party was sent out, but, as it was very dark, could not find it. They went out next night and again missed it. Meanwhile, the mule recovered and went home. Probably, being tight, it thought it had better go to some other transport lines. We are all roaring with laughter at the story.

Two days after writing this letter, Charles McKerrow was critically wounded by a shell burst. His great friend Lieutenant Gosse went to see him and neither man was under any illusion as to the severity of the injury. 'It had been the sight of McKerrow skinning a vole for his little daughter in the trenches by Armentières in 1915 that put it into my head to collect small mammals for the British Museum,' recalled Gosse later. 'Whenever McKerrow and I met, which we did as often as we could, we used to talk about animals and birds, and there was no one in the whole division I liked better or admired more.'

Captain McKerrow died on 20 December and was buried the same day.

1917

The War in 1917

Throughout 1917 the Germans fought only a defensive war in the west. It was a considered policy but dictated by necessity. In Germany, economic mismanagement and an Allied blockade caused industry to falter through a lack of raw materials. Civilians, too, were becoming heartily sick of the war as food shortages caused widespread hunger and little good news arrived home from the front. The Allies were also tiring of the war. The unrestricted U-boat campaign was causing shortages in Britain as well, and meat rationing was introduced in April 1917. However, Britain's capacity to wage war was still sound, and troop levels on the Western Front were reaching their zenith.

April 1917 was a significant month. On the 6th, America officially joined the war against Germany, a boost to Allied morale. Three days later an Anglo-French offensive against the enemy met with mixed results. The British attack, as with so many previous offensives, saw initial success but slowly lost momentum as German resistance stiffened. The French offensive was a dismal failure, leading to a mutiny in French ranks and a near-fatal collapse of morale among its forces. For the rest of the year it would be British and Empire troops who would carry the war to the enemy, first at Messines where the Allies had remarkable success in a battle of strictly limited objectives. Then, at the end of July, an offensive was launched at Ypres, but in rapidly deteriorating weather it quickly became bogged down. The scope of this battle was far larger than that at Messines, but such grandiose schemes had so far failed to bring the results expected and once again a monumental battle of attrition ensued, in which losses on both sides were broadly comparable.

The final offensive of the year, in November at Cambrai, saw the British deploy almost five hundred tanks in the initial assault. The Germans were thrown back and church bells pealed in England in celebration. It was somewhat premature. After ten days a German counter-attack threw the British back to their start lines and beyond. The fighting ended, as did the year. It had been the most difficult one of the war for everyone.

The Natural World in 1917

Any notion that the war could be won in one great strike had been scotched for good on the Somme. The high hopes and ideals with which Kitchener's Army had embraced the opening of the battle had suffered their own form of agonising attrition. The war would be won by grit, determination and grim endurance. And with that awareness there was nurtured a dull hatred of those species that made profit out of man's loss, a loathing of all the creatures that made life a misery for men already in torment. The bloated rats and lice, the disgusting maggots and bluebottles, all tugged relentlessly at the soldiers' morale. Rats that stripped the carcasses of man and beast alike; lice that goaded soldiers into a frenzy of bloody scratching; maggots that wormed their way out from the eye sockets of the dead; and the flies that settled in a great blue cloud on any dead flesh – the same flies that also thrived on faeces and food. It was enough to revolt any man. The maggots would have their way, but the flies were exterminated with flypaper or a rolled-up newspaper, lice by the pressure of two thumbs or a candle run up the seam of a shirt, and rats bayoneted, shot, clubbed and kicked. Not that any of these schemes brought anything but the mildest relief, but it gave soldiers enormous satisfaction to get their own back; even enemy gas shells might almost be welcomed if only to see the rats slowly stagger and die, eliminated for at least a few hours.

In contrast to the soldiers' loathing of these creatures came a love and pity for their own animals. Many men marvelled at their own indifference to the suffering of fellow soldiers, but they could not abide the inevitable yet grotesque cruelty meted out to animals press-ganged into service. Despite the work of the Army Veterinary Corps and a number of animal welfare charities working on the Western Front, 1917 was by far the worst year for 'wastage' among both horses and mules. Losses among these animals had been a little over 14 per cent in 1916. This figure jumped to 28.5 per cent in 1917, with the suffering greatest during the fighting at Arras, when unseasonably cold weather continued well into April. As one anonymous officer of the artillery wrote of that battle, 'Horses perished like flies. You could count them nearly by the score on the road – fanciful word! – and the battery to which I was attached lost seventy fine horses from exposure alone, apart altogether from shellfire. One bitter morning, eleven were reported stone-dead in the lines.' It is a sobering statistic that only a quarter of all horses lost in the war died from enemy action. The biggest killer was 'debility', which in the majority of cases meant exposure, exacerbated by hunger and disease. In April alone 'debility' was the prime reason why 20,319 animals were evacuated to veterinary hospitals.

There was little the men could do. For those in close contact with horses, the artillery, the cavalry and Army Service Corps, their responsibility to the animals was not only institutionalised in military law (their animals' needs came before their own), but was forged in the depths of their shared adversity. The death of a horse brought men to their knees, tears coursing down their faces. Theirs was a bond that might be broken but never forgotten.

The terrible unremitting hardship felt by soldiers in 1917 meant that wildlife, when seen, was enjoyed with undiluted delight. Birds in particular gave them great joy, and utterly disproportionate efforts were made by some men to protect nests, eggs and any newborn young from predators such as rats, and from any unnecessary disturbance by fellow soldiers. Only damage inflicted by shellfire was left to chance.

Soldiers' Memories

The winter of 1916–17 was one of the coldest in living memory, frequently touching -20° Centigrade. Almost everyone was exhausted by the interminable bad weather. Wild animals eked out a living from anything they could find, but they too were weak and often became easy pickings for the troops billeted nearby; partridges especially could be too exhausted even to fly. For men brought up in the countryside, like Private Davies and Trooper Clouting, hunting food had never been easier.

Lt Bernard Adams, 1st Royal Welsh Fusiliers

Private Davies appeared with glowing though rather dirty face holding up a large hare, that dripped gore from its mouth into a scrunched-up ball of *Daily Mail* held to its nose like a pocket handkerchief.

'Look here, Dixon,' I said.

'Devil's alive,' exclaimed Dixon. 'Then you've got one. By Jove! Splendid! I say, isn't he a beauty?' And we all went up and examined him. He was a hare of the first order. Tomorrow he should be the chef d'oeuvre in B Company mess at Morlandcourt.

'How did you get him, Davies?'

'Oh! Easy enough, sir. I'll get another if you like. There's a lot of them sitting out in the snow there. I was only about fifty yards off. He don't get much chance with a rifle, sir.' (Here his voice broke into a laugh.) 'It's not what you call much sport for him, sir! I got this too, sir!'

And lo! And behold! A plump partridge.

'Oh! They're as tame as anything, and you can't help getting them in this snow,' he said.

At last the dripping hare was removed from the stage to behind the scenes . . .

'Wonderful fellow, old Davies,' added Dixon. 'In fact, they're all good fellows.'

'He's a shepherd boy,' I said. 'Comes from Blaenau Ffestiniog, a little village right up in the Welsh mountains. I know the place. A few years ago he was a boy looking after sheep out in the hills all day; a wide-eyed Welsh boy, with a sheepdog behind him.'

Trp. Benjamin Clouting, 4th (Royal Irish) Dragoon Guards

Several of us used to go down to the river for a walk, and it was there that we watched a Frenchman catch ducks, with snares made of horse hair. These snares caught the ducks that walked along the embankment, but far more roamed closer to the river, and could easily be picked off with a rifle. There were so many that at times it was possible to dispatch two or even three in a row, if we got down low enough to the ground.

At first we shot ducks close to the river's edge, picking them out of the water at arm's length. However, it was clear that richer pickings would be had if we could get out on to the river itself. By this time the ice was too thin to walk on at the edges, so we improvised a canoe out of three barrels scrounged from a farm. Cutting them in two, we placed three halves in a line and, with two planks along the side to keep everything sturdy, nailed the boat together. A lance corporal sat in the front, and I sat in the back, then with two spades to paddle the craft out into the river, we collected the ducks we had shot, dropping them into the middle compartment.

As we did this, the Military Police turned up and called us in, arresting us as we landed. There had apparently been several casualties from bullets ricocheting off the ice and wounding soldiers. An order banning such actions had been posted, but no one had told us.

Pte Arthur Alexander,
1/14th London Rgt (London Scottish)
Our observation post was in a farmhouse some distance from the front line and we had a shelter just behind it. I helped to build this with sandbags and logs. We kept a fire going continuously and made ourselves as comfortable as was possible under field conditions. The wood we scrounged from round about the farm and even pulled up the floorboards to keep 'the home fires burning'. Corporal King shot a blackbird here and gave it to me. This I plucked and cleaned and then roasted over the fire. Not much of it, but it was tasty nonetheless. Between four of us it only amounted to a taster each, and we wished it had been a chicken.

Lt Andrew McCormick, 182nd Labour Coy
This morning we are again back to wintry conditions. There has been a light shower of snow, followed by a hard white frost. Silver is now the contrasting colour in place of gold and, of course, that spells starvation and misery for the poor birdies. Our bird board is becoming increasingly popular. Birds arrived in the following chronological order –

1. Robins
2. Chaffinches
3. Hedge sparrows
4. Blackbirds
5. Thrushes
6. Yellow yorelings and
7. Bluebonnets.

For some time past I have noticed pheasants making inroads on our all too rapidly disappearing artichokes and green vegetables. I ordered a pea-shooter to be sent to me. It has arrived and little spitfire things which deal out dastardly sudden death to birds have also reached me. This morning, on looking out of the window as I dressed, I noticed three grouse feeding amongst the cabbage and nearer me – almost under the window – a covey of six partridges, driven by stress of weather to risk their lives in close proximity with the homes of men, crept warily along the pathway picking up whatever edibles they could find. Had the pea-shooter been at hand, up it would have gone to my shoulder and one bonnie birdie with blood staining its pretty feathers would have tumbled dead on the frost-bound ground. But the pea-shooter was downstairs – the window could not have been opened without giving warning to them – and moreover I recalled that on the last occasion I killed a bird – a beautiful woodcock – when I saw the blood dripping from its speckled breast I vowed that I would never kill a bird again.

The partridges fed on and then disappeared round the end of the garden hedge and one by one the grouse rose, flew over to the rough park, and then stretching out their wings softly landed – calling as they did so 'Go-way-back-back-back-back'. Little did they dream that they had had a very narrow escape. Had I fired, I might have got a bird and frightened the others away from the vegetables, but then, apart from breaking any vow, I might have defeated the very object I had in view in placing the bird board there – namely to add to the happiness of the birdies by feeding them, and to our, and our friends', delight, in seeing these beautiful creatures – the handiwork of God – constantly enjoying themselves in our view.

Capt. D.P. Hirsch VC (post.), 1/4th Yorkshire Rgt (Green Howards)

The snow seems to change the whole landscape. The old landmarks stand out sharply. You recognise the well-known tree or skeleton of a tree. But otherwise everything is the same. It's very weird and wonderful, this wide and practically unbroken expanse of snow, covering the numberless shell-holes, with hardly a sign of human life visible to the eye.

There are a lot of moles here. I saw a corporal catch one the other day. Then he dropped it and it was out of sight in the hard ground in a moment. They are wonderful wee beasties. I never dreamt they could burrow at such a rate.

The great battles of attrition at Verdun and then on the Somme had severely eroded the fighting capacity of the German forces in the west. The German army had too few men to hold a front line that bulged into enemy territory so, over the autumn and winter, a new defensive position was constructed, known as the Hindenburg Line. This line, characterised by deep belts of barbed wire and concrete bunkers, was felt by the Germans to be impregnable. Then, in late February, they suddenly withdrew to their new strategic position, relinquishing the Somme battlefield to the Allies almost overnight.

The following month a young officer, Lieutenant Fildes, returned to the front. His service on the Somme had ended in sickness and a spell of recuperation in England. Once more he was on the Somme battlefield but this time he was free to look around him and he was stunned by what he saw. The weather had improved, and the deep frost that had covered the land had finally gone.

Lt G.P.A. Fildes, 2nd Coldstream Guards

Setting forth once more, by a route that passed through the heart of the Somme country, we had been gradually confronted by a terrible panorama. From the open door of our goods van, we were able to realise more than ever before the magnitude and fury of the struggle of the previous autumn. In every direction, as far as the horizon stretched, a desert of brown shell-ploughed slopes and hollows, and scattered upon the face of this landscape, clumps of splintered poles, gaunt and blackened by fire, marked the sites of former woods and copses . . .

Such a region as this, exceeding the limit of our vision in every direction, presented a scene surpassing human imagination. It haunted one like a nightmare. Neither of my companions accompanying the draft had served in France before, but, like most people, they had read newspaper accounts of the Western Front. Now, however, they were amazed. Seated beside them in our van, even I was enthralled by the passing spectacle, but it did not prevent me from noting their murmurs of astonishment. Their feelings were hardly to be wondered at, for, though familiar with the Somme, I, too, had not realised until now the degree and extent of its awful ruin. Life – human, animal and vegetable – had been engulfed; not a leaf, hardly a blade of grass, no sound of bird, greeted us; all was done and finished with. Here indeed was the end of the world . . .

Everywhere around us a wild confusion seemed to have upheaved the land, leaving behind it an ocean of rubble heaps. French helmets battered to shapeless lumps, and Lebel rifles red with rust, lay in the stiffened mud, scattered among the countless refuse of the British and German armies. In many craters lay great pools of bright-yellow water, whose stagnant surface disclosed many a rotting corpse. Coils of wire, like bramble thickets, ran in and out of the sun-baked hummocks, fluttering bleached tatters from their barbs. Close at hand, the mangled fragments of a machine gun protruded from a reeking mound, and beside it lay a human skull, picked clean by birds. Everything was encased by a monotone of mud. Here, as we turned from side to side, odours assailed us at every breath, while a profound silence intensified the dreadful melancholy of the scene.

A/Capt. Eric Mockler-Ferryman, 29th Brigade, RFA

The whole country was a series of large crump holes touching one another. Most of the holes were full of slimy green water, and here and there we came upon human skeletons. With the exception of a few salvage parties there was not a soul to be seen. It would be impossible to live in such an uncanny place. It made me wonder if it was worth losing so many lives to gain these expanses of mud and desolation. One felt just as if one had been through a prehistoric country, and expected to see weird birds and animals, mammoths, pterodactyls and the like.

As Lieutenant Fildes reached the furthest extent of the 1916 battle-field, he climbed a low ridge. What he saw was nothing more than he had seen in England or from the train that had brought him up from the Channel ports, but in comparison with what he had just crossed, the sight of nature, or rather normality, undisturbed and seemingly peaceful, was almost unreal.

Lt G.P.A. Fildes, 2nd Coldstream Guards

North and south, the monotony of the ridge merged into an obliterating atmosphere, wherein the devastation, subdued and toned by the sunlit vapour, was not so much in evidence.

But now we had arrived upon the summit. The skyline before us lurched lower at every step; still all that we could see was a wide expanse of blue sky. Then the ground fell away, and the distant landscape confronted us. For an instant the prospect held one spellbound, so thrilling was its revelation, so placid its majesty. At first I was only conscious of the exclamations of those nearby, for even the attention of the men was centred on what lay ahead. Stretching for miles, bounded by the far horizon north and south, a glorious vision rose to greet us, a riotous pageant of shimmering colour. The low ridges opposite blazed under a mantle of sunlit grass, and scattered upon them, trees, flecked with vivid shoots, spread forth a lacework of slender boughs. Wheeling in a multitudinous swirl in the middle distance, a flock of crows flapped slowly on its way, while at the foot of our slope, a group of mottled roofs was half concealed by branches. Behind all these, displaying a widespread carpet of unblemished pasture land, glowing in the full radiance of the sun, the country undulated into the distance, luxuriant with verdure, scattered spinneys, and a patchwork of fields, and revealing at every point the freshest tints of an awakening world.

Greedily we feasted our unbelieving eyes, scanning the far perspective of the land until baffled by the distant haze. So suddenly had it appeared that it seemed at first only a mocking mirage. But no – still it lay there inviting contemplation. There lay spring in all her vastness and all her splendour.

On 9 April, the Allies launched their spring offensive close to the town of Arras. 1917 was to be the year when, on one front or another, the Allies slowly ground down the enemy's will to fight. The battle opened just as the weather turned. Winter was back with a vengeance.

Capt. James Dunn, RAMC attd. 2nd Royal Welsh Fusiliers
7 April

I sat on a tree stump in the peaceful park of a big white château, with the sun just looking over the tree tops, and a few small deer grazing, and some blackbirds and thrushes singing from the purple undergrowth. Nothing was there to remind me of the war except the enormous thudding of the guns 12 miles away. We had been told that we should move into our final concentration area tomorrow – Easter Sunday! Sitting there alone I felt happy, contented and confident. And the men, I thought, have seemed cheery, and almost elated, the last day or two. But they were always at their best when they knew they were 'for it'. There was a chance of a 'Blighty one' for them, anyhow.

The air turned chilly, and the sun was a glint of scarlet beyond the strip of woodland. And away on the horizon that infernal banging continued . . . 'The sausage machine', I think we used to call it.

Sgt Rupert Whiteman,
10th Royal Fusiliers (City of London Rgt)

Breakfast was ready to be drawn from the cookers by 3.30 having been brought en masse to platoons. Here was another hopeless business trying to distribute boiled bacon to every man by the

light of a miserable guttering candle, with hands stiff with cold
and the wretched candle being blown out by the chill wind every
few minutes.

Hot tea made everyone feel twice the man he was before, and
by the time breakfast was finished, dawn was breaking – a very
cheerless sort of dawn, however. What a strange feeling there
seemed to be in the air that morning, a lull before a terrible
storm, for it wanted just one hour before the opening barrage –
the 4.50 'Zero'.

It was inexplicable, this nervous tension; even the horses and
birds seemed to be imbued with the knowledge that hell was to
be let loose before very long. There seemed to be a strange hush
hanging over every living thing, man, bird and beast . . .

It was perhaps 4 o'clock [in the afternoon] and the sun sinking
low when we received the order to open out into artillery forma-
tion, and to advance over the ridge. On the true summit of the
slope at last! But where was that inferno of crumping shells and
smoke indicating the firing line? It was certainly far from being
obvious. The ridge turned out to be a plateau some 400 yards
across and beyond that a gentle downward slope. The country was
open in front, undulating, and covered with long grass – yes, real
grass and some real live trees here and there. Very few shell-holes
seemed to be visible.

Where on earth were the troops supposed to be in front of us?
Not a living soul was to be seen, not a single shell burst.

Directly in front and ¾ mile away could be seen a line of strongly
constructed trenches and just this side and running parallel with
them, a roadway with a line of trees on each side. This trench
system, we soon learnt, was the 'Brown Line', into which we were
to stroll, reassemble, and from there start our part of the business.
It did not look like a battlefield but more like a piece of peaceful
countryside. Here and there a hare could be seen coursing through
the grass, evidently wondering what had brought such a host of
Cook's tourists to that region.

We wondered just as much as the wretched hares. 'What is happening?' everyone asked his neighbour. Two miles off, over the undulating grassy country and beyond the Brown Line, could be seen a village crowning the summit of a circular hill, with its red-roofed cottages peeping out from amongst the green foliage of trees, altogether a very picturesque view. This village was Monchy – our objective.

These pleasant scenes would rapidly alter as artillery from both sides set to work. It was close to the village of Monchy-le-Preux that one of the last cavalry charges was made on 11 April. Whereas tanks could withstand machine-gun and rifle fire, horses were no match for entrenched artillery and infantry.

A/Capt. Douglas Cuddeford, 12th Highland Light Infantry

An excited shout was raised that our cavalry were coming up! Sure enough, away behind us, moving quickly in extended order down the slope of Orange Hill, were line upon line of mounted men covering the whole extent of the hillside as far as we could see. It was a thrilling moment for us infantrymen, who had never dreamt that we should live to see a real cavalry charge, which was evidently what was intended. In their advance, the lines of horsemen passed over us rapidly, although from our holes in the ground it was rather a 'worm's eye' view we got of the splendid spectacle of so many mounted men in action. It may have been a fine sight, but it was a wicked waste of men and horses, for the enemy immediately opened on them a hurricane of every kind of missile he had. If the cavalry advanced over us at the trot or canter, they came back at a gallop, including numbers of dismounted men and riderless horses, and – most fatal mistake of all – they bunched behind Monchy in a big mass, into which the Boche continued to put high-explosive shrapnel, whizzbangs and a hail of bullets, until the horsemen dispersed and finally melted away back over the hillside from where they came.

'Sammy', the mascot of the 1/4th Northumberland Fusiliers. This dog went with the regiment to France in April 1915 and was wounded and gassed during the Battle of Ypres the following month. The dog always accompanied the battalion into the trenches and was buried by shellfire on several occasions. He later served on the Somme.

German soldiers pose for a picture after a successful rat hunt in the trenches. Both sides enjoyed killing as many rats as they could, often using dogs, ferrets or burning cordite to force rats to bolt from their holes. The rats pictured are rather small compared with many.

Canadian troops chase and attempt to club rats in Ploegsteert Wood. This was as much a pleasant pastime for soldiers as it was an attempt to curtail the rat population.

His prowess with a rifle confirmed, this German soldier stands proudly over his kill, which includes three hares, a pigeon and several pheasants.

Men of the 19th Reserve Division, May 1916. The stag's head has almost certainly been removed from the walls of a French house and transported to the line.

A pigeon released in good weather conditions was a useful and quick aid to communication with headquarters. However, not all men knew how to handle pigeons properly, and in wet weather or fog the birds could refuse to fly, become lost or be shot by the enemy.

A group of soldiers from different regiments pose with their pigeons and pigeon baskets.

A messenger dog with a tube attached to its neck in which to carry reports back to headquarters. Airedales were found to be among the most reliable dogs but a variety of breeds was used on the Western Front.

Wounded horses arriving at the veterinary hospital at Neufchatel. The ambulance had been bought and presented to the Army Veterinary Corps by the Royal Society for the Prevention of Cruelty to Animals (RSPCA), one of several civilian organisations deeply concerned with the welfare of animals during the war.

A more primitive method of transporting an injured horse for treatment. The 'side-saddle' seating arrangement for the driver is very unusual.

A German soldier searches his clothing for lice while relaxing well behind the front lines. Lice infestation in clothing caused the victim almost unbearable itching.

'Nobby having a short chat' reads the caption. 'Chatting', or searching for lice, was an almost universal occupation, for few soldiers found a cure for the dreaded pest.

FIGHTING FLEAS (?) IN FLANDERS

4TH DIVISION

FLIGHT OF FLEAS FROM FLANDERS

WITH BEST WISHES.

Xmas 1914.

For fleas read lice; it was to attempt the eradication of these pests that the men are having a bath while their clothes are steamed in a boiler. Most men found that within hours of retrieving their clothes the itching began again.

Men of the Queen's Regiment with a dog captured from the Germans during the fighting around Ypres in October 1917. Note the men on the right carrying pigeon baskets.

A private named in the original caption as Jock Manuel retrieves a magpie from a German machine-gun position captured during the fighting around the Somme town of Peronne in September 1918.

A poignant picture of a soldier playing with a kitten in the snow, December 1917. Many cats and dogs were born in the trenches and knew no other life. Others turned feral and crossed no-man's-land to opposing lines in search of food.

The handwritten caption on the drawing reads:

a Cat & the family in the Trenches

The only inhabitants of a ruined farm near the front line

(The cat had evidently been hit by a shell fragment for one of its paws was missing.)

One of the strays left behind, as drawn by Herbert Gibson of the RAMC. The caption states that the cat 'had evidently been hit by a shell fragment for one of its paws was missing'.

An abandoned dog in the German-held village of Irles. Such dogs attached themselves to passing battalions in a desperate search for food and affection. Others were aggressive and unpredictable and were shot.

Two rather unkempt canaries, tame or exhausted enough to accept a temporary perch on the end of this officer's cigar. The same officer appears in the picture below, holding the cage.

Canaries abandoned in the French village of Neulette. Many such creatures were rescued or released to fend for themselves by retiring British soldiers when other units were engaged in the intensive operation to halt the German offensive of 1918.

Two horses lying dead on the battlefield. The horse on the right is rapidly swelling but reasonably intact, albeit with its forelegs blown off. The other has taken a direct hit and its entrails are exposed.

A mule rescued from a slow and squalid death in a shell hole. Another is still stuck fast while a third is already dead. Over a quarter of a million mules and horses died on the Western Front.

Eingefangenes herrenloses Vieh.

German soldiers taking away abandoned cattle. As the war continued there was a sharp reduction in the quality and quantity of their food supplies from home, and fresh meat was bought or simply taken from civilians in France and Belgium.

British soldiers taking a moment to milk an abandoned cow near the French town of Meteran. During the Allied retreat such opportunities were crucial in giving men the energy to keep moving.

Thousands of men owned dogs at the end of the war, but military-imposed transport restrictions and the financial cost meant that most were unable to bring their animals back to Britain. A few men sought to smuggle home a beloved pet but not many managed to evade the rules.

1920: home and happy, a Machine Gun Corps mascot wears the cap of his master.

Following the Armistice, a horse looks at the rusting hulk of a tank. After thousands of years, the invention of the armoured vehicle signalled the beginning of the end for the horse on the battlefield.

The Wounded Chum.

A CASE FOR THE BLUE CROSS.

"JUMBO."

The Property of Lieut. E. H. Rouse Boughton, XV. King's Hussars.

Throughout the war, organisations such as the Blue Cross fought valiantly on behalf of wounded animals at the front. After the war it continued its work saving exhausted animals that had been sold to farmers and returning them to peaceful retirement in Britain.

Jumbo: 'doing my bit in aid of the Red Cross Fund'. This mascot, belonging to an officer in the 15th King's Hussars, with his cap and cape was an obvious attraction to the public.

'Ragtime' wearing his master's medals. This horse served throughout the Great War and finally returned to England in 1924, where he regularly paraded in York to raise money for less fortunate animals.

They left a number of dead and wounded men among us, but the horses seemed to have suffered most, and for a while we put bullets into poor brutes that were aimlessly limping about on three legs, or else careering about madly in their agony, like one I saw that had the whole of its muzzle blown away. With the dead and wounded horses lying about in the snow, the scene resembled an old-fashioned battle picture. Why it had been thought fit to send in cavalry at that juncture, against a strongly reinforced enemy who even then were holding up our infantry advance, we never knew. Cavalry may still have their uses in some kinds of warfare, but for a large force of mounted men to attempt an attack on the enemy positions that day was sheer madness.

Sgt Rupert Whiteman,
10th Royal Fusiliers (City of London Rgt)

Who were those mounted men riding up the slope to Monchy from the Arras side? They were only occasionally visible but there seemed to be a lot of them, several hundreds at least. Soon the glorious truth dawned on us, they were the cavalry!

The very word sent a thrill through one. We were about to witness one of the most thrilling episodes of the war, to watch them ride through the village, down the slope on the other side, across the valley and then in amongst the advancing Germans yonder in the dip with sword and lance. Another disappointment: we saw them enter the village but they were soon lost to sight amongst the houses. Expectantly we waited for them to reappear on the other side; waited five minutes, then ten, but no, not a sign of them.

Hideous thought! They must have halted in the village!! Of all places on the Western Front in which to halt cavalry, Monchy should have been the last. The village was developing into an inferno more and more every quarter of an hour, for the Germans were concentrating all their artillery there in the hope of being able to recapture it.

All their artillery, I said, but that was not strictly correct for *we* were getting a fair share along the sunken road. We soon began to see evidence of casualties amongst the cavalry. Those poor old horses, they commenced to come out of the village in all directions, riderless, reins flying in the wind, manes and tails stiff with terror, some limping and wounded, others galloping, down the slopes from the village to the north, the south, east and west.

Lt Col. Cecil Lyne, 119th Brigade, RFA

The difficulties of writing are great, however I'll have a try. The actual fighting has eased off a bit just now, but we are still pushing forward and feeling our way to the next German defensive line, weather has hindered us beyond belief. The hardship of open-air life these days is trying, to say the least. I am wearing more garments than I have done the whole of the winter, the horses need a bit of extra care, especially those who have come from stables and warm standings. There are many hundreds of dead horses along the roadside, mostly due to the criminal folly of clipping them.

This morning I started with ammunition at 10 a.m. to go 3 miles. I have just returned at 6 p.m. A giant tractor with a 6-inch gun had stuck in the middle of a gangway. An Army Service wagon had tried to pass it, slipped off the track and became embedded up to the wheel tops; further on another lorry had got mixed up with a water cart while in various places pack animals mired to the neck were being dug out (in many cases a bullet was the only thing), ceaseless rain, cold winds – one has ceased to hope for anything better. As I said before, there are times when one's sins rise up against us. One of these times is when by feats of endurance you have extricated a wagon in front of you from a morass, your own leading wagon steps off the track, and into a shell-hole from which all the King's horses and all the King's men are powerless to move it.

Capt. James Dunn, RAMC attd. 2nd Royal Welsh Fusiliers

The side road was packed with the coming and going of units, detachments and oddments of men – wounded and unwounded, guns and vehicles of all sorts. Adding to the density of the throng was the cavalry, all over the place: again brought upon the scene by hope disdaining experience . . .

There were dead and dying horses by the roadside. The severity of the winter, short rations and the exertions of concentration, had told on the transport animals. Division, housed in huts in a sandpit off the road, directed me to Blairville. All its transport was there, and the surface had been churned into a lake of mud . . . A robin, a yellowhammer and, I think, a woodlark made an odd little group on the roadside, sitting on a snow-sprinkled heap of sweepings. There was not a twig or a spar for them to perch on. With heads sunk in their shoulders, they looked in utter dejection on the busy road and the devastation around them. The Germans have razed everything that stood or grew on the strip of country from which they retired.

Pte Sydney Fuller, 8th Suffolk Rgt

Quiet with more snow. A robin perched on our dugout chimney and allowed us to touch him – he did not appear to be at all afraid of human beings. Perhaps he had shell shock, or it may have been that he was loath to leave the warmth of our chimney.

Perhaps it was just a case of familiarity; perhaps, in adversity when hunger is the main concern, even the birds found a way to dispense with their normal reserve. Either way, many birds appeared not to mind the close proximity of soldiers. Such a response was very gratifying to men who sought out any opportunity to repay such trust.

Pte Charles Raven, Manchester Rgt

The colonel announced that we had to return to the line. We had had two days in rest and the march up was not a happy one.

Indeed, a more irritable battalion could hardly have been found
– tramping back from the peace of the hinterland, past the wreck
that once had been Arras, over the tail of that accursed ridge, and
on, when darkness came, into a poisonous row of Boche dugouts,
verminous within and shell-visited without . . . And then in the
morning the miracle happened.

Headquarters was in an old signallers' station, and its entrance
was festooned with German wires and decorated with insulators.
On one of these, a pair of swallows was building. Those birds were
angels in disguise. It is a truism that one touch of nature makes
the whole world kin: those blessed birds brought instant relief to
the nerves and tempers of the mess. They were utterly fearless,
flying in and out among the sandbags, making the nest ready for
its treasures. Personally I was fascinated with observing the feathers that they brought for its lining – nearly all kestrel's and grey
partridge's: my companions staked large sums on the date of the
first egg's arrival: we all regarded the pair with devoted affection.

Never was a nest so protected. Elaborate rules were composed
and placarded for its welfare. The nest was on no account to be
touched, or, except once daily, inspected. For inspection, a trench
periscope or shaving mirror was to be used, and the result, since
money would change hands over it, was to be officially verified.
No one was to wear a tin hat near the nest, and strangers were
to be warned by the gas guard of its position. When the battalion was relieved, the nest and the rules regarding it were to be
handed over as trench stores, with a special request that details of
its progress should be fully chronicled and reported . . .

When the Boche celebrated Whit Sunday by an extra dose of
'morning hate', our chief anxiety was lest a stray fragment might
'casualty' the birds. No one could be downhearted when the early
stand-to was terminated by the carolling of the cock, and we
rushed back to see whether the hen had laid overnight. Blessed
birds, they were an allegory of the part which nature can play for
her eldest children when their birthright of toil presses heavily.

And for me at least they revived ancient joys and heralded many hours of rest and stored refreshment.

Capt. James Dunn, RAMC attd. 2nd Royal Welsh Fusiliers
In the wasted area the swallows, missing their ancestral eaves and rafters, set to building in our lean-tos. A pair has nearly finished a nest in the small run-up tin hut that houses HQ. Two strands of wire belonging to our predecessors' mess bell support the nest. To let the bell be taken away, we cut 18 inches out of the circuit, after fixing the wires to the frame of the hut securely with screws. These beautiful creatures, with such plain faces, are most interesting to watch at close quarters. They made themselves quite at home among us, went on building, and accepted help in adding daubs of clay.

Pte Hugh Quigley, 12th Royal Scots
There are some contrasts war produces which art would esteem hackneyed or inherently false. In a corner of the roof, a swallow had built its nest before we entered into possession. At that time there were no doors nor windows to prevent ingress and egress, so that it was quite natural for the mother to choose this site. It had the main charm of being sheltered from the weather. Now, as the result of our efforts, only a small square hole lay open. Yet, from early in the morning until dark the mother whizzed through to the corner, hovered at the entrance for a second, and then darted across to the nest. Quite a beautiful incident! Then the young ones left and sprawled along a narrow cornice, each to receive his share. All the while a great confusion of chirruping and cheeping. Her labour finished, the mother disappeared with a graceful swoop into the open. The delightful thing about it all was the trust placed by the birds in our kindliness, and we never disappointed them. The picture rung of home, had a tang of the domestic that rendered it sacred, as sacred as a porcelain Madonna in a wayside shrine.

Pte Thomas Williams, 19th King's Liverpool Rgt

The pleasant glow of warm sunshine after months of winter gloom gave one a queer, restless feeling. There we were, burrowing like human moles in the mud while the ring doves were mating in the woods and the hawthorn buds would soon be showing green. The utter folly of this terrible killing game was never more strikingly apparent . . .

There was a sweet freshness in the air which one often associates with the first day of spring. Partridges were calling from the grime-covered grass in front of our wire and the notes of a thrush came floating across from a wood behind the German trenches.

Presently a faint rustling noise could be heard out in front. The dead thistle stems swayed to and fro and the long grasses quivered. Something was moving, but at first it was impossible to make out what it was. Soon, however, the rustling became louder. Flashes of white showed up every few seconds. It seemed as though a small dog was leaping about in the tangle of rank herbage. I remember thinking that it might be a fox terrier. On the Somme one had come over to us from the German trenches. What else could it be? At length the rustling noise ceased and I became aware of two sharp eyes looking out from the forest of grasses. The mystery creature was a stoat, an exceptionally large specimen in snow-white winter dress. He had evidently been attracted by the rats and was performing a good service in lessening their numbers.

While I stood watching the strange spectacle of a white stoat hunting trench rats, a magpie arrived on the scene. Perched on one of the barbed wire stakes, the bird commenced to scold while the stoat chattered back angrily. So engrossed was I in this little drama of the wild that for a short space of time I had almost forgotten about the war! However, the sharp crack of a rifle shot came to break the spell. The magpie flew off and the stoat vanished on his quest for more rats.

The shot had been fired from the enemy's lines. Several more followed in quick succession. Overhead a flock of grey geese were winging their way northwards. They appeared to be well out of range, but the marksman was blazing away in the forlorn hope of bringing one down.

In one way, birds offered men in the trenches something that no other animal could: a link with home that was more precious than anything else to a soldier. While dogs, cats and stoats were land-locked, birds were free to leave the battle zone at any time; they were at the war but not of the war. This link with home was never more tangible than in spring when soldiers watched migrating birds, speculating as to their ultimate destination: Britain perhaps, and a moment's rest on a garden gate or chimney pot in London, Leeds or Glasgow. Other men's thoughts were perhaps less focused and a little more ethereal. Birds to them meant freedom and freedom also meant home.

Pte Thomas Williams, 19th King's Liverpool Rgt

Following the geese came a couple of lapwings and then about half a dozen more. It was the call of spring. In a few hours' time those same lapwings might be wheeling over English fields. I watched them go by in scattered pairs, small parties and larger flocks. All were journeying in the same direction. My thoughts went with them to the level fens of East Anglia and the North Country mosses that I knew so well.

I was still watching the lapwing flocks passing overhead when the relieving sentry appeared. It seemed scarcely possible that the two hours could have slipped by so quickly. Back once more in the dugout, I dozed off to sleep. My dreams were of English fields, horses at work ploughing and the spring cries of the peewits . . .

Lt Henry Lawson, 10th Manchester Rgt

My second choice was the next watch from dawn to breakfast. My reason? To be in solitude in the glow of the early morning sun when I could watch the wildlife in no-man's-land. I saw and heard larks, partridges, pied and yellow wagtails, occasionally quail and once a pair of kestrels hopelessly confused by the anti-aircraft shells bursting around them. Those were hours of happiness as though the whole realm of nature was mine. Closing my eyes, I might entrance myself into the belief that I was still at home in Surrey fields on a golden May morning.

Pte Charles Raven, Manchester Rgt
Birds haunted my dreams. Sleep meant for me a visit to one of the bird-crowded islets that my mother had pictured in my nursery days. From the restless horror and hideousness of the war zone I could slip away to the imagined wonder of wave-washed rocks and the clamour of sea fowl and the eggs lying bare upon the ledges or bowered amid sea pink and campion: I knew them in those days as I know my home.

Pte Thomas Williams, 19th King's Liverpool Rgt
A sniper's bullet hit the wire just in front of our post. The whine of the ricochet had scarcely died away before another sound was heard, a sound which one would least expect in such a situation. It was the song of a bird.

Starting at first with a subdued chattering, the voice soon became wonderfully sweet and loud. If I had any doubts as to the identity of the singer they were quickly dispelled when a breath-catching torrent of pure, liquid notes were poured forth. I could scarcely believe my own ears, but there was no mistaking that passionate burst of music. It was the nightingale's inimitable crescendo.

Modern students of bird psychology tell us that the nightingale's song is one of joy, not of melancholy sorrow as the poets would have us believe. This may be so, but few nature lovers, however practical in their studies, could fail to have been impressed with the sweet sadness of that lovely music rising and falling over the war debris of no-man's-land. One could not have wished to hear a more fitting requiem for those who had made the Supreme Sacrifice on this gruesome, moonlit battlefield.

Standing alone with the stars glittering overhead, the beautiful verses of Keats and Matthew Arnold came to my mind. But my thoughts did not linger over the poets' vision of pain and death. Like the skylark's carol, Philomela's voice filled me with a great joy and hope. Some day the war would end, and, if God willed, I might be left alive. I might be spared to hear once more the nightingale's song, not amongst crumbling ruins and water-filled shell-holes, but far away from the thunder of the guns, in Hampshire woods and in Surrey lanes.

During the nights that followed I listened intently for the lovely contralto bird voice. Each night the song sounded sweeter and louder as the rifle or machine-gun fire grew in intensity. Just as a stone thrown into the reeds will start a sedge warbler singing, so the whine of the spent bullets on our wire seemed to incite the nightingale. The more active the snipers, the more vehement became the notes from the hidden bird.

With the obvious exception of rats and perhaps mice, no other wild creature is mentioned more in soldiers' memoirs or diaries than birds. Not only their singing but merely their presence acted as a balm for men bereft of affection and contact with loved ones back home. And birds offered something spiritual too, not necessarily religious, more intangible, perhaps, but understood by many who were there.

The ability to soar above all the filth and blood on a battlefield was something any four-legged animal might have envied, stuck as so many of them were between opposing forces or tethered to a limber or gun. Aggressive, feral dogs and cats in no-man's-land reminded soldiers only of their own unalterable predicament.

Pte Harry Patch, 7th Duke of Cornwall's Light Infantry

You looked out into no-man's-land between the firing points, and all you could see was a couple of stray dogs looking for something to eat to keep alive. I thought, 'Oh well, I don't know, there they are out there, two stray animals, and if they found a biscuit to eat they would start a fight over who should have a bite. Well, what are we doing that's really different? We're fighting for our lives, just the same.'

Capt. John Marshall, 468th Field Coy, RE

The woods were infested with packs of dogs from the destroyed towns and villages. They had run quite wild, but picked up a good living from the bones thrown away by soldiers. These packs contained the most curious assortment of the canine species that one could imagine: pugs, Pomeranians, Dalmatians and dachshunds, nearly all long-haired and bushy tailed, looking most extraordinary, when running in a pack in search of food.

Pte William Golightly, 1st Northumberland Fusiliers

We had a forward post in front of our trench with the Lewis gun on it. We had managed to camouflage it pretty well and the Germans hadn't spotted it. I remember looking out one night through a little hole and I saw a pair of eyes looking back at me. God almighty! Do you know what it was? It was a bloody cat. It scared the living daylights out of me. There were domestic cats, lost or abandoned and left to run wild, and they survived by eating off the dead, fighting with the rats for food.

Throughout the war, each side attempted to dominate by frequently raiding opposing trenches or by aggressively patrolling no-man's-land at night. At the same time, as part and parcel of protecting the trenches, listening patrols were at work while working parties mended the barbed wire in front of the trenches; on all of these occasions it was critical that near-silence was maintained so as not to alert the enemy. However, working in silence naturally magnified all other sounds, sounds that brought a man on patrol out in a cold sweat.

Pte Thomas Williams, 19th King's Liverpool Rgt

It was exceedingly dark when the patrol ventured out. We heard them scramble through our wire and then, without the slightest warning, a perfect hubbub of loud, wild calls broke the stillness of the night. Flares were sent up from the German trenches; a machine gun started to cackle and soon the bullets were coming from all directions. When the firing had died down the party made a decidedly hurried return! They tumbled back into the trench excited and breathless as though the devil himself had been after them. The sudden and unexpected medley of calls had sounded almost unearthly in the pitch-black silence of the night.

When safely back under cover, every member of the patrol laughed heartily, especially when they realised what had been the cause of the disturbance. In crossing a swampy patch of ground they had nearly trodden on a party of wild duck! It is, of course, a well-known fact that flighting duck will descend to almost any splash of water at night-time and this habit probably accounted for their presence in front of our wire.

2/Lt John Gamble, 14th Durham Light Infantry

For a day or two, a large black dog had appeared occasionally, running about on the German parapet and behind the lines. It was only when he was able to escape the vigilance of the Boche in the trenches, evidently, that he managed to take these little trips, as he was invariably hauled in by unseen hands, or unheard coaxings. He was quite safe, however, as we never fired at him, and it was novel to see a dog running about amongst that inferno.

Well, on Tuesday night, I was out between the lines with an NCO, a grenadier, and another man, reconnoitring the ground . . . when the NCO touched my arm to get my attention, and silently pointed in a half-right direction. There we distinctly saw someone moving. We were of course quite prepared for meeting an enemy patrol similar to ourselves, and were fully armed to the teeth. The movements were under a broken-down tree near the German line, and we could clearly see black-looking figures running about. Everything was very dark and quiet, and a flare light had not been sent up for some time. We waited and waited, on high tension, but still they did not approach us, and I was just wondering whether we ought to stalk them, when up went a brilliant flare, lighting up the whole surroundings. We kept absolutely flat and still, but with a gentle, imperceptible movement I raised my head, and saw that black dog, calmly examining something which had probably been thrown out of the German trench – possibly meat or other wasted food, as he appeared to be in an eating attitude.

When I got back, and related the experience to the other officers over a cup of hot cocoa, we simply screamed, and the following morning when the animal appeared on the parapet for a few moments, he was greeted by laughter from everyone who knew about it.

Pte Robert Renwick, 16th King's Royal Rifle Corps

I had a mate called Jim Morris from Macclesfield. About half a dozen of us were sent out on a reconnoitring patrol to try and get a prisoner, and we met a very heavy German patrol. Jim said, 'I'll give out such a yell they'll think there's a battalion coming.' He did, and the Germans scattered, but we collared one prisoner and a dog. I suppose the dog was meant to smell our scent and warn of our approach. When we got back into the line, the bombing officer was on duty and he said, 'Halt! Who goes there?' And Jimmy shouts, 'King's Royal Rifle patrol, a prisoner and one dog, sir.' We adopted the dog. Once Jerry's mascot, now it was ours.

It was not beyond the wit of most men to muse about how man, so predominant a species in the world, did not dare to stick his head above the parapet while animals had the right to pass freely from one side of no-man's-land to the other, as happy to be friends with the Germans as the British. Such thoughts no doubt occurred to German soldiers too, and perhaps with this in mind a dog was used to offer a peace that, sadly, no one could take up. Private Voigt recalled hearing the men

*comment about the incident, revealing a surprising sense of kinship
with the enemy.*

Pte Frederick Voigt, Labour Corps

I reckon Fritz is a bloody good sport. We ought ter shake 'ands 'an
make peace now. Peace at any price, that's what I say . . . I tell yer
a thing what 'appened when I was in the line. We 'ad a little dog
wi' us an' one night she must a strayed inter Fritz's trenches. The
next mornin' she came back wi' a card tied round 'er neck an' on
the card it ad: 'To our comrades in misfortune What about Peace?'
I reckon that was a jolly decent thing ter say. Jerry wants ter get
'ome to 'is missis an' kiddies just as much as what we do!

Pte Christopher Massie, 76th Brigade, RAMC

The war dog is subject to every other condition of war except
discipline. So he is not a soldier. He is always deserting from one
regiment and joining another; hiding himself among the French
or Belgian civilians. He has been known to go over the top with
the first wave of our infantry and return again – a prisoner – among
the German prisoners, laughing mightily as though this was one
of the best jokes in the world. The war dog is a gypsy, a vagabond,
a loveable scoundrel, affectionate when he is hungry, disdainful
when he is full, a born thief, an artful rogue, a prodigal who is
always sure to turn up at the killing of the fatted calf.

*Massie did not have a pet. Some dogs remained utterly faithful to their
owners, and the feeling was mutual. For men on both sides of the line
who were fortunate enough to have the full affection of their pet, the
bond was total.*

Lt Andrew McCormick, 182nd Labour Coy

When we were at Quéant I noticed a strange wolf-like dog with a
coat of yellowish tinge. It always stood at a spot near to which had
been a Boche hospital. It seemed to be wearing its heart out looking

for its master. I coaxed and cajoled it on many occasions, but it was averse to eating anything until I had gone away from the food. I had made progress, however, for on one occasion it took cheese from my hand. It was touching to see that dog daily returning to the same spot and looking longingly for its master – loyal and devoted to its own yet intractable and regardless of the stranger. I had determined to try to find out what was on the collar of this one I saw at Quéant with the patient, devoted look in its eyes, but the exigencies of war gave us another hurried move forwards and I often wonder how the faithful wolfhound solved its problem; and hope that it met with good treatment for its constancy to its old masters.

Maj. Neil Fraser-Tytler, D Batt., 149th Brigade, RFA

Soon after we were back in action, fate dealt us a cruel blow. My Irish pointer, which had joined us a month previously, was reclaimed by one who declared himself to be the rightful owner, so off went Mehal-Shahal-Hash-Baz, which was his name for short, meaning in Hebrew 'rending and destruction', and right well did he earn his name if ever he was left in a dugout alone!

A rumour which I did not contradict got round the battery that I was prepared to give a large sum for the dog if returned to me on our march away from here, at a safe distance from Henin Hill, so the many professional and unprofessional dog stealers in the battery set to work to effect his recovery from his home about half a mile to our flank. By day, however, the dog was carefully guarded, and at night kept securely tied up in a dugout in a trench. The plans tried were many and various. Individuals carrying telephones and pretending they were signallers looking for an imaginary battery at night asked the guard of the dog for directions, while another gang came up from the wagon line and with Red Indian stealth tried to stalk the sentry and get into the dugout unobserved. Others again started sapping up a disused trench hoping to tunnel into the trench, and it was only our move out of the locality that brought to an end these pious efforts.

Lt Andrew McCormick, 182nd Labour Coy

I was sitting in the mess one night when one of my corporals flung a puppy inside the door, remarking in the most casual sort of way – 'a souvenir for you, sir', and before I could even thank him the door had closed. It was a dear wee Manchester terrier, black with brown points. It certainly brought brightness and liveliness into the mess. It was chameleon-like in its movements. It captivated everybody about the place – but still it was my dog – and my dog I was determined it would be. One day about a fortnight after it had thus been gifted to me, I was walking along a road when a lorry drew up. An NCO hopped down, saluted, and as he said, 'Excuse me, sir, but you've got my dog', he picked it up. I observed the dog struggling to get away. I said, 'How long have you lost the dog?' He said, 'About a fortnight, sir.' I said, 'We've just had it a fortnight and we're very fond of it', and he said, 'And I'm fond of it too, sir.' I thought, well, I'll see whether you are or not – and so I said, 'Would ten francs be any use to you?' He said, 'I'll be glad to let you have it for that, sir.' And gladly I paid him the filthy lucre, for I thought that anybody who could part with that dog for 7/6 [seven shillings and sixpence] should never have the privilege of keeping a dog.

Like all soldiers' dogs 'Teddie' was made a great deal of, but she repaid it all many times over. She fed as and when she pleased, and even made free with my bed – although she knew that my batman banned sleeping on my bed. Often when I came in late, as I turned on my flashlight I would see where the wee doggie had been snugly lying and would just catch a glimpse of her hind legs disappearing into her own box. She loved to sit on my shoulders, and one day an old French woman, seeing her sitting there thus, addressed me: 'Ah, M'sieur, bonne piccaninnie!'

We dubbed the doggie 'Teddie' because she loved to dance round on her hind legs when 'Are you there little Teddy Bear?' was played on the gramophone. Bell, my batman, took a great pride in Teddie. He used to try to undo all the bad habits I taught her. Being a soldier's pet dog, I just felt that she did so much to cheer me I could scarcely do enough for her in repayment. Chocolate at 5/- [five shillings] a packet was entirely consumed by Teddie, and when the magic word 'choco' was uttered she just danced with delight. Bell was firmer with her – at any rate where the bedclothes were concerned. When he caught her on the bed he would look angry and say, 'I'll warm you, my lady', but I'm sure he never had it in his heart to hit her. He used always to say, 'If we have to part with that dog, sir, I'll shoot her first. It wouldn't be fair to leave that dog behind.'

Lt Reginald Dixon, 251st Siege Batt., RGA

Soldiers love animals and will make pets of any strays they find. After the Vimy Ridge battle, the battery I was serving with at that time found in the battered village of Thélus a small mongrel dog that had had its front paw shot away by a shell splinter. The brigade MO had treated it, the wound had healed, and the MO had actually made and fitted a little artificial wooden leg for the little beast. We named him Thélus, because that was where he was found, and he became the battery pet, running around among the guns as if the business of war was his natural milieu.

It was not only French farmers who used dogs in a working capacity. Dogs worked on an official basis in the army, running messages from the front line back to headquarters. Senior commanders had had to be convinced that dogs were capable of carrying messages in battlefield conditions, and after extensive trials in 1916 Airedales were found to be among the most reliable. However, despite this evidence, a large number of varieties were used in France and Belgium with varying degrees of success, although, as a rule, dogs with darker coats were chosen as they blended in better with the surroundings. Each dog was given a name such as Rab, Nipper, Ray and Surefoot, with notes including the name of the handler and the battalion to which they were attached. Records were also kept as to what happened to the dogs. Rab, an Airedale and Ray, a whippet, were killed in service, Surefoot, a collie, was destroyed for 'being useless', while Nipper, an Irish terrier/ Airedale cross, survived the war.

Rifleman Alfred Read, 1/18th London Rgt. (Irish Rifles)

My first job was to take a dog up the line. The idea was to train this one (and others) to bring back messages. Anyhow, they were a complete failure, because whenever a shell came over they would dash into the nearest dugout and sit whining, so that the boys would make a fuss of them, and they would not leave. One dog, a black retriever, was at Bedford House [a destroyed château used as HQ]. The strange thing about this one was that he would never leave the place. As one brigade took over from another, so he would attach himself to the newcomers. He was named 'Wipers' and was a marvel at catching rats. Shortly after, orders were issued that all dogs found within three miles of the front line were to be destroyed, because it was discovered that the Germans had been training some of them to cross our lines. Old 'Wipers' must have known something, because he suddenly vanished.

A number of soldiers referred to this order to shoot stray dogs. Certainly both sides brought bitches on heat into the front line to distract enemy messenger dogs from carrying out their duties.

Sapper Albert Martin, 122nd Signal Coy, 41st Div., RE

We have some dogs that have been trained as message carriers. They go backwards and forwards between us and certain stations in the line. They are fairly big, ugly looking mongrels and they are persuaded to do their work by the prospect of food at the other end. That is to say, a dog that is to do a journey is kept from food for a few hours. From experience he knows that he will get a meal at another certain spot, so as soon as he is released, with the message fixed to his collar, he makes a beeline for grub.

The principle of focusing on food was used in exactly the same way when it came to the army's use of carrier pigeons. Unlike dogs, pigeons had been trusted messengers from the earliest days of the war. By the end of 1915, fifteen pigeon stations were in use on the Western Front but with the introduction of mobile lofts on the Somme, their number had grown exponentially with several thousand available to carry messages during the battle. There were some clear advantages to using pigeons. Unlike dogs, pigeons were less likely to get bogged down in mud and, given their relative size, they made a difficult target to shoot. However, they remained vulnerable to attack by birds of prey and more susceptible to failure and capture in adverse weather.

2/Lt Frank Mitchell, Tank Corps

A squad of officers was marched into the pigeon hut, where a sergeant explained to them, with great detail, how and when to feed a pigeon, how to release it from its basket, how to roll up and attach a message to the clip on its leg, and how to start it off on its journey.

One weary pigeon acted as a demonstrator. Each officer advanced in turn, grabbed the poor bird in one hand, attached the message with the other, and replaced the pigeon in the basket. These lessons were going on all day long, and the wretched bird had become so used to being clumsily handled by scores of officers that it scarcely made a movement, realising perhaps that passive resistance was the wisest plan.

It is interesting to recall that when a pigeon is released with a message from a tank in action, it is thrown downward so that its wings will open out, and it can then rise swiftly and fly away.

Colour Sgt William Meatyard, Plymouth Bttn, RMLI

The artillery had a telephone in the dugout, so that we could soon get a message through to the guns. Pigeons were kept in case of emergency only, the message being fixed to their leg in a small aluminium cylinder. The bird when let loose would make for its loft at Brigade Headquarters. There, by entering its loft, pushing through a trapdoor, an electric bell rang, which told the attendant that a bird had arrived. A fresh couple were then let loose with a practice message, 'Wind S.W.' or something. Only water was given them whilst up in the trenches so that they went quickly for grub. These birds will fly through artillery barrages and even gas, although after a time gas would affect them and for this purpose a sack treated with chemical was kept in the dugout.

Lt Murray Webb-Peploe, 23rd Heavy Artillery Group

I went for a walk with the doctor this evening and we captured a Boche carrier pigeon which was apparently exhausted. It just flopped along in a field and we caught it quite easily. It has a nickel ring on one foot with NURP and some figures on it. Haven't found a message on it so far. I suppose it will have to be sent to the Intelligence Department. We have it in a cage and are feeding it on water, oats and bread. Had another look at it just now and found my servant had supplied the pigeon with a liberal slice of bread and jam!

The bird had become exhausted from flying into the wind and died a few hours later; whether this was from overexertion or jam poisoning, Webb-Peploe was never sure.

By 1917, the British Army was awash with 'schools' giving training courses and lectures on almost every aspect of army life in which it was deemed a course would help with the long-term prosecution of the war. Hygiene and vermin control were perhaps not as high on the agenda as some officers might have liked but even this attitude was changing, as Philip Gosse was about to find out. His role of hunting voles for the Natural History Museum was about to come to an abrupt end.

Capt. Philip Gosse, Rat Officer, 2nd Army

The staff officer quickly came to the point, 'Are you Captain PHG Gosse?' 'Yes,' I admitted, though wondering whatever it was all

about. 'Well,' continued the staff officer, 'am I right in understanding you know all about rats?'

I wanted to learn a little more before giving a definite answer.
So to gain time I replied, 'Well, I know a good deal about birds.'

'That's excellent,' said he. 'You are appointed Rat Officer to the
Second Army and will report forthwith to the Director General
Medical Services to the Second Army at Hazebrouck', whereupon,
without waiting for any further observations from me or bidding
me farewell or even expressing any interest in my bad cold, he
right-about turned and marched out of the room.

In peacetime every man's hand had been against the rat: every
farmer took some means or other to keep him in check, if not to
exterminate him, while most houses had a cat or a dog which also
helped. But when the armies came, most of the farmers left, and
for some mysterious reason the dogs left as well – the French peasants said the English soldiers took them, and not without some
justification, for almost every British battalion was accompanied
by a small pack of mongrel mascots wherever it went. But probably the most important reason for the increase in rats was food.
The British Army was supplied with a vast surplus of rations.
Food, stale bread, biscuits and particularly cheese littered the
ground. Some quartermasters, to save themselves trouble and to
guard against any risk of being caught without enough, would
indent for greater quantities of rations than they required or were
entitled to.

While organising my rat campaign, I had to travel far and wide
over the army area, interviewing all manner of officers from proud
brigadier generals to suspicious quartermasters. The latter were by
far the most difficult to deal with. Not only were they suspicious
– there was nothing about rat-catchers or catching rats in King's
Regulations – but they particularly resented any assumption on
my part that their stores might be better if they were protected
from rats by wire netting. Considering that by this time almost
every quartermaster's store had become so swarming with vermin

. . . it might have been thought that any suggestions to improve matters would be welcomed. But this was far from being the case.

I had to deliver lectures. These began in a quite small way at Hazebrouck, where a school of sanitation for officers had been started and where courses of lectures were delivered by various experts, each on his own special subject. Last but two on the syllabus of subjects came mine, rats; the two even lower on the list being flies and parasites, the experts on which were familiarly referred to as OC Maggots and OC Lice.

At first the lectures were given only to officers, but soon classes were formed for men as well. On a table were arranged specimens I had caught and stuffed of most of the small mammals to be met within or behind the trenches, as well as models and drawings of traps. To most of those who saw these, it came as a surprise to learn how many different animals there were in northern France, believing as they did that the brown or trench rat was the only beast but man to be found in Flanders. Amongst the exhibits were moles, hedgehogs, common shrews, garden shrews, weasels, stoats, polecats, bank voles, subterranean voles, orchard dormice, wood mice, harvest mice, rabbits and pipistrelle bats. My lecture came in time to be looked upon as a sort of drawing-room entertainment much in the way conjurers and ventriloquists are, who give refined entertainments at children's Christmas parties.

It was a pleasant surprise to find how keen these soldiers were on natural history. At first, I feared they would be bored with anecdotes about birds and beasts, but the majority seemed very interested. After one of the lectures on rats a middle-aged man from a Yorkshire regiment told me how, quite recently, he had entered a wrecked church at Ypres in search of some wood to make a fire with. He found and pulled some down behind the ruined altar, and in doing so uncovered a large bat asleep. After carefully examining the bat he put it into a box, and afterwards laid the box near the fire he had made. After a while, the warmth of the fire – this happened during very cold weather – awakened the bat, which began to scramble about in the box, so the soldier let it out and it flew away.

This little anecdote had a sequel. Ten minutes later the soldier who told me about his large bat brought up to me another soldier, to whom he had never spoken before but who had overheard us talking. The newcomer, after explaining to me that he was 'fond of animals', produced a grubby little pocket diary and showed me this entry for 2 January 1917: 'Saw today a large bat flying about the streets of Ypres. Probably disturbed by shellfire.'

Whatever Gosse taught the men, all soldiers learnt by merely watching others and attempting to replicate what they saw: whatever the methods, they all came under the broad umbrella of 'ratting'. In ideal conditions, when there was plenty of food, one pair of rats could produce 880 offspring in a year, so the rat population was always ripe for a cull, and a good old rat hunt appealed to men whose pent-up aggression was often stifled by repetitive duties or inactivity. Ratting was almost a social occasion.

Trp. Benjamin Clouting, 4th (Royal Irish) Dragoon Guards

Ratting took place either around deserted farmhouses or among holes in a hedgerow. A whole afternoon could be taken up, packing cordite into the holes before the rats were smoked out in their dozens. Earlier in the war, ratting had been something of a laborious exercise, as cartridge cases were emptied from hundreds of bullets to get enough cordite to prove effective. By 1917, when more shells were available, it was possible to get hold of a shell case, or, better still, the cordite that was packed separately to fire the big guns.

Howitzer cordite gave off a nasty green gas and was packed into a hole from which a trail of cordite was drawn. Once the trail was lit, a clod of earth was quickly packed around the cordite in the hole, forcing the fumes down the tunnels and the rats out. There was a great deal of excitement as we laid into the rats with sticks and clubs, scattering them squealing in all directions, as we killed just as many as we possibly could.

Rifleman J.A. Johnston, 13th Rifle Brigade

There was a regular warren of rat holes at the back of the house, so we got some straw, a pile of bricks and our swords [bayonets], and in a body proceeded to wage war. Stuffing the straw down most of the holes, we set fire to it and stood guard over the ones that remained to wait for the rats to bolt. We did not have long to wait for first one rat came flying out of a hole, then another would make a dash, and we were soon kept busy. Not many escaped, and when the numbers tailed off and it seemed we had accounted for them all, one of our party noticed a big rat, old and cunning, who was about a foot down a hole filling it up with his body so that the smoke could not reach – and was watching us out of two beady eyes, waiting for us to go before he came out. We could not make the rat come out so, at last, one of the men traced the line of the run and, measuring the ground off until he was over the rat, drove his sword through it and succeeded in killing it. We accounted for 23 rats that afternoon.

2/Lt Edmund Fisher, 36th Div., Ammunition Column, RFA

I have just adopted an enormous French foxhound. I saw him by the side of a road ratting with some navvies. He is without exception the most accomplished ratter I have ever met. He wanders along in a nonchalant way till he finds one. He then marks by an intense gaze of a second or two; after this he strolls round to discover the bolt hole. Then to see him dig is an education, his eye ever in the bolt hole. When he gets near the rat, he just pats with his paw so as to deal promptly when he bolts. Though he is a great lumbering fellow he is about 6 times quicker than any terrier I have met and quite often catches them in the air. He caught 27 yesterday, today about 15. The ratting is much too easy in these shell-holes. Usually a stroke or two with a pick is enough to bolt them. They are generally about the size of rabbits, which

makes it easier still. Today one escaped and ran along under the
duckboards. These are boards arranged to act as paths in the mud,
joined together. We had no idea where it had gone to but the old
boy winded it and trundled along about 50 yards of duckboards,
and caught it as it bolted to get under a hut. He is red under the
eye like a bloodhound, and sleeps in my bed. I must try him on a
hare later on when I get some time.

Capt. D.P. Hirsch VC (post.),
1/4th Yorkshire Rgt (Green Howards)

In the doctor's dugout here there are some swallows nesting and
the rats have, *for the second time*, eaten their young, and they are
now starting again for the third in the same place, poor little
devils! Talking of birds, I managed to shoot a sparrow in the
trenches yesterday. It keeps your eye in! We are very bothered
with mosquitoes and flies just now too. Some chaps have their
faces swelled to most awful shapes.

*The nonchalant way in which Captain Hirsch mentioned shooting a spar-
row to keep his eye in would have appalled men like Thomas Williams
and Charles Raven, but, with death so commonplace, why should anyone
have worried too much about the cause of a small sparrow? Killing was the
currency of the day. Nevertheless, while the killing of innocent animals was
widespread, some men were embarrassed, others bitterly reflective over such
senseless behaviour, especially when it was by their own hands.*

Lt Henry Lawson, 10th Manchester Rgt

There was an unexpected incident when my platoon was performing an exercise under the inspection of a general. There had been
a divisional platoon contest, which my platoon had either won or
had obtained a place in the final before the competition was abandoned for lack of time.

That may have been the reason why we were put into the
particular exercise that became our undoing. We were given live

ammunition and we had to manoeuvre up a grassy hillside for about one thousand yards, targets being placed on the face of the hill. There was a small group of cattle grazing between the starting point and the targets, to which I paid no attention. All seemed to go reasonably well. On arrival at our destination the general began to make some observations and comments of approval until suddenly he stopped and said, 'What is the matter with that cow?' I looked round and sure enough there was a cow collapsing and falling to the ground. The general then exclaimed, 'And there is another one!' I could only hang my head in shame.

Others may have been in the exercise, but there could be no doubt that my platoon was responsible. We had to pay a heavy compensation to the farmer. I have no recollection whether we had the beef! Naturally I was ashamed at the cruelty to the animals. My own investigation did not reveal the culprits. Possibly after months in the trenches in a quiet sector the men had been unable to resist the opportunity afforded by a living target. I include the episode merely to demonstrate the great difference between town dwellers and countrymen, who would never have done such a thing.

Capt. Philip Gosse, Rat Officer, Second Army

The battery commander, a major, invited me into his dugout where he produced a bottle of whisky and two tin mugs. We talked of various things, trying to find some subject or interest in common. As I began to think about leaving, a little mouse came out of a hole in the wall and began to dart nimbly about the floor. The red-faced major swore, kicked a boot towards it, and the little mouse vanished as suddenly as it had appeared. The major cursed the mouse, declaring it was always running about like that, and wished he could get rid of it. I offered to rid him of it, if it really bothered him, and so the next day I brought one of my mousetraps, baited it with a piece of cheese, and set it near the hole in the wall. The whisky bottle was brought out again, and the major and I sat drinking and smoking, when all at once, the major whispered, 'There it is!' I looked and there was the little mouse. It was exciting to sit very still and watch it. More than once it seemed to be making straight for the trap, but each time, as it drew near, it turned in some other direction.

The excitement became intense. The major and I dared not move or whisper, and our pipes went out. Then once again the mouse approached the trap, and seemingly getting wind of the cheese, drew closer still and remained motionless, listening. Then suddenly it seized the bait in its two tiny paws and began to gnaw hungrily at the cheese. Click went the trap, which sprang high into the air as the spring was released, and fell clattering down on to the floor, with the little mouse beneath it.

I went and picked up the trap and showed the major the little soft body, quite warm, the cheese still between its minute, sharp teeth. I felt a curious feeling of pride that by my own ingenuity I had outwitted it. But this sensation did not last for long, and began to ebb away while I held the little limp thing in my hand. After all, I reasoned with myself, it's only a mouse, and it annoyed the major. But all the same I wished I had not killed it. Bother the major, why on earth had I told him I had a mousetrap; why had I not told him to catch the mouse himself if he wanted to? But it would never do to let him see how I was feeling about it; he would despise me for a sentimental fool. I finished off my whisky and turned to say goodbye. The major was holding the little mouse in his hand, and surprised me by saying, 'I wish now we hadn't killed the little chap. I believe I had grown quite fond of him.'

Pte Thomas Hope, 1/5th King's Liverpool Rgt

Gaily we swagger along until, getting tired of the monotonous zigzag of the communication trench, we climb out on top and enjoy the beauty of the countryside so far as the morning mist will allow.

A mole, taking his morning airing, darts off at our approach, and before we realise it we are after him. Backwards and forwards he dodges, escaping the swipes we make at him with our sticks, by a hair's breadth. We are oblivious to everything else in the excitement of the chase after a poor, frightened mole. A lucky stroke and I knock him over. Picking up the kicking animal I give him another tap over the head. The convulsive movements gradually stop, and the little furry body lies inert in my hand.

'Got you, my beauty,' I exclaim breathlessly after my exertions.

'Look at his little piggy nose. Funny sort of creature, a mole.'

Mac comes over and looks at the body. A trickle of blood comes from its mouth and drops on my upturned palm, leaving a little crimson spot in the centre of my hand.

'Poor little blighter, such a soft silken coat' – and Mac softly strokes the tiny creature from which I have knocked out all the life.

'What're you going to do with it, Jock?' inquires Webby, 'we can't eat moles. There's only one bite anyway.'

'Oh, I think I'll start saving them up,' I reply. 'A hundred or so and I could have a nice fur cardigan.'

It is the first mole I have ever seen, and I am rather taken with the idea of a fur jacket made of moleskins.

I tie the body by the tail to my stick and begin to wonder. After all, what can I do with it? Whatever prompted me to chase and kill it? I must be a bloodthirsty brute. If only I had thought before I made the fatal stroke. Poor little inoffensive mole, its life was as precious to it as mine is to me.

Signalman J.C. Aird, Benbow Batt., RND

Raining. German plane brought down. Usual artillery fire. Rat hunting at 1 a.m. Killed a fine hawk in mistake, noticing his form on the parapet. Have kept his wings in memoriam.

In 1915, natural description involved simple wonderment at mother earth in all her glory rather than any contrast to wholesale destruction.

*By 1917, such descriptions had subtly changed, drawing out the differ-
ence between nature where it survived and the general vista of desolation. Different too, perhaps, are the descriptions of wildlife, descriptions
now tinged with a greater feeling of war-weariness and a longing for
a resolution to the conflict.*

An anonymous officer in the Household Bttn

In England there seems to be a general belief that nothing but every
imaginable hardship and horror is connected with the letters BEF.
People see only bully beef, dugouts, shell-holes, mud, and such
like as the eternal routine of life. True enough, these conditions
do prevail very often, but in between whiles, they are somewhat
mitigated by most unexpected 'corners'. The other day we took over
from a well-known Scottish regiment whose reputation for making
themselves comfortable was well known throughout the Division,
and when I went to examine my future abode I found everything up
to the standard which I had anticipated. Standing on an oak table
in the middle of the dugout was a shell case filled with flowers, and
these not ordinary blossoms, but Madonna lilies, mignonette and
roses. This vase, if I may so term the receptacle, overshadowed all
else and by its presence changed the whole atmosphere, the perfume
reminding me of home, and what greater joy or luxury is there for
any of us out here than such a memory?

After having duly appreciated this most unexpected corner, I
inquired where the flowers had been gathered, and was told they
had come from the utterly ruined village of Fampoux close by. At
once I set out to explore and verify this information. Sure enough,
between piles of bricks, shell-holes, dirt, and every sort of *débris*,
suddenly a rose in full bloom would smile at me, and a lily would
waft its delicious scent and seem to say how it had defied the
destroyer and all his frightfulness. In each corner where I saw a
blossoming flower or even a ripening fruit, I seemed to realise a
scene belonging to this unhappy village in peaceful times.

I meandered on through the village until I struck a trench

leading up to the front line: this I followed for a while until quite suddenly I was confronted by a brilliancy which seemed to me one of the most perfect bits of colour I had ever seen. Amongst innumerable shell-holes there was a small patch of ground absolutely carpeted with buttercups, over which blazed bright red poppies intermixed with the bluest of cornflowers. Here was a really glorious corner, and how quickly came memories of home! No one, however hardened by the horrors of war, could pass that spot without a smile or a happy thought. Perhaps it is the contrast of the perfection of these corners with the sordidness of all around that makes them of such inestimable value.

2/Lt John Gamble, 14th Durham Light Infantry

There are moments, sometimes hours, when right at the seat of the greatest of wars, close behind the firing line, near where there have been many thousands of lives lost in the fiercest fighting of the war, one can close one's eyes and imagine all is peace again. At times when all the infernal engines and machines at the command of the armies are subdued for a few minutes, one may realise that all the frightfulness man can invent will never kill nature. Listen, now, to the birds singing over in those trees, which are rustling gently in the mild western breeze, as they have done for hundreds of years; and that little stream which has so often run with blood since the war commenced, still makes its merry music, as it bubbles over the little stones towards the canal waiting to receive it.

Close your eyes with me here, and listen to nature gently protesting that she still does, and always will, hold sway; that war will not continue for ever, and soon she will reassert herself in the stricken land, and with the aid of time, gradually cover up and remove all the appalling signs of the forces which have endeavoured to upheave her.

Such well-written prose could capture a moment, it could hint at greater, more substantial thoughts, but for the officer who wrote it there was also the reality of a war to be won. The diary would be put away, the letter closed, and the daily work of leading a company or battery resumed. With men constantly on the move, there was a continuous circulation of animals between units. Horses and mules were frequently traded, particularly among the artillery and service corps, keen to eject a horse that caused problems but which might settle down with another team. Theft, however, was a major cause of loss. This frequently exercised the minds of officers keen to recover a favourite horse from among dozens of others serving with another unit, all of which could look pretty much the same.

Capt. Graham Reid, 1st Field Squadron, RE

I saw Captain Alexander Arnold, who had been Riding Instructor at Chatham, several times. He came over to tea and did a bit of horse swapping with the squadron. We had some Australian RFA lines near ours and had to keep a very strict lookout on our own horses and saddlery. One night when two bombs fell near the line, several of our horses got loose, including one of Alexander's chargers which, when we had rounded everything up, was missing. Keeping watch next day at the watering point, Alexander saw his own horse being ridden by a lanky Australian gunner, who was one of the large watering party. Alexander went up to this man and politely told him that he had his (Alexander's) horse which had got loose the night before. The Australian replied, 'Not a bit of it: I've had this horse ever since I came over, and that's three years ago: Sammy, I call him.' On Alexander pointing out that Sammy had 'RE98' branded on his forefeet the Australian looked down and then quite naively remarked, 'So he has: I forgot that, sir. You'd better take him.' He was not in the very least embarrassed.

Maj. Neil Fraser-Tytler, D Batt., 149th Brigade, RFA

I took a different route from the battery in order to lunch with the North Irish Horse, and also to pick up a horse hidden there for certain reasons during the last two days. The battery had quite a successful march, picking up a horse and two mules and having only one horse reclaimed, also a nice looking young setter joined them on the road, which will be useful for partridge shooting further north. Owing to all batteries grazing their horses in large herds in the open clover fields, a good many had changed hands, so every outgoing battery is carefully examined by those who are anxious to reclaim their horses.

Lt Richard Talbot Kelly, 52nd Brigade, RFA

We noticed while grazing our horses that numbers of other horses from units other than our own were also being grazed, and one particular bunch of horses used to be sent out in the charge of very few drivers, who then promptly went to sleep and took no further interest in the proceedings. Now there were amongst these horses one or two beautiful beasts in the pink of condition and we felt it would be nice to acquire them, so one day we arranged a little stampede and in the muddle that ensued quickly whisked away all five of these coveted 'gees'. We rushed them back to our own wagon lines and set the farrier and his staff on to trimming them up with the clipping machine and to restamping the numbers on their hoofs.

Looking back on it now, it seems a thoroughly immoral act, but by this time the British Army had become expert scroungers, and scrounging a horse or two we felt was just as legitimate as scrounging RE material for a dugout. Two days later two officers came round and asked if we had found any stray horses. We said we had both lost and found some horses two days previously in the stampede, but if they liked they could come and look round our lines and see if they could recognise any of the horses they had lost. They walked round, but either the horses we had collected were not theirs or they failed to recognise their own beasts and they went away empty-handed.

Driver Charles Keller, RHA

We moved a long way back and built some stables and thatched the walls and roof with straw. It was quite warm for the horses but it couldn't have been very well built because the first high wind that sprung up blew it away. We were able to hang on to most of the horses but some did break loose. Those that got away we couldn't do anything about before daylight and it took several days to round up all of them. Some of them were more than thirty miles away. Some were found hidden in farmers' stables and they didn't want to give them up. Others refused to allow us to check their barns and we had to get the local police. We had a few horses that were balky [perverse] and troublesome and, although we saw them, we didn't bother to pick them up as they were more than a nuisance when we used them to take up ammunition. They would no doubt soon lose their balkiness when the farmer hooked them to a plough. The farmer would see that the balky one earned his oats. They weren't as kind to their animals as were the British soldiers.

French farmers were realistic about the purpose of an animal on a farm. There was no room for sentiment when the living was hard, made harder still by a war which stripped the countryside of most young agricultural workers. Most soldiers out on rest were, if so minded, happy to watch the work, although antagonisms between farmers and soldiers were as frequent as they were perennial.

Pte Hugh Quigley, 12th Royal Scots

There is a curious self-containedness in the life of a French peasant. Even the farm stock fraternise in a strange way. Yesterday the good wife (who waddles along as if cut through at the waist, bust and hips wobbling in different directions) brought in a cartful of dried bean-stuff. It seemed to be a delicacy, for first a brown cow slipped up and tore off a mouthful, then a calf, then an old grey mare and foal, until the cart was completely surrounded and the

old wife lost to view. Quite a fine picture! Cows, horses, a loqua-
cious sow, an infinity of white hens, ducks, and, bringing up the
rear, a troop of half-grown turkeys.

Pte Arthur Alexander, 1/14th London Rgt (London Scottish)
Nearby was a small farm where we could buy fresh milk. Sometimes
we would have to wait while the woman milked the cows before
we could be served, so it was then quite warm and unquestion-
ably fresh. Whilst waiting to be served, I was surprised to see how
close the cattle were to the inmates of the farmhouse. One had
only to open the living-room door, which room, by the way, had
in it a great old four-poster bed, and you walked into the cow-
stall and saw the cows bedded down. This was much too close
to my way of thinking but they thought nothing of it and were
evidently accustomed to eating and sleeping in close proximity to
their cattle. I am afraid it would horrify most English folk.

Rifleman Aubrey Smith,
1/5th London Rgt (London Rifle Brigade)
I had a wordy argument today with a man who tried to hit my
horse because he imagined he was being forced into the mud beside
the road. I also had trouble with a fat old wench who swore at me.
One of her fowls flew through the mud, spraying my face with
slosh; as I was in a bad temper I gave vent to my wrath by chasing
the offending chicken up the road. The owner happened to see the
chase and ran after me, jabbering away nineteen to the dozen and
shaking her fist, which led to retorts in equally strong language
conveying, however, nothing to her unreceptive mind . . .

   We were in a typical Flanders area where the billets were farms
– miles from any shops or canteens and surrounded by an almost
impassable flooded waste. This was the place where we joined the
remainder of the transport, the section sharing a barn with about
two dozen fowls. From the noise they kicked up it would appear
that they were the original and lawful owners and their protests

became so loud in the early morning that nearly everyone hurled mugs, boots and other missiles at the rowdy roosters. The civilian owners of the farm, as one might expect in these parts, were surly and resentful. As if we were out here for a beanfeast, deliberately choosing to live with their livestock and sleep on their smelly straw! As if we were occupying their filthy barn for the love of the thing! We were no happier than they – we, who were far from our homes and would shortly be enduring hell at Ypres. The least these mercenary old peasants could do was to be grateful to the British for keeping the Germans from their doors.

Ypres: other than a brief excursion into the town in October 1914, the Germans had been held back on the edge of a tight salient that contracted and expanded according to which side had been on the offensive. The town itself had slowly succumbed to enemy fire, the beautiful Cloth Hall was a smouldering wreck as was the cathedral, while the town's ramparts were shell-pitted and sandbagged. Yet in the moat there was still life.

Capt. James Dunn, RAMC attd. 2nd Royal Welsh Fusiliers
Ypres is a ghost: the grubby little town will have to be rebuilt, every house, from its foundations. The ramparts are scarred, but stand. Only the moat is unchanged. On its calm surface there floated, so stilly as to make scarcely a ripple, two swans preening themselves languidly in the brilliant, oppressive sun of a fine day.

A month later the swans were still there, but their circumstances had worsened.

Cpl G.W. Durham, 3rd Div., Cyclist Coy
One wretched pair of swans, the last of a big flock, still has a nest in the moat. Someone tried to get the eggs one day, but suddenly realising that he was being shot at by our sentries, he wisely

desisted, as they had made pets of the birds and would have shot him as calmly as a rat. Both the birds are crippled.

The cuckoo sings on the rampart, so do the blackbirds and thrushes. The birds take no notice of war at all and will sing over a battery while it is firing.

Capt. James Dunn, RAMC attd. 2nd Royal Welsh Fusiliers
The cob, a great beauty, appears to have been wounded; one of the digits of his left wing looks as if it had been broken and had set badly. These birds have become legendary. Their appearance at the Menin Gate foretells a peaceful day, their disappearance, no one knows whither, portends a bombardment.

Chaplain Thomas Tiplady, Army Chaplains' Dept
For three years the storm centre of the British battle front has been at Ypres. Every day and night it had been the standing target of thousands of guns. Yet, amid all the havoc and thunder of the artillery, the graceful white form of a swan had been seen gliding over the water of the moat. It never lacked food, and was always welcome to a share of Tommy's rations. [Then] a shell burst near the swan, and it was mortally wounded.

Somehow the swan seemed a mystical being, and invulnerable. It was a relic of the days of peace, and a sign of the survival of purity and grace amid the horrors and cruelties of war. It spoke of the sacred things that yet remain – the beautiful things of the soul upon which war can lay no defiling finger. Now it had gone from the water and Ypres seems more charred than ever, and the war more terrible.

On the last day of July 1917, the British offensive at Ypres began in earnest. The battle lasted over three months and the general morass in which it was fought came to symbolise in the public consciousness the misery of that conflict.

Lt Col. Cecil Lyne, 119th Brigade, RFA

Had I a descriptive pen I could picture to you the squalor and
wretchedness of it all and through it the wonder of the men who
carry on. Figure to yourself a desolate wilderness of water filled
with shell craters, and crater after crater whose lips form narrow
peninsulas along which one can at best pick but a slow and precarious way. Here a shattered tree trunk, there a wrecked 'pillbox', sole
remaining evidence that this was once a human and inhabited land.
Dante would never have condemned lost souls to wander in so terrible a purgatory. Here a shattered wagon, there a gun mired to the
muzzle in mud which grips like glue; even the birds and rats have
forsaken so unnatural a spot. Mile after mile of the same unending
dreariness; landmarks are gone, whole villages where hardly a pile
of bricks amongst the mud marks the site. You see it at its best
under a leaden sky with a chill drizzle falling, each hour an eternity,
each dragging step a nightmare. How weirdly it recalls some half-
formed horror of childish nightmare, one would flee, but whither? –
one would cry aloud but there comes no blessed awakening. Surely
the God of Battles has deserted a spot where only devils can reign.

Think what it means, weeks of it, weeks which are eternities,
when the days are terrible but the nights beyond belief. Through
it all the horror of continual shellfire, rain and mud. Gas is one
of the most potent components of this particular inferno. Nights
are absolutely without rest, and gas at night is the crowning limit
of horrors. The battery that occupied the position before we came
was practically wiped out by it, and had to be relieved at short
notice, and the battery that relieved them lost 37 men on the way
in. You can imagine how bucked I was when they handed me out
these spicey bits of gossip on the way up. I daren't risk more than
three men per gun up here at the same time and only two officers
besides myself; at the moment they are rather sorry for themselves
after last night's gas stunt, and doing unhelpful things to their
eyes with various drops and washes. I've got a throat like raw beef
and a voice like a crow.

Pte Hugh Quigley, 12th Royal Scots

The landscape has no salient features of its own; everything blasted to mud – railway embankments, woods, roads confused in shell-holes and mine craters. Trees are only skeletons, and masses of obscene ruins mark farms or houses. You look in vain for a wood where such is marked on the map. The only way at night is to bend down close to the ground and gaze at the skyline for black shadows of pillboxes; by those shadows you find your way. Or, to remember a road once shown, the oddest details must be noted – a solitary length of rail or wire, a dud shell, three stakes together, a fragmentary hedge, a deserted waterlogged trench, dead men lying at various angles, and the position of pillboxes in relation to the track followed. The most exciting time I spent was in hunting B Company Headquarters across this monotony of mud and water. I think I must have visited the whole Division before finding it, artillery as well as infantry.

Long gone were the wandering farm animals of 1915 and 1916, gone were the weasels and stoats parting the long grass, gone were the feral dogs and cats; insects survived, but they went unnoticed. If, as Lieutenant Colonel Lyne suggested, even the rats had 'forsaken' the land, then it was indeed desolate. Only the fearful creatures forced up to the line to work were regularly seen: horses and mules.

Pte Thomas Hope, 1/5th King's Liverpool Rgt

We become conscious of a sound totally different to that of shrieking bursting shells. We listen more intently and can pick it out quite easily from the general babel of noise. It has a rhythm about it which at first I cannot place, then suddenly it dawns on me: it is the thudding of hoofs.

'What the hell's that, Jock?' shouts Webster. 'Do you hear it?'

'It's the horses, Webby. Look, there's two of them.'

Rearing and plunging, the terror-stricken beasts come out of the hell of shells and smoke. With necks outstretched they gallop

on, making straight for the trench and the barbed wire in front
of it.

'The wire, Webby, they'll be on it in a minute.' . . .

We wave our arms and shout, but our voices can't be heard
above the noise of shelling, and there is a tanging of wire as the
half-crazed animals gallop into the tangle of cruel barbs. They
rear and kick and plunge deeper into its depths, making every
movement a torture to them, and very soon they are a mass of
lacerations right up past the flanks. One viciously snaps at its
tormentors only to toss up its head with a cry almost human, its
mouth dripping with blood.

Hopelessly we try and get at them, but have become so
entangled ourselves that at each movement the wire tears our
flesh, yet the piteous cries urge us forward, until we get to
within four yards of them, but can get no further. We are close
enough to see the mess they are in. Both are bleeding freely
from dozens of ragged tears, while one has a huge slice out of
its hindquarters.

'What the hell do we do now, Jock?' Webster inquires. 'We'll
never get them clear of this lot, they're too well anchored.'

'We'll have to try, we can't shoot them without an officer.'

'Officer be damned, Jock. I'm going back for my "Bondook"
[rifle].'

As Webster struggles back to the trench for his rifle I speak
gently to the two animals and try to stop their frantic struggles,
but they are beyond control of human voice. Foam appears at
their mouths, while steam rises from the blood that trickles from
dozens of places on their torn bodies.

At last Webster is laboriously working his way back.

'Try and quieten them, Jock,' he urges. 'Get hold of that one's
head and give me a chance.'

'I can't, damn you,' I reply irritably, as my foot becomes entangled and I trip over sideways on to the ragged wire.

'Well, look out,' yells Webster.

Only four yards separate him from the beasts, but as if they know what is about to happen, they rear and plunge more violently, as Webster tries to take aim.

It takes three shots before the first sinks limply down on to its couch of barbed wire, and by now the second animal is struggling desperately in its terror, but by good luck Webster's second shot gets it between the eyes. It flops instantly and it's all over – poor, hard-working, uncomplaining friends of man.

Chaplain Thomas Tiplady, Army Chaplains' Dept

On two miles of road I have counted a dozen dead mules and burial parties are sent out to put them out of sight. One night, alone, I got three dying mules shot. The road was crowded with traffic, yet it was difficult to find either an officer with a revolver or a transport driver with a rifle. I had to approach scores before I could find a man who had the means to put a mule out of its misery; and we were within two miles of our front. So rigid is our line of defence that those behind it do not trouble to take arms. Even when I found a rifleman, he hesitated to shoot a mule. There is a rule that no horse or mule must be shot without proper authority, and when you consider the enormous cost of one, the necessity for the rule is obvious. I had therefore to assure a rifleman that I would take full responsibility for his action. He then loaded up, put the nozzle against the mule's forehead and pulled the trigger. A tremor passed through the poor thing's body and its troubles were over. It had come all the way from South America to wear itself out carrying food to fighting men, and it died by the road when its last ounce of strength was spent.

Pte Christopher Massie, 76th Brigade, RAMC

The mule is not so mysteriously beautiful as the horse. When he is wounded he walks away from the battlefield in the direction of the field hospital. The humour of this situation is crowded out by its simple pathos. Men and mules, broken in battle, dragging

themselves back down the awful road to Ypres. Often the mules
are bandaged with the men's first field dressings. There is the same
'fed-up' expression in their sad eyes, the same selfless humility – a
humility which gives one the impression that men and mules are
rather ashamed of their wounds.

The warhorse will stand wounded at his post. I remember
coming down from Messines one misty dawn and finding a horse
standing by the body of his dead mate. He stood quite motionless as I patted his strong neck. 'All right, old chap?' I asked. He
looked at me with those mysterious eyes of sorrow, like a mother's,
and turned his head away. I looked over him and found a long
gaping wound in his stomach. And then, when I had found it,
he ventured to glance at me once more, as if he would say quite
simply, 'You see, my friend, it is all over.'

Pte Thomas Hope, 1/5th King's Liverpool Rgt

We come across many wounded and dying horses. They are scattered all over in shell-holes, and at our approach attempt to get
up and off, as if they mistrusted the very presence of a human
being. One poor beast with back broken tries to haul its useless
hindquarters along, while others just lie where they have fallen,
colouring the sodden earth with their lifeblood. A few are still
galloping aimlessly about, foam-flecked and wild-eyed – victims
of man's ruthlessness.

. . . Dawn at last, and we plod wearily back for our spell of
uncertain off-duty.

Standing near the debris of guns and limbers is a solitary horse
gently cropping leaves from a low-lying hedge. At our friendly
words it trots towards us as if pleased to have our company, but
not sure of its welcome – poor faithful beast, how ill you are repaid
for your staunchness.

I have long since become accustomed to wounded humanity.
Their plight evokes pity and the desire to help, but a wounded
animal leaves me with a feeling of loathing, loathing towards

myself and the civilised humanity which I represent. Too often have I seen reproach in the eyes of a dying horse, and outraged frailty in the flutterings of a wounded carrier pigeon.

We may understand; they never can.

The fighting at Ypres was so awful, the conditions so evil, that few men mentioned wildlife; there was no beauty in the Salient in 1917. Entire battalions sent into attack floundered in mud as the unremitting and unseasonal rain flooded the low-lying ground. Men struggled and they died. If messages were sent back, it was pure luck if they arrived. Sometimes, if the situation were not so tragic, it could almost have been funny.

2/Lt Alan Goring, 6th Yorkshire Rgt (Green Howards)

We had a very busy time, for naturally there were snipers all around us and bullets zinging about all over the place. I was left with just a handful of men, all that was left out of those three platoons, so I wanted to send a message back to see if we could get a bit of help from the artillery. We had two pigeons in a basket, but the trouble was that the wretched birds had got soaked when the platoon floundered into the flooded ground. We tried to dry one of them off as best we could and I wrote a message, attached it to its leg and sent it off. To our absolute horror, the bird was so wet that it just flapped into the air and then came straight down again, and started actually walking towards the German line about a hundred yards away. Well, if that message had got into the Germans' hands, they would have known that we were on our own and we'd have been in real trouble. So we had to try to shoot the pigeon before he got there. A revolver was no good. We had to use rifles and there we were, all of us, rifles trained over the edge of this muddy breastwork trying to shoot this bird scrambling about in the mud. It hardly presented a target at all.

Well, we did manage it but that still left the problem of trying to get the message back. We did everything to dry off that other bird. We had one man called Shuttleworth, a well-meaning chap, but very awkward. If there was a piece of barbed wire that everyone else had avoided, Shuttleworth fell over it. If there was a shell-hole that everybody had skirted, Shuttleworth fell into it. Shuttleworth, anyway, was the one who suggested that if we had a cooker with us we could have toasted the bird over that a bit until he dried off. Eventually, we did something nearly as ridiculous. We huddled round this bird and blew on its feathers. As a matter of fact we did get it dried off, but we made jolly sure it *was* dry before we sent it off with the message.

Lt Norman Dillon, 20th Tank Bttn, Tank Corps

Each tank had two pigeons, and often they carried news of vital importance. During an attack in the Salient, one of my friends, Wagstaff, reached his objective, and, taking pity on his pigeons, fed them on seedy-cake and whisky. Soon after, his tank got stuck on a tree stump and although the tracks went round, it was immobile. So he tried to send off a pigeon to report his predicament. Opening a port over a track, he pushed the pigeon out but it sat on the track and refused to move. So they started the track, thinking that it would carry the bird forward and it would then fall off and fly when the track doubled under. But the pigeon was having none of this, and, no doubt hoping for more whisky, started keeping station by marching against the flow of the track.

Pte Thomas Hope, 1/5th King's Liverpool Rgt

Idly I watch the pigeon man and officer fix messages to the legs of two pigeons, then free them, and up they soar. One second they are there, thirty feet above the ground, the next they have gone, just disappeared. A feather or two floats down gently, and the pigeon man makes off for another pair of birds. He had only been gone three or four minutes when a lance corporal pokes his head round the traverse shouting, 'Duggan's hit, sir.'

'Badly?' inquires the officer.

'Dead, sir, a shell got him.'

'Had he the birds with him?'

'Don't think so, sir; didn't see them.'

'All right, corporal.'

Then turning to me. 'See if you can get those pigeons and bring them here.'

'Very good, sir' – and off I go.

There's very little semblance of trench left, and I have to crawl past the spots where the parapet has been blown down, over dead bodies, and past wounded who groan when I knock up against them. I step over Duggan's body, he's dead all right, and further along in a little niche cut out of the trench side I find the wooden cage with the two pigeons. I wait a little as three shells fall in quick succession on the trench just ahead, then make a bolt back to my own section.

One of the birds is taken out. Poor creature, it is cooing away as if it was in some quiet country loft, or at some village race meeting. The message is soon fixed and up the bird goes. I watch it until it is lost to sight, but the lieutenant keeps his glasses trained on it, then as he lowers them:

'It's down, we'll have to send a runner.'

The battles of 1917 tested the British Army to an extraordinary degree, sapping men of much of their resilience. They had little left to live on except the comradeship that bound them to their friends and the love they had for their animals.

Lt Andrew McCormick, 182nd Labour Coy

I recall one of the things which pleased and cheered me most of anything I saw during the war. I happened to be on a railhead one day when wounded horses from the line were being entrained. I saw a man leading along a horse that was severely wounded in several places. He could not have shown more consideration for a human being than he did for that horse. After every few paces he succeeded in coaxing the animal along, he placed his shoulder under the animal's jaw and allowed it to rest its head there. I was so much struck by that soldier's humane conduct that I went forward to him and said, 'Your kindly treatment of these animals is most praiseworthy and I have seen nothing finer in the war.' He seemed pleased but excused himself for his tender heartedness by saying, 'Well, sir, how would you feel if you was both deaf and dumb and could not make known the pain you feel?'

Further along the railhead I saw another officer standing, and I repeated what I had told the soldier. By slow degrees the soldier and his horse came right opposite where we were standing. To my surprise the soldier said to the officer, 'This one is not quite so bad as the last one, sir', and then I felt glad that I had not failed to praise that kind, thoughtful soldier to his own officer.

Cpl Robert Evans, 36th Div., Signal Coy, RE

I remember only too well working with several others for hours in the darkness in a desperate effort to save a pair of beautiful draught horses who were gradually sinking in the mud. As this was happening well within range of the German machine gunners, we had to work in darkness while their driver spoke quiet endearments to his horses, to encourage them.

It was a heartbreaking, horribly long-drawn-out, losing battle, and gradually we knew that they were doomed. Poor tragic driver! I have never forgotten you; you, who had looked after them for so long and loved them so much, now wept, heartbroken, and who shall wonder that you wept?

Lt Charles Bennet, 162nd Brigade, RFA

Just as I finished my last letter to Mary a shell fell in the middle of one of our teams wounding five mules, two of which had to be shot. The poor driver who had one of the mules was heartbroken at its death. By some merciful chance no one was wounded, except that driver whose ear was cut: he didn't mind that because the death of his mule absorbed him: he kept on saying 'and he was my donkey, my donkey' poor fellow. They do love their animals.

Driver Herbert Doggett, RFA

Our ammunition wagon had got up and it had only been there a second or two when a shell killed the horse under the driver. We went over to him, tried to unharness the horse and cut the traces away. He just kneeled and watched this horse . . . A brigadier came along, a brass hat, he tapped this boy on the shoulder and said, 'Never mind, sonny!' This driver looked up at him, just for a second or two, and all of a sudden he said, 'Bloody Germans!' Then he pointed his finger and he stood there as though he was transfixed, stood there like stone. The Brass Hat said to his captain, 'All right, take the boy down the line and see that he has two or three days' rest.'

When an animal was so badly wounded that there was no possibility of it continuing in the team, it had to be abandoned to an uncertain future. Not knowing what would become of a treasured horse or mule was worse than knowing it was out of its misery.

Rifleman Aubrey Smith,
1/5th London Rgt (London Rifle Brigade)

Very early the next morning I went out on to the lines to see the old horse who had been my mainstay for over a year and a half. There he stood, with his mutilated leg swathed in the rough and ready bandages that had been applied by lamplight, his brown eyes looking sadly at me, as much as to say: 'What have I done to deserve this?' Chrisp had said that he would be of no further use and would probably have to be shot; did he instinctively know this as he rubbed his old nose against me?

I thought of his good points, not his jibbing qualities, in that moment; how he had taken me all through the mud and squalor of the Somme at the expense of the flesh he had put on in the blessed days at Third Army Headquarters at St-Pol, and how the third winter, the Battle of Arras and Ypres had all seen Jumbo ready at any time to pull his share even though it was sometimes such a bore to start off!

After I had handed over my pair I had watched them with a fatherly interest, even to the extent of putting down more than their fair share of hay while on picket! Now, I was really upset at the thought of parting with Jumbo.

After an early breakfast, the other horses were taken off the lines and hooked in their limbers. Leaving Ben in someone's charge I crossed over to my old friend again and stood by him until the last moment, a lump rising in my throat.

'Goodbye, Jum! You've been a faithful old pal and I shan't forget you. Yes, the old Grey's leaving you. So am I. Let's stroke your nose for the last time.'

'Get mounted.'

'Goodbye, Jum!'

He begins to fret and whimper. Gordon rides past. The Lewis gun limbers are moving off down the brick-laid slope into the road, brakesmen are ready waiting their opportunity to slip half their impediments on to the limbers. Taking a last look round, I see the other unit preparing to take possession of the deserted lines. I also see a solitary horse, head erect as far as his chain will permit, plunging against the rope and prancing to and fro – on three legs.

1918

The War in 1918

Six months after the United States entered the war, Russia under the new Bolshevik government sued for peace with the Germans. The Tsar's regime had been overthrown and so, in a sense, had his war. Peace with Russia released a million Germans from the east to fight in the west – a piece of undoubtedly unpalatable news to the Allies in France and Belgium. If Germany could force a wedge between the Allies, throwing the British back on to the Channel ports, there was just a chance that the war could be won.

It was not until mid-March that Germany would be in a position to strike and, with the knowledge that an offensive was on the way, the Allies prepared in detail to meet the onslaught. When it came, helped by a fortunate spring morning mist, the German troops caused havoc among the British front-line soldiers. The speed and penetration of advance were so fast, so deep, that many British gun batteries miles in the rear were overwhelmed before they started firing.

Within three weeks, Douglas Haig, the Commander-in-Chief, issued his 'backs to the wall' address to the men. Such was the seriousness of the situation that every man was expected to fight it out with the enemy, and that included cooks and transport drivers. As the British retreated, so canteens and dumps of food and supplies were burnt to stop them falling into the hands of their enemy. However, not all canteens were destroyed. German soldiers, poorly fed and hungry, were astonished at the sight of the quantity and quality of the foodstuffs available to them. The food did a lot to stave off their immediate hunger but it helped to undermine morale, too.

The German forces were eventually held in front of Amiens, but, rather than battering away at the same position, the Germans switched their attack to the north, to Armentières and then Ypres. Once again their success, though startling at first, soon ground to a halt. The German forces simply did not have the military infrastructure and the necessary supply lines to maintain the momentum. Energy was dissipated and, when attacks were made elsewhere, it was clear that the failure of the German effort in the west was approaching.

By mid-1918, the Americans had already taken to the field in force and had suffered many casualties too, but there was an almost infinite number of fresh units to come. German morale began to crack. When the British and Empire troops launched a well-planned and well-executed counter-offensive in August, the great swathes of prisoners taken were testament to the enemy's rapidly eroding will to resist. So many prisoners were boys, so many old men, far too many with poorer quality, worn-out equipment. Allied artillery was now predominant and barrages cripplingly heavy and sustained, while the assimilation of all arms into one combined operation was not only technically possible but could at last be implemented. Many Allied soldiers predicted that the end of the war was coming, fewer that it would in the end come so rapidly.

The Natural World in 1918

Most historians agree that, with the benefit of hindsight, it is clear that German chances of delivering a knockout blow against the British and French in 1918 were in fact small.

Nevertheless, the ferocity of the German strike opened up the Western Front in a way not seen since the earliest days of the war. The tactics had moved on. Terms such as rapid infiltration, elastic defence and all-arms operations were all the rage and for good reason: they worked. Yet despite the advances on almost all fronts, in tactics, weaponry and communications, there was something unnervingly reminiscent of the fighting in 1918 compared to that of 1914. There was the rapid retreat, civilians thrown once more on to pavé roads, belongings and all, farm animals let loose, hungry soldiers, large tracts of battlefields that looked, on first viewing, untainted by war.

Armies were on the move, and, while modern weapons such as tanks were critical to the breaking of enemy defences such as the Hindenburg Line in September 1918, it was the cavalry that came to the fore, once more harassing the enemy. It was the horses, not the tanks, that ended the war, dragoons and hussars charging enemy positions close to Mons just as they had done in August 1914.

Unlike 1914, the advantage now lay with the Allies. The Germans were put to flight, not quite as relentlessly as the British Expeditionary Force four years before, but in a prolonged and exhausting retreat nevertheless.

Sandwiched between the German March Offensive and the Allied advance to victory, often known now as 'the last 100 days', was a time of stability, a brief period when both sides held a collective breath and took stock of the situation. It was the summer and once again nature flourished and men appreciated the beauty of butterflies and the flight of beetles in an attractive countryside. Yet when the decisive move came and the Germans fell back, there was a different mood. The old battlefields of the Somme that the Germans had fought so hard to capture just months before were relinquished quickly. The ground near Arras and in front of Ypres was given up too, taking the Allies to land not seen since 1914. But the men of 1914 had long gone and the war was now fought predominantly by young lads of eighteen and nineteen, led by officers not much older. Open warfare to them was a curious spectacle. It ran counter to anything they had ever read in the newspapers and to a degree it ran counter to what they themselves had seen. Soldiers found themselves in fields and barns, in ditches and lanes full of vegetation, deer crashing through the undergrowth in the Forest of Nieppe. The dead were now to be seen lying in a verdant countryside, in country gardens and châteaux grounds where bees hummed and birds sang. It seemed unnatural to many soldiers and a violation: the dead belonged to a war-torn battlefield, not here.

When the war was over, Allied forces moved to the Rhineland to begin an occupation that would continue for more than a decade. Elsewhere, soldiers, with the enforced help of German POWs, helped with battlefield clearance and wondered at their freedom to move over a terrain that had kept them underground or in trenches for so long. The sullen grey that covered the Ypres and Somme battlefields slowly turned to green, animals reappeared and the battlefield pilgrims began to arrive in their hundreds and then their thousands.

Soldiers' Memories

It took a full year's service in France before a spell of leave was granted to an other rank or NCO, while officers had a more generous leave allowance owing to their greater responsibilities. Such were the numbers on the Western Front that even 1 per cent of soldiers receiving leave would correspond to 20,000 men being processed and shipped to England and back again each week. The administrative process was convoluted but thorough and, if nothing else, men were supposed to be free from vermin before setting foot on the leave boat. Even those who were given permission to proceed away from the front line for leave in France were checked over, men such as Sergeant William Rigden who received a three-day pass on Christmas Eve 1917.

Sgt William Rigden, 196th Siege Batt., RGA

The 24th was a glorious day, cold but bright. I had been keeping away from the [gun] pit and the last week I tried hard to keep a thick wall between myself and any possible shell splinters. I received passes and went to the ADS [Advanced Dressing Station] to pass the doctor. We had to be certified free from disease and lice.

He was a jolly stick and after sounding me said, 'Any livestock, sergeant?' – 'No, sir', I said. 'Bet you a bob you have,' he smiled and I bet he would have won, although I had new clothes and had had a jolly cold bath.

On his return there was a new addition to the battery, a pig bought as food for some unspecified time in the future. Its home was a dugout where it was nearly drowned in a flood and slightly gassed before the battery was ordered to move. At this point a carpenter 'knocked up' a wooden pen and the pig, squealing its objections, was loaded on to a lorry for transfer to a muddy farm where the battery would be billeted.

Sgt William Rigden, 196th Siege Batt., RGA

The lorries could not get within half a mile of the farm so everything had to be carried over a field. The pig was a bit of a nuisance and we all took turns, sometimes pulling in front, sometimes pushing behind until at last we got him into an old stable.

We were troubled somewhat by Boche planes dropping bombs in the evenings. Several fell in the fields near our farm but none did us any harm. The poor old pig had another narrow escape: the Boche dropped a bomb one evening which destroyed the building next to his stable. He was not hurt but managed to get out of a hole made in the wall. We chased him half over Belgium before we caught him again.

Bringing him back across one field, we found our way barred by a dyke full of water. We could not find a way over in the dark and we didn't want to go around if we could help it. We found a narrow plank that just reached over. I went over first and caught the end of a rope we had attached to his lordship. I hauled on this while others pushed the pig from behind. We almost got him over when he slipped over into the dyke. It cost no end of labour to get him out and when we finally got him to his stable, he squealed all night. In the morning the major said, 'If you don't soon kill that pig then I shall.' We managed to get permission to keep him until he got a little fatter by bribing the officers with a promise of a big joint when we did kill him.

Just as men were not supposed to go on leave with any wildlife, pets or lice included, so they were not meant to return with any, either. After a fortnight's leave in England, Major Hardwick was on his way back to his unit. He was not, however, travelling alone.

Maj. A.G.P. Hardwick, 57th Field Ambulance, RAMC
With much trepidation and misgivings, I left Newquay this
morning by the 9.30 train – the aforesaid fears being on account
of a pair of ferrets that I was taking back to France to fight the
rats. I had arranged by wire for Alan [his brother] to meet me at
Paddington if he got leave from the gunner school at Weedon. I
could not get a carriage to myself at Truro, and so I had to put the
'menagerie' out in the corridor, as their smell was a bit stronger
than their bite!

Alan was at Paddington all right, resplendent in a white band
around his cap and a new pair of spurs, and so he was eminently
fitted for the post of 1st whip and I allowed him to carry the
pets. We then took a taxi to the Regent's Palace and found that a
double room had been reserved for us – but, oh, no! No animals
were allowed in the hotel. However, by going round to another
door and walking in as if we were carrying 'a present for a good
boy' we managed to smuggle the beasts up to the bedroom. I had
a pocket full of bread saved from lunch and so we gave them a
good feed of bread and tooth-water at once and strapped them
down again.

Alan was called at 5 a.m. as he had to catch a dashed early train
at Euston and so he had his breakfast upstairs: I bagged all his
milk and so the ferrets had a grand breakfast. They made a devil
of a row during the night, scratching away at the box and squeak-
ing so much that I quite expected to hear of a complaint from the
next-door neighbour.

*Major Hardwick managed to conceal his ferrets all the way to France,
where he found his Division near Cambrai.*

Maj. A.G.P. Hardwick, 57th Field Ambulance, RAMC
We went to the 'Aux Huitres' and had a gorgeous dinner of
oysters and lobster whilst waiting for the car. Arrived at Péronne;
we decided to stay the night with the MAC [Motor Ambulance

Convoy] people. They were delighted with the ferrets which they persuaded me to let loose in the mess – but they were not quite so pleased when the little beggars 'forgot themselves' in all four corners of the room!

It was an inauspicious start. However, two days later the ferrets made amends.

Maj. A.G.P. Hardwick, 57th Field Ambulance, RAMC

Beautiful weather. Had the ferrets out for a trial run amongst the shell-holes. The old buck is dashed good and almost immediately got first blood. He killed a decent-sized rat in a blind hole and we had to dig them out. It was only a trial run, as they had had a huge breakfast, but it shows that they are all right.

It was March 1918 when Major Hardwick returned to France. In stark contrast to just twelve months before, the weather was beautiful and unseasonably warm. The British Army was on tenterhooks for the German offensive, long anticipated, was expected at any time. There was an uneasy peace before the inevitable storm. While preparations were being completed to withstand the enemy onslaught, normal routine was observed, and orders correcting any perceived slackness in the ranks were issued.

Pte Frederick Voigt, Labour Corps

The sergeant major blew his whistle and shouted: 'Listen to the Orders.' He held a bundle of papers in his hand and read with the help of a torch:

'Every man must shave once in twenty-four hours. Buttons' (he pronounced it 'boottons', for he came from the North Country), 'cap badges and numerals must be cleaned thoroughly once a day. Box respirators and steel helmets will always be carried. Except when it is raining, greatcoats or waterproofs will not be worn when men are working. Men are forbidden to smoke while at work.

Pigs in camp are army property and will eventually be consumed by this Coomp'ny. It is therefore not only, er, reprehensible, but also against their own interest if men tease these pigs and pull them about by tails and ears or feed them with unsuitable food. Offenders will be severely dealt with.'

Sgt William Rigden, 196th Siege Batt., RGA

We killed the old pig and had pork for breakfast, pork for dinner, pork for tea, pork for supper, pork before retiring, all night and all day. I never dreamed there was so much meat on a pig, for there were ten of us at him, and, besides, the officers had a large joint. And this for a solid week.

Pte Frederick Voigt, Labour Corps

Our lives had become unspeakably monotonous, but the coming of warm days banished much of our dreariness. The hazy blue sky was an object of real delight. I often contrived to slip away from my work and lean idly against a wall in the mild sunshine. At times I was so thrilled with the sense of physical wellbeing, and so penetrated by the sensuous enjoyment of warmth and colour, that I even forgot the war.

At the bottom of the woodyard was a little stream, and on the far bank clusters of oxlips were in bloom. Here we would lie down during the midday interval and surrender to the charm of the spring weather. It seemed unnatural and almost uncanny that we should be happy, but there were moments when we felt something very much like happiness. Moreover, it was rumoured that leave was going to start. How glorious it would be to spend a sunny May or June in England!

A/Capt. Kenneth Jones, 1/5th Welsh Rgt

The sunsets have become very remarkable lately, and we have all turned out to view them. A few days ago I was watching a fine one, which suddenly struck me by its resemblance to something

I had seen before. Looking carefully, I saw it all clearly. By some freak of nature there lay before us a perfect image of the Severn as viewed from Doverow or Frocester, and one of our officers from Gloucestershire saw it too. There was a long bluish purple stratus cloud, just like the hills of the Forest of Dean, and then some light-coloured twisting clouds, touched with silver, made a perfect river, whilst the land in front of us was level and low. What more could one want, save the reality?

We have been having the most gorgeous summer weather for nearly a month now. In fact, it is almost like August. The larks are singing their hearts out up above, and nature is bursting with pride and delight down below. The willow catkins light up the small copses, and the bees are working as hard as we are. Long may it last! No doubt 'big things' are in the air, but unless the Hun is quick, he won't get much chance. He is very quiet at present, although our guns are hammering away all day and every day with their eternal thunder. I often pity him! All the same, quiet on the Hun's part is not nice, and so we are all on the *qui vive*. Something will have to go bang this year.

Pte Frederick Voigt, Labour Corps

Once a fortnight we paraded for our pay outside one of the bigger sheds of the yard. As a rule, I was filled with impatience and irritation at having to wait in a long queue and move forward step by step, but now it had become pleasant to tarry in the sunshine. One day, when we were lined up between two large huts, a deep yellow brimstone butterfly came floating idly past. It gave me inexpressible delight, a delight tempered by sadness and a longing for better times. I drew my pay and saluted perfunctorily, being unable and unwilling to think of anything but the beauty of the sky, the sun and the wonderful insect.

It was time to go back to work. But I cursed the work and decided to take the small risk and remain idle for an hour or two. I went to an outlying part of the yard and sat down on a patch of long grass and leant back against a shed. The air was hot and several bees flew by. Their buzzing reminded me of summer holidays spent in southern France before the war. I thought of vineyards and orchards, of skies intensely blue, of scorching sunshine, of the tumultuous chirping of cicadas and grasshoppers, and then of the tepid nights crowded with glittering stars and hush except for the piping of tree frogs.

'Before the war, before the war,' I repeated the words to myself. They conveyed a sense of immeasurable remoteness, of something gone and lost for ever. But I wouldn't think about it. I would enjoy the present. But the calm waters of happiness had been ruffled and it was beyond my power to restore their tranquillity. I began to think of many things, of the war itself, of the possible offensive, and soon the fretful rebellious discontent, that obsessed all those of us who had not lost their souls, began to reassert itself . . .

Some distance ahead was a farm of the usual Flemish type, a thatched roof, whitewashed walls and green shutters. Nearby was a little pond with willows growing round it. In the field beyond, a cow was grazing peacefully. The sky seemed a deeper blue through the willow branches. The tender green of the grass was wonderfully refreshing to the eyes. The cow had a beautiful coat of glossy brown that shone in the sunlight. I abandoned myself to the charm of the little idyll that was spread out before me and forgot the war once again.

And then all at once a gigantic, plume-shaped, sepia-coloured mass rose towering out of the ground. There was a rending, deafening, double thunderclap that seemed to split my head. For a moment I was dazed and my ears sang. Then I looked up; the black mass was thinning and collapsing. The cow had disappeared.

I walked into the yard full of rage and bitterness. All the men had left the sheds and were flocking into the road. Some were strolling along in leisurely fashion, some were walking with

hurried steps, some were running, some were laughing and talking, some looked startled, some looked anxious, and some were
very pale.

We crossed the road and the railway. Then, traversing several
fields, we came to a halt and waited. We waited for nearly an hour,
but nothing happened and we gradually straggled back to the yard.
Some of us walked to the spot where the shell had burst. There was a
huge hole, edged by a ring of heaped-up earth, and loose mould and
grassy sods lay scattered all round. Here and there lay big lumps of
bleeding flesh. The cow had been blown to bits. The larger pieces
had already been collected by the farmer, who had covered them
with a tarpaulin sheet from which a hoof protruded.

The next day more shells came over, and the next day also. The
big holes with their earthen rims began to dot the fields in many
places. No damage of 'military importance' had been done. Not
even a soldier had been killed, but only an inoffensive cow.

*Fortunately for Frederick Voigt, he was serving near Ypres and was
nowhere near that part of the line about to feel the brunt of the German
assault. Information gathered from German prisoners pointed to the
21st being the fateful day and the front line east of the Somme battlefield being the target.*

Driver Dudley Gyngell, 58th Divisional Army Column, RFA
20 March

Awoke this morning to a glorious sunshine and blue sky with
fleecy white clouds. Although bearing very many signs of the
strife – this place [Corbie] seems pretty peaceful and rather holi-
day-like – I fancied however that I heard a distant rumbling, but
I must have been mistaken.

21 March

I am sitting at my window looking out into the garden. It is a
wonderful morning of bright sunshine and golden shadows. An

old Frenchman is tending his flowers. He came to the window: 'Bonjour, Monsieur – I have picked you some violets to send to your sweetheart' and he handed me a fragrant little bunch. Suddenly an ominous sound vibrated through the air – the German guns – the villagers gathered in the streets and listened with questioning faces. It is a sound they have not heard for months.

There was a jingle of spurs in the tiled hall and Shirley hurried in. 'Pack up at once and stand by to move.' So something had happened.

At 5.30 a.m. the Germans opened up a massive hurricane bombardment, and, with the advantage of a morning mist, their infantry advanced, bypassing strongpoints in a surge that would take them deep into British lines. The policy of rapid infiltration ensured that Allied forces were thrown into almost immediate confusion before an adequate defence could be made, negating some, though by no means all, of the preparations made to repel the attack. Beforehand, the Royal Engineers had supplied both pigeons and dogs to the front line to aid communication, but for different reasons they proved ineffectual.

Signaller Bert Chaney, 1/7th London Rgt

One by one our telephone lines were smashed. We endeavoured a number of times to repair them, going out into the barrage, creeping down communication trenches trying to find the ends of the wires, but in that mist and in that barrage it was a hopeless task, and we had to get back to our dugout thankful to be in one piece. Looking across in the direction of our visual communication system on the mound, we saw that it was impossible to see anything: the Aldis lamps were unable to penetrate the mist, even the telescope did not help.

Dashing down into the dugout, I scribbled two similar coded messages on the special thin paper, screwed them up and pushed them into the little containers that clip on to the pigeon's leg. I and one of the boys, each carrying a pigeon, crept up the steps and, pushing the gas blanket to one side, threw our birds into the air and away they flew. We watched them as they circled round a couple of times and then they swooped straight down and settled on top of our dugout. We retrieved them and tried once more, but those birds refused to fly. We knew so little about homing pigeons we could not understand why. Those birds had been trained to fly direct to their loft, in that mist they would not fly on a blind course and would not start until they could see their loft. So down into the dugout again and another message was written and put into the small pouch attached to the dog's collar. Leading it to the entrance, I gave it a parting slap on the rump, at the same time shouting firmly, 'Home, boy! Allez!' I watched it for a minute or two as it trotted off, then dropped the gas blanket back. Even while we were still sighing with relief, a wet nose pushed the blanket aside and in crawled the dog, scared out of its wits. All our efforts could not budge him, we pushed and shoved him, pulled him by the collar to get him moving, but he just lay down, clamped his body firmly to the ground and pretended to be asleep. He was a lot smarter than we were.

All we could do was swear a lot, give him a kick or two in the hope of moving him but without success. We eventually took the message from his collar, put it on the other dog, and tried to send that one on his way. Whether he was more timid than the first dog, or sensed its fear, he would not even move. He dropped flat on his stomach and there was no shifting him. Once again we went through the pushing and pulling, but it was no good. So ended all our wonderful preparation for keeping communications going during an attack. Within a few minutes of its commencement we had become entirely isolated.

Pte Albert Bagley, 1/6th Northumberland Fusiliers

The volume of firing got so fierce that at last flesh and blood could not stand against it any longer. As if by some instinct, every man threw himself down flat, burying his face in the soil as best he could for protection. For my part I was lying flat and wondered how long I would be like this, for the soil was sticking to my lips and I felt a tickling sensation under my face. Raising my head as high as I dare, I saw that the tickling was caused by a beetle worming his way. Oh, how I wished then that I was a beetle, or at least could be so small.

Lt Leonard Pratt, 1/4th Duke of Wellington's Rgt
A shell landed ten yards from my doorway. It was a dud, then another hit the ground four yards away, it sent a great spray of earth and mud up to the skies, and left a hot sulphur smell in my nostrils. I looked down at my feet, and saw a worm climbing my breeches. I picked it up and threw it away into the trench, remarking that it was a *bit premature* for there was life in the old dog yet!

Cpl Eric Harlow, 10th Sherwood Foresters
My recollection of the next few days is very hazy. We marched endless miles and held positions while other units went through and then we in turn leap-frogged back through them. We passed through the whole of the Somme battlefield we knew so well. We lived to some extent on the country and I remember participating in the slaughter of a very old tough cow and trying to disembowel it and cut up the meat into joints. Also I plucked some fowls and ducks and had very little sleep. My head was painful where the weight of the helmet pressed.

The advance had been so rapid that, although the casualty figures for the first day's fighting had been enormous, a large proportion had simply been overrun and taken prisoner or, like Bert Chaney, they were cut off 'in a small pocket of peace', as he described it, and were waiting for events to unfold.

Signaller Bert Chaney, 1/7th London Rgt
We no longer needed the dogs and I sent them back with a coded message just to get rid of them. They were now only too pleased

to go, being cooped up in a dugout was not their idea of a good life. I wondered sometimes if they ever found their kennels, which I am sure were by then in the hands of the enemy. The same thing applied to the pigeons though they had to run the gauntlet of some trigger-happy Jerries as they flew off, doing one complete circle to get their bearings before flying away west as straight as a die.

The defensive infrastructure had more or less collapsed and the war regained a fluidity not seen for four years. Once more civilians took to the roads, piling all they had on to carts and prams. The soldiers could not help but feel pity for people turned out of their home perhaps for a second time.

Maj. Cecil Lyne, 119th Brigade, RFA
Early in the war the Hun had overrun their once prosperous farm, driven off their cattle, killed all their stock and left them destitute. Then the tide flowed back; for 3½ years they had scraped and toiled till twelve fine cows stood in the stall, pigs, poultry, etc; their crops were all in and the old man had just put down 1,000 francs' worth of artificial manures. Every penny in the world was in that farm, and suddenly the crash came. Father, mother and eleven children, they had to leave everything. Poor old Grand-père of 80 was left behind. Twenty-four hours later that farm was given as one of my targets, but I never fired on it.

What I've been telling you is such a pitiably incomplete fragment, just a glimpse here and there of the tragedy of it all, impossible to describe, but never to be forgotten.

Capt. James Dunn, RAMC attd. 2nd Royal Welsh Fusiliers
We passed eighteen dead horses and two broken limbers, the result of a direct hit which exploded the ammunition in a limber. For much of the way we were passing the country people clearing out.

A woman, still in her second youth, very fat and quite composed, shared a cart with a breeding sow and a caged parrot; an ageing woman, wan, patient-looking, stooping, led the horse. The day was hot and the march trying; the men got fed up with being told – 'it's only one kilometre more' – they ached with every weary pace.

Trp. Arthur Bradbury, 2nd Dragoons (Royal Scots Greys)

In one considerable village we scattered a flock of sheep, evidently all abandoned in extreme haste. These unfortunate sheep seemed inclined to move out with the troops and I could see in the eyes of my fellow troopers a hungry look, in spite of the stringent penalties against looting. We halted briefly on the hilly slopes above the village and witnessed the slaughter of a sheep by two of our troopers who used their bayonets. This unlucky animal was summarily divided and tied to our saddles, which dripped with blood as we rode. We contrived to get some of it cooked when we halted for the night.

Pte Thomas Hope, 1/5th King's Liverpool Rgt

Evidence of these hurried departures are scattered all over. A perambulator with buckled wheels nobly strives, with the aid of its broken spokes and rusty framework, to defeat the attempts of its load of children's underclothing to flutter away on every friendly breeze after its youthful owners. A dilapidated harmonium is visible, miserably exposing its innards to all who pass the gable end of the little parlour in which it had once been the pampered, well-dusted hallmark of snobbish village respectability. A more gruesome object, a kennel, with long rusty chain and rain-washed skeleton of a dog, the neck bones encircled by a sodden leather collar. As I gaze on it I inwardly hope the faithful animal was killed before its master fled, or, if not, that his bones lie rotting the same as his dog's.

Capt. Harold Pope, 1/2nd Lancs Heavy Batt., RGA

Things seem a bit more settled for the moment, though there was a bit of an alarm yesterday, and we were ready to move at short notice. We are using a deserted château as a mess. A very fine house with everything left behind. We use all their plates and dishes and everything. The owner has a magnificent aviary of rare foreign birds, also ostriches and emus, in his grounds. Most of them will die of starvation, I'm afraid.

Capt. John Marshall, 468th Field Coy, RE

Doctor Foster and myself spent the best part of two days going round the town letting out dogs from premises – the owners of which had locked them up, leaving the dogs in charge, with the idea that they themselves would return in a day or two. We had several stiff climbs, up walls and trees, to get at some of these animals – and then they generally received us as burglars in a most ungrateful manner. Doctor Foster rescued a parrot that called itself Coco. The bird bit him twice on the nose, so that he had to wear a bandage. It could swear beautifully.

It appears that despite his truculence Coco was taken as a pet or mascot of the unit, for Captain Marshall records that 'after many journeys' the bird ended up living in Birmingham after the war. Just how he got it home is not revealed.

Pte Albert Bagley, 1/6th Northumberland Fusiliers

The officer turned to me and asked if I wanted anything to eat. He pointed out to me a chap who he said would see me all right. The man was only too pleased, and on diving his hand into a sandbag, he withdrew a loaf, a lump of cheese and then his water bottle. Imagine my surprise when, putting my lips to the water bottle, I found it contained fresh cow's milk. On asking my new friend where he had obtained it, he told me that nearby was a farm where all the animals were still installed.

It wasn't very far and I was surprised at looking round to find the place intact, and all the animals still fastened up. Our first visit was to the hen house, and my friend searched the nests for eggs quite methodically, just as if he were the owner. He then searched one of the hens and, before I knew, he had rung its neck and laid it on a corner. He then took me into the place where the cows were and proceeded to give them a feed of hay and then calmly got a petrol can and started to milk the cows until at last he had the can full. He also filled his water bottle and also another, which belonged to the officer to whom he was batman, which explained why he could wander off where he pleased. He then filled a sandbag with potatoes. We then returned, he carried the hen and sack of potatoes, and I the can of milk and the two water bottles. On reaching our destination he proceeded to light a fire and two hours later I was carrying roast chicken, boiled potatoes and milk to the officer in the trench. On returning to the fire, I was greeted with a meal of the above delicacies.

Lt J.R.T. Aldous, 210th Field Coy, RE

All the way up the road, and in fact all over the countryside, houses and whole villages were on fire, lighting up the whole district. One most pathetic side of the war which was very much in evidence was the dreadful fate which the livestock on the farms had to suffer: when the owners of these farms cleared out, they were in such a hurry that they left all their livestock tied up in the barns with the result that many were killed by shellfire, many were burnt in the farms, and those which escaped starved to death in their sheds. On our way up, the air was full of the cries of those miserable animals and the smell of burnt flesh was easily recognisable in some of the roads as we passed along.

Capt. Philip Ledward, Headquarters, 23rd Brigade

The brigade had already suffered heavily and everyone was gloomy. One of the first casualties had been 'Jane', the brigade headquarters'

cow. She was acquired and served with the 23rd Infantry Brigade
for three years. During all that time she gave milk, often in the
most depressing situations. All through the time we were at
Passchendaele she stood in mud and never saw grass, but she continued to give milk. Her 'man' was from the Devons, a thorough yokel
who could manage her like a horse. When we made long moves we
used to give him 100 francs and send him off into the blue, and he
used to drive Jane by easy stages through the back areas to our new
objective. All our mess servants came from the Devons and they
knew how to make Devonshire cream – that was what we used to
do with her milk, drinking tinned milk the while in our tea. She
was at once a boon and a distinction and was much mourned. She
and her faithful man were killed by a shell near Villers-Carbonnel
and fortunately it was instantaneous.

*The Germans were finally stopped at Villers-Bretonneux, a few miles
east of Amiens. Their advance had taken them fifty miles to the west
but the decisive breakthrough had eluded them. In early April, the
Germans renewed their efforts further north, but once again, after
prodigious expenditure of men and munitions, the attack petered out.
Men taken prisoner during the spring and early summer saw the
evidence that the entire German offensive, for all its apparent might,
was in fact increasingly ramshackle and held together by a shoestring.*

L/ Cpl Thomas Owen, 1st South Wales Borderers

Three others joined me. They also had staggered from the sham-
bles of no-man's-land, and we bled from various wounds all along
that pitiless road to the rear. How we escaped the shelling I know
not. German transport wagons lumbered past us at intervals, the
drivers whipping the horses to a mad gallop. Here and there,
dead or dying horses lay among the splintered ruins of shafts
and wheels. The very road was greasy with blood. Yet even as the
horses fell, the poor brutes were dragged to the side of the road
and the matter-of-fact Germans whipped out knives and cut long

strips of flesh from their steaming flanks. Heaps of intestines lay in the ditches.

Pte George Gadsby, 1/18th London Rgt (London Irish Rifles)
We had not been on the march long when we realised what a terrible state Germany was in. The roads were blocked with transport, two and three motor cars were lashed together and pulled by the power of the front one, and vehicles (not much better than orange boxes on wheels) were packed so heavily that they creaked under the weight. Although we realised what privations confronted us, we could not but raise a smile as we marched along. The Germans' transport reminded us of a travelling circus. Behind each cart generally followed a cow, whilst on the top of the loads could be seen a box of rabbits or fowls. A motor car came dashing along the road, evidently containing German staff officers. They were wearing their high coloured hats and resembled proud peacocks rather than soldiers.

What a pandemonium! Now and then a troop of dusty cavalry mounted on boney ponies passed us on the way, whilst a battalion of infantry led by martial music (which did not sound much better than the noise made by a youngster kicking a tin can along the road) advanced to the front with stooping heads looking particularly fed up and worn out.

Pte Frank Deane, 1/6th Durham Light Infantry
We were marched off back across our trenches and onwards, behind the German lines. That night we spent out in the open, then marched further back. I became quite cheerful because they seemed to have such a ramshackle lot of transport, an old harvest cart being pulled by a donkey, a mule and a horse. I didn't see any motor transport, so I thought, well, if that's the sort of equipment they've got, they won't last long; I felt quite optimistic.

Chaotic and exhausting though the retreat was, it was not without its humour, black, odd or simply bizarre.

Signaller Bert Chaney, 1/7th London Rgt

Very heavy siege guns, each with a team of at least a dozen horses, were being pushed back, the gunners whipping and cursing their mounts for not moving fast enough, the gunners telling us as they passed that the Germans were advancing fast. Amidst all the chaos, two horses attached to a swanky private carriage came trotting smartly down the road, two Australian soldiers sitting side by side on the driving seat, one wearing a black silk topper and flourishing a long whip, while the other sat beside him holding aloft an open umbrella. They also were retreating but they stopped long enough to tell us that they had no intention of letting this smart equipage fall into German hands if they could help it, saying, 'It's too good for the bleeding Hun.' Then off they went, the driver raising his hat in salute, oblivious to all the shells that were falling around, some very close indeed.

Lt J.R.T. Aldous, 210th Field Coy, RE

Bullets seem to come from a house in front of Vieux-Berquin and some more as enfilade fire through a gap between two houses on the left of our line. One amusing incident was that after the first house had been hit a very fat and old pig crawled out of the building and sat down a few yards away, turned round and looked at the house. He remained like this all through the bombardment as he was too fat to walk away, and sat there watching his former home burned down to the ground.

Capt. John Marshall, 468th Field Coy, RE

We took with us a brindled terrier named Jack, which had attached itself to Kelly, our cook. During our stay at Fouquières, this Kelly, hearing that a pal of his had got drunk and had received a black eye fighting a Canadian, set out with another man, accompanied by the faithful Jack, to try and find their friend. The first thing they did was to visit all the estaminets and not unnaturally imbibed too much liquor. This led to a heated argument as to the whereabouts of the missing man, which culminated in a fight between Kelly and his friend, in the course of which Kelly also acquired a black eye.

Kelly had false teeth, and, to avoid their being damaged, he removed them, placing them on his coat before the fray commenced. The dog took them away and buried them, they could not be found that day, but on the following day the faithful hound, on being led to the neighbourhood, dug them up.

Ever since the start of the war, the British soldier had proved himself adept at balancing his responsibilities to the army with the pursuit of his own interests and requirements. When it came to hunting, British soldiers continued la chasse *whether it was deemed legal or not: fishing with grenades, riding down a partridge, chasing a hare across a field. These activities had not always gone on far from the front lines or out of sight of the enemy. Second Lieutenant Frank Mitchell recalled one incident which took place shortly before a tank attack in the spring of 1918.*

2/Lt Frank Mitchell, Tank Corps

Captain Brown, called 'Tiny' because he stood over six feet high, was explaining various points of the attack to his tank commanders. There was a slightly serious look on his kindly face. He was Irish, a shy and modest man with a passion for fishing. He had brought his fishing rods to France with him, and wherever he found a pond, stream or river which might possibly contain a fish, he angled eagerly and with tremendous patience. His talk was of shooting and hunting, and of the wonderful fish he had caught on the Blackwater. He had been my section commander at Villers-Bretonneux, and this morning, as he talked, I remembered vividly an incident in that earlier battle.

Captain 'Tiny' Brown had been running in the open, from tank to tank, under heavy machine-gun fire, and at last he had been obliged to take refuge in a trench with the infantry. Just then there came a lull in the German attack, and Tiny, who was gazing anxiously over the parapet through field glasses, was amazed and delighted to see two brown forms creeping along through the grass in no-man's-land.

He bobbed down, excitedly called the sergeant of the infantry platoon, and thrust the glasses into his hand. 'Look out there, man, and tell me what you see!' he commanded eagerly.

Very cautiously the sergeant peeped over the top. 'Why, it's only a couple of birds, sir,' he said in surprise.

'Yes, my boy, two fine partridges! What a stroke of luck!' Tiny's face lit up with joy; he had forgotten all about the war. He borrowed a rifle, and then made a sporting offer to the sergeant.

'Now, sergeant, we'll both take shots at the partridges, shooting alternately. I bet you five francs I get them first.'

The sergeant was naturally taken aback; he hardly expected that kind of shooting in the front line, especially when the Germans might attack at any moment. No doubt he considered this excited tank officer utterly mad, but nevertheless he thought it wiser to accept the offer.

The curious contest lasted some time, for a third party entered into the game – German machine gunners in a wood behind them. Every time a steel helmet showed above the parapet, machine guns opened out in disapproval, so the rivals were forced to be very wary; but eventually the birds rose into the air, and thereupon Tiny brought them both down.

Maj. Neil Fraser-Tytler, D Batt., 149th Brigade, RFA

Yesterday the Germans deigned to turn a machine gun on to me. I was out shooting partridges with the new Irish pointer which I have annexed, and must have come a little nearer to the precious line than he quite approved of. Probably he considered pursuing partridges in no-man's-land during April contrary to the laws of the Hague Convention! So he splashed some bullets about in an aimless fashion till I removed myself to a quieter spot . . .

A month later, Major Fraser-Tytler tried his luck again.

Maj. Neil Fraser-Tytler, D Batt., 149th Brigade, RFA

The enemy, with the exception of their professional snipers, are harmless with their rifles. The other night, when I was pursuing a wounded partridge on a grassy slope within 700 yards of the Hun main line and in full view of them, not a single shot was fired at me, except a few rounds of Hun whizzbang shrapnel, which burst as usual harmlessly high in the air. Curious when one thinks of the South African War, with accurate rifle shooting up to 1,500 yards.

As things are quiet at headquarters, the colonel has been spending several afternoons with us sniping from our Observation Post, and, his home being in the midst of the best partridge country, I have frequently been over there for joint drives, utilising the orderlies and spare signallers as beaters, so neither partridge killing (forget the month) nor Hun killing (always in season) has been neglected.

The Germans launched their final attacks in May 1918 before, exhausted by their efforts, the front lines settled once again. But there was a difference. In the past the Germans had been able to withstand Allied counterattacks, giving ground only inch by inch. No longer. When the Allies regrouped to launch an offensive of their own, there would be neither the morale nor the uniform strength in depth to resist. In the meantime there was a short hiatus in which both sides could appreciate the summer weather and the wildlife that once more flourished in countryside that had been occupied and farmed until just weeks earlier.

Lt Cyril Walker, 18th Div., Signal Coy, RE

We remained for a month holding the line between Albert and the Ancre. Not a strenuous front on these midsummer days – no

worries beyond occasional shelling near the main road and by the
batteries. The poppies have taken a new lease of life and flour-
ish in tangled tracts with vetch, cornflowers and blue masses of
suckory; great yellow swallowtails flit everywhere, and fritillaries
and little blues and browns. All the country is open and chalky
under a baking sun. The grasshoppers' chirp becomes unsupport-
ably insistent, and little coveys of quail whistle by your feet in the
ripening corn, or get up and fly when flushed by a dog.

Pte Wilfrid Edwards, 15th London Rgt (Civil Service Rifles)
The front lay west of the old Somme battlefields, in more or less
undevastated country, and a period of relative quiet supervened.
There was a front-line trench on the slopes above Albert, in standing corn over the chalk, which was memorable in a number of
ways. A typical sequence of events on quiet days was as follows:
at 'stand-to' an hour before dawn, the darkness of no-man's-land
would become musical with the songs of skylarks, which continued until sunrise. When the sun was well up, a bevy of swallow-
tail butterflies would appear, fluttering over the trench and perch-
ing on the wild carrot that was flowering on the chalky rubble
of the parapet. We had ample opportunities for observing these
lovely insects: we could almost rub noses with them! Curiously, I
do not remember seeing any other butterflies here, though white
admirals and marbled whites were common elsewhere. Despite
bursts of shelling and small-arms fire, and a nasty smell of phos-
gene among the corn, they all appeared in mint condition. They
ignored us, and we them for the most part, though one or two
went home to younger brothers, folded up in green envelopes.

Lt Cyril Walker, 18th Div., Signal Coy, RE
The 12th Division relieved us in the line and we went to Querrieu
on the Ancre to prepare for active battle on the Somme. The
weather began wet but became hot again. The lazy Somme
tempted with its cool, reedy backwater and shady poplars. The

hills by it are hot and chalky with scattered juniper bushes and gay wild flowers where great swallowtails flit and settle. Golden orioles call and fly in packs about the high woods and Australian soldiers battle or bomb for fun in the cool river while their mules graze in the deep watermeadows.

Even where the trenches ran through the old Somme battlefield to the north, there was a poignant beauty to be appreciated when the all-too-evident scars of the land were softened by a new natural growth.

Cpl Fred Hodges, 10th Lancashire Fusiliers
One day I picked a bunch of red field poppies from the old grassy trench and put them in the metal cup attached to my rifle. They quickly wilted in the hot sun, but in any case I don't think the idea would have appealed to my officer if he had seen them. Most of the boys and men I was with apparently found no pleasure in flowers, but I was acutely conscious of them growing there in the midst of all that man-made destruction. Only field poppies and a few other wild flowers, but the persistent charm of nature in such conditions during that period of May, June and July 1918 was more poignant than it had ever been before in my life, or since.

That spring and early summer, I was often conscious of the great contrast between the man-made ugliness and horrors of the war-torn countryside, and the fresh, unchanging harmony and beauty of nature. Certainly I have never lived so close to nature since, nor been so acutely aware of life. Between wrecked villages, the crops lay ungathered, and nature, uncontrolled by man, was a riot of scent and colour; oats and barley mingled with blue corn-flowers and red poppies, with the song of a lark in a blue sky. This contrast was almost too much to be borne.

In our daily lives in towns and cities, we live with our senses half asleep, but in those fields near Albert, where for nearly four years death reigned, I was never more alive. Even at night, when on sentry duty under the stars, which I seldom noticed when living in a town, I was intensely aware of the orderly arrangement of the stars compared with the disorderly scene all around.

L/Cpl Frank Earley,
1/5th King's Own Yorkshire Light Infantry

I am in a narrow trench about four feet deep, and my dugout is a hole scooped out of the trench side and roofed over with a piece of corrugated iron. When, at night, we settle to rest, and hang up the oil sheets at the openings, and light our candle, we are comfortable and happy. You must know that we have good companions – fine big earwigs, who run about the walls all day and night. They are much bigger than those you know at home, and look very fierce. I like to watch them crawling about and running out of the way of the big field spiders. See what grand amusement I have!

For all its evident beauty and variety, the natural world brought its own complications and dangers. It had been two years since men held trenches that were within a stone's throw of abandoned farm animals and most of the men serving in 1918 would simply not have had the length of service to remember how strange cracks and rustlings put the hairs up on the neck.

Pte Christopher Haworth,
14th Argyll and Sutherland Highlanders

Two men are standing on sentry at each end of the bay, while Scott is resting, too cold to sleep, on the fire step. The other members of the section are in dugouts at the rear of the trench. It is uncomfortably quiet; a cloud passes over the moon, and our small world is plunged into darkness, but the blackout is momentary, as a high wind speedily moves the small cloud onwards, leaving the moon to shed its silver-green light on us. A cock crows in the distance.

'Kick me, Chris,' says MacDonnell, full of surprise. 'Am I standing in a trench or in a country farmyard?'

Another cock answers the call, and one of the sentries, half turning so as to see into the trench, is much perturbed and calls to me, 'Those blasted birds'll give our position away if they keep on screeching like that.'

I do not reply to his remark, as I believe it myself; not that a feathered rooster will inform the enemy of our whereabouts, but it is making a noise, a clarion call, and our tired, frightened and nervy minds hang on to the idea that the cock will arouse the sleeping enemy and cause him to blow us to the moon.

Now a dog barks, the echo ringing across the sleepy and frosty air. The cock crows again, the other bird answers, and another cloud – a much bigger one this time – completely obscures the moon. Silence once again, and MacDonnell and I resume our walking.

A whitish-grey light is gradually appearing in the sky: the moon now is entirely blotted out, heralding the approach of dawn and once again the call of the cock pierces the air. Suddenly the quietness is broken by a screeching whistle, and a heavy shell lands *Crump! Bang! Wallop!* behind our trench, followed immediately by four more. The sentry turns and stares at me, but says not a word about the cock, although he has his suspicions that the old bird has brought this trouble upon us.

Pte Henry Irving, 2/4th Gloucestershire Rgt

Twenty paces away, slightly to our left, was part of a building with a small farm with a wooden lean-to on the nearest half wall end. We creep, listen, creep, listen and so on like stalking cats. The only terrifying thing now was broken tiles over which we had to creep. Soon all three of us were lifting the largest pieces of tile out of the creeping line. More creeping and listening. It seemed like a lifetime getting to that wooden lean-to but we did, stood up and prepared for any sudden intrusion but none came, that is probably why I am writing this . . .

A few more Jerry parachute flares, he was getting the wind up, then in the distance we could hear a cock crow, and to really put us on the alert and ready, we could hear something moving about and cracking the tiles which littered the ground. The safety catch is off and bayonet is on to surprise anyone who might be snooping for a take over. In a case like this, surprise attack at close quarters is the best, especially in the dark. The tile cracking came nearer and came round the corner of this half-demolished small farm when, all of a sudden, grunt and another grunt and the sound of four or five piglets out for an early day with mamma. Thoughts turned to gammon rashers but the mother would squeal blue murder especially as she had some offspring and so we waited for the lot to get out of our way.

Thoughts of gammon rashers: no matter where he was, no soldier ever felt he was fed enough by the army. Civilian-run estaminets had traditionally been the place for a Tommy to buy his egg and chips, often at inflated prices. After four years of war, civilians were hard-nosed and savvy as to the laws of commerce and savvy too as to the ways of British troops and their capacity to help themselves.

Pte Christopher Haworth, 14th Argyll and Sutherland Highlanders

Milk can be obtained from the one cow on the farm, but no free issue. Having purchased *du lait*, my section scouts around the farm in the hope of locating chicken or other treasures which might be put to good use when darkness falls. We are like primitive man now, and if we are unable to purchase necessities, we 'scrounge' them, which to the mind of the serving soldier is quite legitimate as it often happens that money is worthless. On this farm, however, there is nothing to scrounge: troops have been here before, and Madame understands the psychology of the British soldier, and locks the cow up at night in case she strays. This is a wise precaution, for if Madame left it in the field at night it would be cooked meat by the morning. When a fellow has not tasted meat since he left England, and is hungry

– and we are always hungry – it becomes a natural instinct to kill the cow . . .

We enter a house for a meal of *pommes de terre frites* and *oeuf frite* – a plate of chips and one egg – one franc. The dining room is dirty – we are repelled by the sight of big black gluttonous flies, a solid mass covering the plates which had been used by others.

'Hell!' exclaims Fraser. 'We can't eat here.'

'It's the best you will get in this godforsaken place, Jock,' says a man who is finishing a meal. 'All the other places are the same – covered with flies – they breed quicker here than lice on a soldier's shirt – and that's saying something!'

We do not like the idea but must feed, and having dined we get out quickly.

The quality of food for officers was incomparably better than for other ranks. Not that officers were less willing to 'scrounge' when the opportunity presented itself, though some were a little less capable than others.

Capt. John Marshall, 468th Field Coy, RE

Crawling through the rhododendrons bordering the moat, I disturbed a pair of roosting swans. Remembering books of the Middle Ages which speak of the swan as an edibility, it occurred to me that I might introduce one to the menu of the mess, so I went in search of a weapon and found a pick helve. Cautiously approaching one of the gabblers, I caught him two strong blows on the neck, but he seemed none the worse for them, and escaped me. Men: in future hit swans on the top of the head.

In July 1918, the Allies launched a series of small actions designed to pave the way for greater success. Tanks were used in great numbers and, with the ground ahead less broken up than in the great battles of attrition of 1917, their progress was often spectacular. For those surviving farm animals out grazing, the appearance of so many tanks must have been terrifying.

2/Lt Frank Mitchell, Tank Corps

As I was walking in front of a tank I heard a strange noise immediately ahead, and suddenly a huge form charged down on me out of the night. As I recoiled, it rushed past me, missing me by inches, and then pulled up abruptly, heaving and panting. Greatly startled, I flashed my torch in its direction, and discovered that it was a poor inoffensive cow, shuddering with fear! Hastily I rushed to the driver's flap, yelling to him to stop, and he pulled up just in time. The cow was tethered to a peg in the ground, and the rope, becoming entangled in the track, had dragged the terrified animal nearer and nearer, in spite of its frantic efforts to escape.

At length the dim outlines of the wood came into sight, and the tanks, like huge toads, crawled into the undergrowth to find hiding places. To enter the pitch-black depths of a wood at night is a weird experience. Branches are cracking and snapping on every side, occasionally a young tree falls heavily to the ground, startled birds flutter by, squawking and crying, the muffled light of a torch sweeps to and fro revealing great trunks standing like pillars in the night.

With newer, ever more reliable tanks, the value of horses on the battlefield was slowly but surely being undermined. By 1918, the condition of the horses being sent from Britain was also being called into question.

Capt. Norman Dillon, 2nd Bttn, Tank Corps

We were supplied with horses, although I can't think why. They were rarely, if ever, used, but provided me with an opportunity for riding. They were frightful brutes, some being broken down polo ponies, or racehorses, or those thrown for purchase by owners at home or in Ireland, happy to part with vicious or unmanageable animals. One of the best refused to jump even a narrow trench, and had a habit of rearing up when we met one of the motor vehicles, which fortunately did not happen very often.

The Australians were good horsemen and were rather proud of this and thought we knew nothing in this respect. We had one horse that nobody could ride because it was a confirmed bolter. But it looked a picture. It was not difficult to arrange an exchange for a less exciting mount, and off they went, pleased at scoring off the Pommies. The next we heard was that one of their experts got on its back, when it promptly bolted and went nearly into Amiens (seven miles) before it stopped.

To cement the partnership between the Australians and ourselves, a small attack at Hamel was staged with 60 tanks. The result was a great success . . . At last the realisation that the tank was a war winner had penetrated the horse-minded GHQ.

After the strains of fighting, the opportunity to recuperate was welcome. For young officers, on whose shoulders great responsibility for the lives of their men rested, time out to take stock and relax was essential.

Lt Henry Lawson, 10th Manchester Rgt

Often we lived in a wood when resting; a lovely little place full of spring and summer scents and sweetness. I was interested in butterflies and moths. Once I found on a stem of grass the most perfect specimen I had ever seen of *Hylophila bicolorana*, a gloriously vivid-green moth with white underwings, having just emerged from its chrysalis and dried its wings. At the time I was talking with our Company Commander, lying in the shade of the trees. I drew his attention to this miracle of nature's beauty and speculated whether it could be a harbinger of peace. I derived comfort, a kind of companionship, from this cycle of natural life within range of the shellfire and the total destructiveness of war.

I have frequently sensed that all mystery finally lies in the order of creation, its development and regeneration. I was fortunate to have been brought up with a sufficient outline knowledge, though elementary, of living creatures to obtain solace and immense pleasure at so tiny a discovery. Such moments were priceless for the recruitment of spirit in preparation for the next round of fighting. The unexpected discovery of this perfect moth, which I have never forgotten, did indeed prove a precursor of the peace we all longed for, but alas only after the heavy losses, many amongst our own company, in the great offensive battles that were to lead to victory in a few months' time.

Pte Wilfrid Edwards, 15th London Rgt (Civil Service Rifles)

In August the Battle of Amiens brought us back into the 1916 battlefield, a sort of desiccated Passchendaele in that summer heat, but with weeds and brambles spreading over the old shell-holes and trenches. Now we were doing what we went out to do, with no time for anything else. The only animals I saw in this waste-land that could be called wild were occasional roving dogs, which we thought might be strays from the German army. And the only beautiful thing I remember seeing was a spray of ripe blackberries gleaming in the early sunlight on the edge of what had been St Pierre Vaast Wood hard by the smoking heaps of empty cartridge cases as we flushed the German machine gunners out.

Pte Christopher Haworth, 14th Argyll and Sutherland Highlanders

Passing a ruined house demolished by incessant shellfire, we see a tiny thing of beauty flourishing amidst this desolation. In the shell-torn garden, the grasses have formed a shroud, nature had triumphed over man's vindictiveness, and standing valiantly like sentinels are several magnificent bright red poppies, graceful in their simplicity.

The Battle of Amiens threw the Germans back across the Somme battle-field and beyond. The German High Command realised at this point that the war could not be won and when the Germans' last great defensive position was breached in September, open warfare resumed. For so long, the wonder of nature had been both in its beauty and its survival

in a wasteland, but now that vision was inverted. It was scenes of
death and destruction in an otherwise unspoilt land that impinged
themselves upon the memory of those who were there.

Lt Henry Lawson, 10th Manchester Rgt

We came to a stretch of open and undamaged countryside – a
marvellous contrast to life in the trenches – and entered and occupied a château, which had been an important headquarters of the
Germans. The lawns were mown, the borders of flowers still in
bloom, lovely in an early autumn evening. But the shock still
lingers in my memory. I went out into the garden to post my men.
There had been a fight by another regiment before our arrival, of
which I had heard nothing; the picture of that fight lay glaring
before my eyes when at each turn of the garden's footpaths we
came upon the bodies of the young men of that regiment shot
down by rifle or machine gun, hardly marked, lying almost as
children resting in sleep, in number perhaps a dozen. Why their
regiment had not covered the bodies was never explained to me
and we had to do what was necessary.

The poignant contrast on the one hand of the immaculate and
peaceful garden and on the other of the sacrifice of such young
lives brought tears to my eyes. That graphic and overwhelmingly
pitiful picture has often been in my mind as I have walked around
the paths and lawns of my own country garden. An episode quite
unforgettable and stamped with limitless grief for the evil of the
world. That fight must have been the most grisly hide and seek
ever played. I once heard a cathedral sermon ending with the
words, 'never forget the garden'. The Bible is full of incidents associated with gardens and I speculated whether the preacher, whom
I knew well, could possibly imagine what garden was indelibly
printed in the mind of this old soldier among his congregation.
So lovely, so beautiful, yet so besmirched and desecrated by a deed
of war.

Cpl Fred Hodges, 10th Lancashire Fusiliers

I used to wonder what the seigneur would say if he could see what had happened to his beautiful château, extensive grounds and gardens and the protecting high brick wall. On one of our working parties, when enemy shells were bursting with loud crashes in the street flanked by the high wall, our officer led us through the village by the back ways and gardens, and I had a good view in the moonlight of the smashed and broken château gardens, greenhouses, statues and summer houses as we hurried through the tree stumps.

Pte Frederick Voigt, Labour Corps

The big bronze bell lay outside the church in two pieces. The cemetery had been churned by shellfire. The tombstones were chipped and broken. One big block of granite had been overturned by a bursting shell and the inscription was so scarred as to be illegible. The stone Christ had been hit in many places. His left hand was gone, so that He hung aslant by the other. Both His legs had been blown off at the knees and His nose and mouth had been carried away by some flying shell fragment or shrapnel ball. All the graves had been thrown into confusion by the violence of innumerable explosions. Bits of bone femurs, ribs, lower jaws lay scattered about. The hip of a soldier who had been buried in his clothes projected from the soil with the brown mass of maggot chrysalids still clinging to it.

Cpl Fred Hodges, 10th Lancashire Fusiliers

We were marching at night towards the front to take part in the next attack, as usual marching on the right side of the road. We were passing a long column of transport wagons coming back from the front. We heard explosions ahead of us as a German plane dropped small anti-personnel bombs. As it came nearer, we realised that it was flying low above the track. We could see the column of men in front breaking up as officers and men ran off the track to the right. We all followed suit, flinging ourselves down about thirty or forty yards from the track.

When it was all over, we stood up, and for some reason that I cannot explain, some of us were laughing as we returned to the track, where we found both men and mules lying dead. We marched on, and soon we reached the forward area.

The moon was rising as we left the track and moved in open order across a very large field of stubble, and here in the bright moonlight, field mice scampered in scores; one could scarcely avoid treading on them. Obviously this area had been cultivated, unlike the Somme fields where no corn had been harvested during the war.

Lt John Nettleton, 2nd Rifle Brigade

I was pretty sure the Boche had withdrawn but, even so, I got the fright of my life when, as we were passing a cottage, we heard the clatter of breaking crockery. My runner unslung his rifle and I drew my revolver. In great trepidation we crept up the garden path as quietly as we could. Then we flung open the door and rushed in – to be confronted with a tiny kitten who was crawling about on the dresser from which he had knocked down a cup. The relief was so great that we both burst out laughing.

Lt Reginald Dixon, 251st Siege Batt., RGA

It is not possible to remember where I found my kitten. I know that we had been on the go in the final push that beat the Hun out of France in 1918, on the go for days and days and nights and nights, pulling our guns out, pulling them into some new position three or four hours later, laying out new lines of fire at first light – for we often moved in at night, and often enough to some farmyard or other that gave some cover to our gunners . . .

On this occasion we had got my own two guns into a farmyard about midnight. The farm was deserted by its owners, who had obviously fled as the tide of battle swept near. By the coming of

the false dawn these guns were in position; as the men were giving
the last heaves on the ropes, I spotted a tiny movement under the
gun carriage, between the huge wheels. I stopped the men for a
moment and bent down to investigate. There, terrified out of its
tiny wits, was a wee kitten. How or why it had got into such a
position no one could guess, but I hauled her out with ease. By
the torches' lights and that of the false dawn, everybody could see
what I had in my hands. Somehow it cheered everybody up. The
men laughed. 'Blimey! It's a bloody kitten!'

I stuffed the poor little thing into my trench-coat pocket,
which was commodious enough, and got the chaps going again,
until the gun was where we wanted it. Then I set off with my
bombardier and some stakes and my compass and when the true
dawn came I had my guns in position and my lines of fire laid out.
I joined the others in the kitchen of the farm which was serving
as a very temporary mess, and got a mug of hot tea and a swig of
whisky from my flask. And not till then did I remember that I had
a kitten in my pocket!

I pulled the little beggar out, unsquashed and with all its nerves
apparently intact. My fellow officers stood around and admired
the mite of tabby fur and whiskers, and made a fuss of her. My
batman swiftly brought a saucer of milk, and there on the kitchen
table by the light of hurricane lamps, surrounded by the rough
kindliness of gunner officers in full war kit, that kitten, without
the slightest sign of discomposure, weighed into that milk, and,
having disposed of it, mewed for more.

'Mr Dixon's kitten' became famous in 251 Battery, and my
batman had the job now of seeing to her welfare. She went along
with us and she thrived right up to the moment when I bade her
goodbye and went off on the quest for my leave warrant.

Pte Albert Lowy, Army Service Corps

A friend who bred wire-haired terriers asked me if I would like
one as a mascot. It was a bitch who, having one blind eye, could

not be 'shown', but was healthy and exceptionally intelligent.
Food for dogs was scarce, and this one could not be provided for
much longer.

I got permission to keep the dog in camp and to take her with
me when we went overseas. It was a little unfortunate that she
took a dislike to the captain, growled when he tried to stroke her,
though she was perfectly friendly towards everyone else. She was
a very good-looking thoroughbred and was much petted. We had
very little drill or other military exercises, so she was always near
me, she learned my family whistle tune, and slept in my ambulance, which she could always recognise although all were new
and exactly similar . . .

She of course sat next to me whenever I went out, and she
became very adept at running off to find the waste-food bins,
where she could eat her fill of the choicest bits, and return to *her*
ambulance usually before I was ready to leave. If it happened that
I was ready first, I only had to whistle, and she would run at once,
she never kept me waiting more than a few minutes.

She was well known at the British hospitals and was friendly
with everybody. Comments were often made to me about having
so handsome a dog, and men would stop me in the street and
ask me how much I wanted for her. I told them that no amount
of money could buy her; she was simply not for sale. Some of
our drivers had picked up stray dogs; there were quite a number
that had been 'lost' by their owners. Peace seems to have reigned
among these mongrels and mine only rarely picked up fleas from
them.

It is more than likely that my life was saved by the fact of my
having her with me during all this time. There was a raging 'flu'
that many army men caught: some died of it, possibly from the
bad conditions in the overcrowded hospitals. I had to take many
such cases, and, not unnaturally, I found myself with a very high
temperature; I shook all over and my eyes ached and I saw everything blurred. Hospital was obviously the right place for me, I

would only have had to 'report sick', but – and it was a desperate 'but' – what would have become of her? I thought of the horrible wet marquees where men were put, and the poor attention they were getting; and I knew that I should not find her when I came out. I decided not to go sick.

That day and the next I managed somehow to keep out of the way of people who might notice my shaking and obvious illness. I had to drive very slowly because I had so little strength in my arms, and the high fever made me anxious lest I should have an accident. I managed those two awful days and then gradually recovered. My dog was saved . . .

There was a period when I was taken off my ambulance to be a dispatch rider. One has to obey orders, however unpleasant they may be. I obtained an extra large knapsack and carried her on my back wherever I had to go. She would sit in it with her head poking out and often resting on my shoulder, enjoying the rush of air: my back-seat driver. This experience of sitting in a sack helped very materially when we left for home [at the end of the war].

Pte Frederick Voigt, Labour Corps

Our new camp lay at the foot of a gloomy hill. A disused trench ran right across it. Rifles, bayonets, bandoliers, grenades, water bottles, packs, articles of clothing and bits of equipment lay scattered everywhere. Barbed wire rusted in coils or straggling lengths. Rusty tins and twisted, rusty sheets of shrapnel-riddled corrugated iron littered the sodden mud. Water, rust-stained or black and fetid, stagnated in pools and shell-holes. The sides of the trench were moist with iridescent slime. Dead soldiers lay everywhere with grey faces, grey hands and mouldering uniforms. Their pockets were turned inside out and mud-stained letters and postcards, and sometimes a mildewed pocketbook or a broken mirror, were dispersed round every rotting corpse. In front of my tent the white ribs of a horse projected from a heap of loose earth. Nearby, a boot with a human foot inside emerged from the black scummy water at the bottom of a shell-hole. An evil stench hovered in the air.

We buried all the dead that lay within the camp lines. Then darkness descended and we crept into our tents. We were lying on wet, oozy clay, thinly covered with wisps of soaked grass and decaying straw where had been a cornfield here a year ago. There were thirteen of us in one tent. We were wedged in tightly, shoulder to shoulder, our feet all in one bunch.

Candles were lit and some of the men sat up and searched their clothes. I was conscious of a slight irritation, but was so tired and depressed that I resolved to ignore it and postpone my usual search to the following day. But as I lay still, trying hard to fall asleep, the irritation increased. At last it became so maddening that I started up in bitter rage. I lit my candle and pulled off my shirt.

'Chatty are yer?' said someone in an amused tone.

'I've got a big one crawling about somewhere,' I answered. None of us ever admitted that we had more than one or two, even when we knew we had a great many. It was also considered less disreputable to have one 'big one' than two small ones.

'It's the Gink's fault 'e swarms with 'em. I was standin be'ind 'im in the ranks the other day an' I saw three of 'em crorlin out of 'is collar up 'is neck. 'E never washes and never changes 'is clothes, so what can yer expect?'

The 'Gink' flared up at once:

'Yer god-damn son of a bitch it's youss guys that never washes. I bet yer me borram dollar I 'ant got a god-damn chat on me' . . .

A long wrangle ensued. Wild threats and foul insults were flung about. But the quarrel, like nearly all our quarrels, did not go beyond violent words. I began to search and soon found a big swollen louse. I crushed it with my thumbnail so that the blood spurted out. I heard several faint cracks coming from the opposite side of the tent and knew that others were also hunting for vermin. I examined the seams of my shirt and found two or three more. Then, to my dismay, I discovered several eggs. They are so minute that some are sure to escape the most careful scrutiny. The presence of eggs is always a warning that many nights of irritation will have to pass by before the young grow sufficiently big to be discovered easily. I thought I had looked at every square inch of my shirt, but I looked at it a second time in order to make sure. I soon found a whitish elongated body clinging tightly to the cloth. Then I found another wedged into the seam. Meanwhile, my neighbour, who had been tossing about restlessly and scratching himself and sighing with desperate vexation, lit his candle and began to search busily. The sound of an occasional crack showed how successful he was.

The night was warm and sultry. A storm threatened and it was necessary to close the tent flap. I blew out my candle and wrapped myself in my blankets. I was unable to stretch my legs because others were in the way. I was hemmed and pressed in on all sides. I felt an impulse to kick out savagely, but was able to control myself.

The stifling heat became unbearable, and at the same time the cold, clammy moisture from the soft, sodden mud underneath began to penetrate groundsheet and blankets. The irritation recommenced. A louse so big that I could feel it crawling along stopped and drew blood. I tried in vain to go to sleep. I heard my neighbour scratching himself steadily. Nor could he find a comfortable position to lie in and kept twisting and turning and moaning. The other men were snoring or fidgeting restlessly. At length a fitful slumber came upon me and a confusion of rotting bodies swarming with monstrous lice passed before my closed eyes. I was fully awake long before reveille, sleepy and unrefreshed, and when reveille came we received orders to move within two hours.

All the evidence was there: the number of enemy prisoners, the inexorable retreat of the German army, the predominance of Allied firepower, yet only a few dared imagine that the war could be close to the finish. In the last weeks, the cavalry had once again asserted itself in open country; a last hurrah in which dragoons, lancers and hussars could harass the enemy, cutting lines of communication. For a few in the infantry, the appearance of the cavalry was a little late in the day as, one by one, village after village was liberated from four years of occupation.

Pte Thomas Hope, 1/5th King's Liverpool Rgt

Seems like the end of the war to me; it's a proper breakthrough at last. And then, most glorious sight of all, the cavalry. How we cheer them as they trot past. This is the first time I have seen mounted cavalrymen so near the front and in full warpaint, tin hat, spare bandoliers of ammunition round their horses' necks, swords and rifles, everything complete. The creak of leather and the jingle of harnesses sound, to my ears, almost like the bells of peace. They canter over a rise in the ground and are lost to view, and I have an uncomfortable feeling that I won't be in at the death after all. If this advance continues, with cavalry streaming through, the war will be over within a fortnight. It's a great feeling chasing the Boche, even at a distance.

Pte Andrew Bowie, 5th Queens' Own Cameron Highlanders

We had fallen out by the side of the road and suddenly we heard the patter of horses' feet and round the corner came a squadron of cavalry. There they were, sitting on their horses, looking proud. And you should have heard the remarks. 'Oh, they've come on their gee-gees to help us finish the war', and 'Oh, they haven't brought their hobby horses with them.'

Pte Christopher Haworth,
14th Argyll and Sutherland Highlanders

Having crawled along for an hour we halt on the side of the road for a rest, which is not very satisfying, as we have to stand. On the side of the road are scores of carcasses of mutilated horses and mules. What a pitiable sight they make! I have always looked upon a horse as a noble animal, and to see them battered and mangled by shellfire sickens me.

'I don't think there's a living creature under the sun which isn't brought into the war,' says one man.

'It certainly looks like it,' I reply.

Pte Frederick Voigt, Labour Corps

We came to a litter of wreckage that had once been a village and then we crossed the main road and entered a little wood, or rather an assembly of scarred tree trunks leaning at all angles, which was crossed by a zigzag trench and all the refuse of battle lay scattered about.

An Australian soldier lay on a low mound. His head had dropped off and rolled backwards down the slope. The lower jaw had parted from the skull. His hands had been devoured by rats and two little heaps of clean bones were all that remained of them. The body was fully clothed and the legs encased in boots and puttees. One thighbone projected through a rent in the trousers and the rats had gnawed white grooves along it. A mouldy pocketbook lay by his side and several postcards and a soiled photograph of a woman and a child. An attempt had been made to bury some of the dead, and several lay beneath heaps of loose earth with their boots projecting. But the rats had reached them all, and black, circular tunnels led down into the fetid depths of the rotting bodies. The stench that filled the air was so intolerable that we hastened to get out of this dreadful place.

Capt. James Dunn, RAMC attd. 2nd Royal Welsh Fusiliers

The people were friendly and kind to us, but they seemed as yet too dazed to realise that the German occupation was actually a thing of the past. They were badly clad, looked sad and emaciated. What they craved was meat. They asked for the carcass of a horse that had been killed in our lines. It must have been a British horse, because all the German horses we came upon had been stripped of the best of their flesh. Seemingly every German on finding a dead horse took out his jackknife, cut himself a steak – preferably from the loin – and put it in his haversack for a future meal. The inhabitants stripped the bones; groups of old men, women and children could be seen round the carcasses.

Capt. Francis Hitchcock, 2nd Prince of Wales' Leinster Rgt
At one point we came on a particularly revolting sight – half a dozen bare-footed women tearing off flesh from a mule, which had been killed some days previously in the advance. They had pulled the skin off the quarters, and with knives and forks were cutting off chunks, and putting them into handkerchiefs. They were ravenous with hunger.

Cpl Fred Hodges, 10th Lancashire Fusiliers
When I reached the back door of the farm, I found a small queue of men waiting, and saw an old Frenchman pumping up water from a well under an old stone sink; it was very primitive. Soon I moved into the stone-floored kitchen and, as I waited my turn, I studied his old wrinkled face, grey hair sprouting out from under a peaked cap. Outside, on the road, enemy shells were bursting, some quite near, but the old man was completely unconcerned as he pumped up water for the thirsty troops. His twinkling eyes and stolid peasant patience revealed an uncomplaining acceptance of the war on his farm; life must go on; British boys were thirsty, so he filled our water bottles.

Trp. Benjamin Clouting, 4th (Royal Irish) Dragoon Guards
Increasing numbers of German prisoners could be seen, trudging back to our makeshift prison cages. Many were ridiculously young and looked as if their world had fallen to pieces. They looked dishevelled, their equipment dilapidated, for their lines of supply were breaking down, and many had been left to scrounge their

own food. At one farmhouse where I stopped right at the end of the war, I found the owners in tears: the Germans had passed through, the previous night, and had eaten their old guard dog, cooking it at the farm.

Pte Dick Trafford, 1/2nd Monmouthshire Rgt

We were capturing the enemy all the time. I wouldn't say young boys, I'd say young men. They were glad that it was ending because from their point of view they would be right for meals, that's what they tried to explain to us, they'd not seen a decent meal in a long time. The only thing they could do had been to kill their horses and use the meat for food.

Lt Col Rowland Fielding, 15th London Rgt (Civil Service Rifles)

On reaching the town, as I found no horse or wheeled traffic other than some belonging to our army, I sent my horses home and walked, so as to be in company with the inhabitants, every one of whom was on foot. No, not quite. I saw a hearse drawn by what could have been called a 'skin': indeed, it was less than a skin. It was a skeleton. That was the only horse or vehicle that I saw in Lille today, left behind by the Germans after their merciless occupation of the city.

The end was almost in sight. The drive north-east had taken the British back into lands they had vacated in the Mons retreat over four years earlier. And with the advancing units were their mascots, cosseted, loved and well fed, despite the onerous speed of advance that was beginning to outrun soldiers' supply lines.

Maj. Richard Foot, D Batt., 310th Brigade, RFA

Another casualty in the Mormal Forest was the loss of the battery pet, a fine fat billy goat. He had been on a wagon that got ditched and, in the subsequent confusion, slipped his halter and disappeared into the wood. He was quite a character, that goat, the pet of the wagon lines for more than a year, waxing plump on the plentiful supply of hay and oats for the horses. He had a mania for tobacco and would rear up and put his forefeet on a smoker's shoulders, snatch a lighted cigarette from the astonished man's lips and eat it with evident enjoyment. He could also be relied upon to butt an unpopular visitor, and his horns hurt with his full weight behind them! We never found him again, though search parties looked for him in the forest for several days. We could only imagine that he had been found, killed and eaten by the local French civilians, who were very short of meat.

Lt Andrew McCormick, 182nd Labour Coy

A little beyond Valenciennes, I was moved to honest laughter when I saw the goat mascot of some unit sitting on the top of a transport wagon with its horns sticking up through a lady's tricky straw hat having on it a large red, white and blue bow. It was a perfect type of the unconscious humorist. But whoever rigged it up in that disguise did a good thing in helping to put so many folks into a mirthful frame of mind.

Capt. John Marshall, 468th Field Coy, RE

The road had been blown up in two places by the retreating Germans, and I had orders to take a party to repair it to enable vehicles to enter the town. The Monmouths' transport was believed to be somewhere in the place and I spent an hour or two searching for it. Eventually I located it in some blown-down cottages. I should not have found it, were it not for the discovery of the Monmouths' pet monkey sitting on a doorstep, unperturbed by the shelling, gravely examining his own features, from every sort of angle, in a cracked piece of looking glass. His owners were in the cellar.

Signaller Bert Chaney, 58th Bttn Machine Gun Corps

On a cold November day a battery of 18lbs galloped past going
hell for leather. Suddenly they made a tremendous swerve left,
through a gap in a hedge, almost overturning in the ditch, into
a field of stubble, the drivers using their spurs for all they were
worth, then making a complete semi-circle. They stopped with
a terrific jerk as the riders hung on the reins, pulling back the
mules' heads and almost piling the guns on to their limbers, the
gun muzzles now pointing in the direction they had been facing
originally. In a few swift movements the mules were uncoupled
and the gun trails dropped to the ground. At a range of less than
a thousand yards they began firing like mad. The thrill of seeing
and hearing those guns going into action was unforgettable, something I had not seen before. I realised how thrilling war must have
been before someone thought up the idea of a stationary war, a war
of attrition, which turned men into moles, living like vermin in
holes in the ground.

Pte Frederick Voigt, Labour Corps

A bend of the road, as it topped a gentle slope, revealed an expanse
of smooth green fields dotted with groups of trees. It did our eyes
good to see trees that were alive and unharmed. Their foliage was
autumn-tinted – until now we had hardly realised that autumn
was with us. A placid river flowed through the meadows. On the
far shore was a town, beyond it a hill crowned by a fine château.
As we walked on, the scattered houses drew closer and closer
together until they formed continuous rows. A civilian passed by,
pushing a wheelbarrow that clattered over the cobbles. Then there
followed a woman with a bundle on her back.

There was something peculiar about the houses. They were
not damaged in the same way as the others we had seen. They
were all roofless and floorless, but the walls were unharmed except
for occasional holes and scars. Then we suddenly realised that
the Germans had stripped the entire street of all woodwork, of

floorboards, of beams and rafters, of doors and window frames, leaving only the bare, empty shells of brick. We turned a corner and entered another street in which the houses had not been rifled. Several were occupied by civilians. Before us, in an open field, lay our camp. Scribbled in chalk on a piece of board nailed across a broken window were the words:

> *'Der Friede wird stündlich erwartet.'*
> Peace is expected every hour.

And then peace arrived. The Armistice left most men somewhat dumbfounded and at a loss what to do. Suddenly there was no objective, no longer a requirement to concentrate purely on the collective aim of victory. Soldiers' thoughts turned to home, and for men who owned animals it turned in time to the thought of how they were going to take their beloved pets. Private Albert Lowy's story was not exceptional, although the final outcome certainly was.

Pte Albert Lowy, Army Service Corps

There is a strict law that any animal must spend four months in quarantine, to ensure that it is not carrying rabies. I wrote to the proper authority for papers, but perhaps due to my being a mere private, I got no reply. I therefore determined to try to smuggle my darling dog back to England.

All the men – several hundred – due for a certain train were assembled at a station. A staff officer, who recognised my dog from having seen her at some hospital, asked me if he could lend me the money needed for quarantine. I told him that I had failed to get the necessary papers, and that I was going to try and take her all the way with me. He wished me good luck. I am sure though that he thought that there was no chance that I could succeed; nor could I see how it was to be done.

During the days in the cattle truck, I practised her sitting in my kitbag being humped on my shoulder, and bumped up and

down, whispering 'shsh' and 'keep quiet' and 'it's all right'. When
we arrived at Cherbourg camp to await embarkation in a day or
so, I carried her in the kitbag, but it was so heavy that I 'fell-out'
and followed the road slowly, my dog walking near me. We, men
going to England, were warned against trying to take dogs with
us, and the tents were watched by officers looking for dogs. She
had to spend a lot of time in my bag, lying quite still, and no one
suspected that an animal was there hidden.

At last we were to be marched to the harbour to embark. Again
the bag became too heavy for me to carry so far, so I pretended to
be a bit lame, and was allowed to follow slowly. My dog of course
walked until we came near the harbour, when she was stowed
away again. I looked so weary carrying such a heavy kitbag, that
the officers, who had discovered several dogs hidden under men's
overcoats, didn't suspect the real cause of my apparent distress was
due to the burden I was struggling under.

I got on board, where the ships' officers were also on the lookout for dogs. I talked quietly to her while looking for a place to lie
down among the men who were packed like sardines on the lower
decks. I used the kitbag as a pillow, not daring to let her be seen,
and so the night passed.

*Unbeknown to Private Lowy, the length of time an animal would have
to spend in quarantine had been raised to six months and the cost of
care set at £14, an amount far beyond the pocket of the vast majority
of other ranks. In time, organisations such as the Royal Society for
the Prevention of Cruelty to Animals (RSPCA) and the Blue Cross
Society heard of the soldiers' plight and approached the government in
order to take over the care and cost of these animals during their months
under supervision. The soldiers deposited £2 with the charity to ensure
that they collected their animals after the requisite time in quarantine
had elapsed.*

*Before any dogs were allowed to come home they had to be taken to
Boulogne to a veterinary hospital. Here they were checked for illness,*

being kept for five days before being sent onwards to England. Boulogne
was the only crossing permitted.

Lt Andrew McCormick, 182nd Labour Coy

When the day came when I had to return to my civilian duties, I made up my mind to get the dog across with the assistance of the Blue Cross Society. I had to travel for the first time by Calais. I was referred to the AMLO [Assistant Military Landing Officer] for information as to getting the dog across. He, an irate old colonel, said, 'It can't be done.' Then I said, 'Why mislead people by allowing paragraphs to appear to the effect that the Blue Cross Society would put them in quarantine and deliver them when the dog was pronounced free of rabies?' 'You should have gone by Boulogne,' he replied. 'But I had no say in the matter, sir,' I argued. He could give no answer but just fumed and stamped about the landing stage. Well, I shall not tell you all that my heart prompted me to do.

I had to turn away sick at heart when I saw Teddie being taken away on the shoulder of an NCO who had promised to look after her for me. Had I cried 'choco' I verily believe she'd have attempted to swim the Channel after me.

From that moment to the day – after repeated inquiries – when I heard that Teddie had gone up the line again with a brother officer must be the 'veiled' period as to my actions with regard to Teddie, the dearest and best of soldiers' doggie chums. Should that officer ever hear of this plaintive story, oh surely he'll send back to me the dog of my heart.

Pte Albert Lowy, Army Service Corps

In the morning we stood on the quayside for an hour, and although this was England, I still did not dare to let her out for some snooper to see her and possibly to be returned on the ship and then turned loose in Cherbourg. We did not get away until early evening. Well, I just had to take a chance and let her out

after so long and patient an imprisonment all night. I walked
her along the platform, trying to spot anyone looking for me and
trouble. I bought some railway biscuits and found water in a fire
bucket, and I kept her as much as possible hidden under my coat
for most of that awful day. At one moment the same staff officer
who had wished me luck touched me on the shoulder and said,
'Well done, I am glad that you have succeeded in bringing her
with you.'

When a train eventually came, every seat and inch of the corridor was packed and jammed with men anxious to get home.
We got out at Wimbledon station; we were to march up to the
Common, a good mile away. Outside the station there was a large
cheering crowd, trams rang their bells and car horns blared. In a
minute I had lost her, as I couldn't lead her in the solid column of
soldiers; she could have been trodden on. At least I was consoled
that she was lost where she would be picked up and given a good
home.

I had to stay in the column and march up to the demobilisation
camp, which occupied dozens of army huts. After an hour and a
half she found me – to our great joy. I tied her up in an empty
hut, and made a bed for her with most of my remaining army
clothes, so that she should know that I was around. I had still to
go through the long rigmarole of being charged for the clothes
that I should have handed in and being handed 'civvies' that only
fitted here and there, and signed the many discharge papers. Then
I collected her and got her home in time for breakfast.

She and our fox terrier, Spot, produced a litter of half-pedigree
pups; their father was not at all thoroughbred, but she didn't
mind anything after what she had been through in the war and
had come back.

Lt Andrew McCormick, 182nd Labour Coy
My poignant soul cry has been answered in a curious way. A colonel whom I had met in the army came to reside near where I live.

When I paid my first call I received joyous greeting at the doorway from a little doggie, the living image of Teddie.

*For most of the larger animals requisitioned for work, there was to be
no joyous and well-deserved homecoming. Horses, mules and donkeys
were assessed before being sold off to farmers, or, if in bad health, taken
to be killed and turned into horsemeat. It was a sad end. Given the
bond between horses and men, there were those who would have preferred
their horse to have had a quick and painless death in action to seeing it
simply rounded up and taken away. For over a year, Trooper Benjamin
Clouting had looked after a horse belonging to a senior officer, and his
friendship with that horse was as natural as it was extraordinary.*

Trp. Benjamin Clouting, 4th (Royal Irish) Dragoon Guards

I often went to a particular café, and as an entertainment sometimes went down with de Wiart's horse, Nancy. Once there, she
would half follow me in, with just her head and front feet through
the door, to the amusement of the customers. Nancy liked being
made a fuss of, and it became a bit of a show. I would ask the
owner for sugar, but withheld it until Nancy kissed me. 'Brassez-
moi' I would say in French, and as I raised my face, she would lean
over and nuzzle her face into mine.

She was a horse that I never had to call. I would just clap my hands
and she would race across the field, giving a sort of chuckle as she
arrived. It was possible to ride her down the road without anything
on her at all, not even a head collar, steering her with the pressure of
my knees. At night, if we were in a barn, she would lie down and
place her head on my legs and I'd put my arm round her neck.

Nancy had a remarkable temperament and, like most cavalry
horses, stood up well to the noise of gunfire. She was killed at the
end of the war when a shell burst almost underneath her, but,
though it seems hard, I was glad. So many of the regiment's horses
were handed over to local farmers at the end of the war, and there
was no knowing what might have happened to her.

Pte Christopher Massie, 76th Brigade, RAMC

The warhorse is honest, reliable, strong. He is a soldier. And I
have written this eulogy of his merits as one soldier might write
of another. I want someone to take his case up and see that he falls
'cushy' after the war. It is only fair. He is a mate of ours – one of
us. A Tommy. Don't ring a lot of bells and forget him. A field of
clover, a bundle of hay, a Sussex meadow, a bushel of apples, a loaf
of bread, a sack of carrots, sunshine and blue hills, clean stables,
and trusses of straw, may they all be his, for he has earned them!
It is only fair.

*It might have been fair, but it is not what happened. Well over one
million horses and mules were mobilised or purchased by the British
Army in the Great War. An indication of the sheer logistical effort this
required is in the War Office's own published calculation that the total
weight of oats and hay sent overseas to the Western Front to feed these
animals exceeded the weight of ammunition of all types sent to feed the
guns, 5.95 million tons and 5.27 million tons respectively. During the
course of the fighting, 225,000 horses and mules were killed, and of the
remainder only 62,000 of the fittest ever returned home.*

Pte Fred Lloyd, Army Veterinary Corps

At the depot, we classified the horses to see what was coming
home and what wasn't. There were three grades, and peacetime
vets were saying which ones were fit to go back to England,
these went into quarantine; the next grade was to be sold to
the farmers, and the others were for food. A terrific lot of the
horses were blind, hundreds of them. They never found out why,
perhaps it was exposure to gas. Some of the time, I was leading one awkward horse and three more that were totally blind.
If they weren't fit, we'd take them by train or, if they were,
we'd take them by road. We used to go right up to Paris with
horses, each man leading four to sell to the French for food. In
the slaughterhouses, we led them on to scales four at a time

and weighed them up. We sold them by weight. It was a bit upsetting.

Within eighteen months of the end of the war, nearly 200,000 horses had been sold and in the end 56,000 were killed. Only later, in the 1920s, did animal welfare organisations attempt to rescue some of those that had been sold. Our Dumb Friends' League bought a number of overworked and emaciated horses that still bore the tell tale broad arrow branding of the British Army. Although not all were returned to Britain, all those found were allowed to live out their lives in comfort.

Until the peace treaty was signed at Versailles in June 1919, thousands of troops remained abroad, either stationed in France, clearing the battlefields, or as part of the Army of Occupation in the Rhineland. For those who signed to stay on in the army, a semblance of peacetime soldiering was restored, while in Britain the first battlefield pilgrimages were organised for grieving families to visit the graves of loved ones. Cemeteries were constructed, and soldiers took stock. For the first time they were free to survey the land in which, for so long, they had lived as worms.

Lt Harold Hemming, 84th Brigade, RFA

In Germany the horsey members of our army decided that they should start fox-hunting. Unfortunately there were no foxes, so they had to descend to a drag-hunt. However, everything else was done in style. They sent to England for their red coats and caps, and managed somehow to collect a pretty comic pack of hounds, appoint a Master of Hounds, etc.

I took part in one of the early hunts. I had acquired a sweet little mare who was pretty good at jumping fences. I only went to one meet and I put up a pretty poor show, and soon found myself all alone and ended up with a bunch of grooms with the 'second' horses. Anyway, I was particularly hostile to blood sports and I decided not to make an exhibition of myself again, even though there was no fox blood being spilt.

Lady Londonderry: visit to battlefields, 1–5 April 1919

Ypres

The shell-holes then, as now, were full of water in which our men had to live. It cannot be described. It must be seen, and even so, no one, fortunately for them, who was not there could imagine or picture for themselves such a hell as it must have been during the fight. We saw nothing alive the whole day except three wild ducks in flight and a grey crow perched upon a tree. Even the insect life seemed to have departed – and vegetation was in a moribund condition. No fresh green tufts of grass or bright-hued mossy patches, only dull blotches of grey weeds. There was no hum or whirr of insect wings or chirping of grasshoppers – just absolute silence and stagnation.

Somme

The village had always been a very unhealthy spot during the war and was commonly known by the name of 'Funk' Villers. It was not a pleasant habitation to take a siesta in or stroll about. We left the car and walked over to the Hun lines by Gommecourt Wood. They were still in splendid order and very deep. We investigated a very deep dugout with several rooms in it . . . These trenches gave one a far clearer idea than any others which I had seen of the life led below ground during the day when visits above ground could only be nocturnal. We wandered right through Gommecourt Wood past trees and shrubs which before the war would have been bursting forth in bud full of promise of coming spring but which in fact were lifeless, silent witnesses testifying to the tragedy that had been remorselessly going on around us for months . . . Nature itself seemed moribund and mutely reproachful of mankind who had made this terrific mess and muddle. I know I cannot adequately transplant my feelings into words. My last impression, as it was my first, of the battlefields, was the feeling of death pervading everything around us.

Anonymous British officer, 1919

Yesterday I visited the battlefield of last year. The place was scarcely recognisable. Instead of a wilderness of ground torn up by shells, a perfect desolation of earth without a sign of vegetation, the ground was a garden of wild flowers and tall grasses. Nature had certainly hidden the ghastly scene under a veil of many colours. I was specially struck by a cross to an unknown British warrior which stood like a sentinel over the vast cemetery of the fallen in last year's battle, now hidden under the dense vegetation. Most remarkable of all was the appearance of many thousands of white butterflies which fluttered round this solitary grave. You can have no conception of the strange sensation that this host of little fluttering creatures gave me. It was as if the souls of the dead soldiers had come to haunt the spot where so many fell. It was so eerie to see them – the only living things in that wilderness of flowers. And the silence! Not a sound, not even the rustling of a breeze through the grass. It was so still that it seemed as if one could almost hear the beat of the butterflies' wings. Indeed, there was nothing to disturb the eternal slumber of this unknown who was sleeping his last sleep where he fell. A contrast indeed to the hideous crash of battle of a short year ago.

Anonymous member of the Wicks family [sister] visiting the grave of L/Cpl Christopher Wicks, 31st Motor Ambulance Convoy, 1921

The cemetery is beautifully kept, and an English gardener and two subordinates (both English ex-soldiers) attend to the graves. It is laid out with military precision . . . the graves are in a long row, with just room to walk before the crosses on well-kept newly planted turf. A little rectangular flowerbed is made in each long row, and hardy flowers are planted at the foot of every cross. Marigolds, daisies and Michaelmas daisies are in full bloom every-where, and in the photograph of my brother's grave daffodils are blooming.

This St-Pierre cemetery is not so utterly military as those scattered everywhere in the open country – many we saw afterwards in the Valley of the Somme and on Vimy Ridge, and nearly to Ypres, were about two acres in extent, carefully fenced and a large notice board with the nationality and number prominently displayed and no habitation of any kind near for miles. At such places the countryside was laid waste, and the utter desolation and barren outlook can only be seen to be believed. Just a wilderness with many enclosures with little white crosses. It is terrible, and only three years' weeds and rank grasses cover the landscape for miles.

Former Capt. Stephen Graham, 1st Scots Guards

From Albert to Bapaume, from Fricourt by Carnoy and Maricourt to Longueval and Ginchy and Le Transloy, a pleasant day's walk now. There is the incomparable Somme silence, a silence achieved by the tremendous thunderous contrast in history, a silence from the stilled hearts of the dead, a deafness and a muteness. Then when the mist disperses, and the sun lifts his awful radiance o'er the scene, there are audible the lowly orchestras of flies and bees. The rags of horses' skeletons lie on the roadway, and beside a ruined direction post a clean-picked horse's skull has been placed on the stump of a tree. Lifting one's eyes to the view, there rolls forth to the horizon vast moors empurpled here and there and with gashes of white on wan green wastes. An organised tour by car whirls past upon the road raising phantom hosts of white dust. It will do the whole Somme campaign in an hour and bring up safely at some French hotel where hot lunch and foaming beer persuade the living that life is still worthwhile.

Former Pte James Hudson,
8th Queen's Own (Royal West Kent Rgt)

It was 1923. A travel agency sent me a brochure about trips to the battlefields and, on the spur of the moment, I thought I would go. This was on the Monday and I travelled on Friday.

There was only one other old soldier on the coach. We got to know each other and together we walked into the cemetery at Passchendaele, Tyne Cot. It was a lovely summer day, quiet and peaceful, and at the back of the cemetery was a young Belgian fellow with a single plough drawn by a mule, one of ours, for it had an arrow stamped on its backside. The peace, the quiet, the scene had both of us damn nearly in tears. We parted and we were left alone for some time before we could pull ourselves together a bit. It brought back so much.

Looking back, many soldiers found it hard to see in their mind's eye anything beyond the unmitigated horror of trench warfare, and that is entirely understandable. After all, if they ever spoke about their war, if they ever answered questions about their service, it rarely, if ever, involved flowers, beetles and butterflies. Yet there was beauty there, and in abundance; moments of true spiritual exhilaration and wonder that could have been overlooked only by the most unimaginative of men. Undoubtedly the presence of wildlife helped to save men from complete despair and gave them a scintilla of hope for the future that was, perhaps, all that was needed at that moment to keep them going. For a lucky few whose love of nature was a deep personal pursuit, its presence was a godsend. That some of these men recorded the natural world in the way they did, in letters, diaries and memoirs, has helped recall a side to life on the Western Front that was, in its own way, as life-saving to their souls as any phial of morphine, bandage or pill was to their bodies.

Former Pte Thomas Williams, 19th King's Liverpool Rgt
Looking back on the varied experiences of trench life on the Western Front, it may seem strange to think that some of us still treasure one or two really pleasant associations with no-man's-land. Who, for instance, can forget the red glow of early dawn over the enemy's lines and the larks singing in the morning sunlight? Men in mud-stained uniforms of khaki, field-grey and

horizon-blue listened with never-failing wonder to those sweet notes. In many places, to show one's head above ground was a decidedly risky business, yet the skylarks soared fearlessly. So long as the larks sang, there always seemed to be hope.

Former Capt. Philip Gosse, RAMC

Some of my readers may find fault with me for having comparatively little to say about the 'horrors' of war and so much about the beasts and the birds. The title might well have been, 'A Solace of Birds', for without the birds I dare not think how I should have got through the war at all. One friend, after reading my manuscript, asked if I could not include 'more horrors', even at the expense of some of the birds, but I told him that in any case I could remember no more 'horrors', though of birds I remembered so much. The mangled corpse is forgotten, but the warbler with its nest and eggs is remembered. I think the reason for this is largely that at the time the 'horrors' were so beastly, so ugly, that one got into the habit of putting them aside by concentrating on the birds, so that now, after many years, the memory retains the birds and to a large extent has got rid of the rest.

Acknowledgements

I would like to thank the wonderfully supportive staff at Bloomsbury, particularly Bill Swainson, the senior commissioning editor, for his encouragement and enthusiasm, and Emily Sweet for her exceptionally keen editorial eye. I am also very grateful to Nick Humphrey, Ruth Logan, Anya Rosenberg, David Mann, Lisa Fiske, Polly Napper and Andrew Tennant for their support in helping to nurture *Tommy's Ark* all the way to publication. I would also like to express my gratitude once again to Richard Collins for his excellent editorial comments and careful reading of the text, helping to iron out many small queries.

Once again, a special mention must be made of my good friend Jeremy Banning. His remarkable research skills and unflagging energy have helped make this book not only possible, but much richer in material. I should also like to thank Stuart Arrowsmith, who, once more, was very generous in lending me photographs from his collection taken by Sgt Harold Bisgood, 2nd London Regiment; Andrew Read and Steve Chambers for images from their own extensive and impressive photographic collections; and Stewart Simpson for the image from his archives of Jacko the monkey. I am also very grateful to Taff Gillingham for reading through the text; his Great War knowledge and expertise is truly to be envied. My gratitude must also go to Jim and Sarah Burnham, who came up with the title *Tommy's Ark* over dinner, trumping all other contributions such as *Your Country Needs Zoo* and *Not Fur-gotten*. Thanks also to Peter Barton and Simon Jones for pointing me in the direction of some superb quotes about the service of canaries and mice underground, and to Nigel Steel at the Imperial War Museum who also proffered some very sound advice on sources. My gratitude is due to the Royal Welsh Fusiliers Museum and to Brian Owen and my friend Anne Pedley for granting permission to quote extracts from Captain James Dunn's *The War the Infantry Knew*. I also appreciate the support of Vic and Diane Piuk, Mark Banning, Matt Dixon, Caryl Williams, Iain and Donna McHenry, David and Judith Cohen, Peter Wright, and Ken Prowse.

Especial mention should be made of my wonderful agent, Jane Turnbull, whose duty of care knows no bounds and who has always offered sage advice and been totally supportive of all I have done: thank you once again, Jane.

My warmest thanks must go to my family: to my mother, Joan van Emden, who, as always, has been wonderful and a tower of editorial strength. I remain deeply in debt to my wife, Anna, whose support grows greater as deadlines loom and who, when the pressure is on, steers our three-year-old son away from my study door.

I would like to thank the following people for permission to reproduce extracts from diaries, letters or memoirs written by their Great War relatives: Gill Pullinger (for extracts from the diaries of Arthur Alexander); Laurence Martin (extracts from the diary of Albert Martin); Tim Hardwick (extracts from the papers of A.G.P. Hardwick); Jean Harris (extracts from the memoirs of F.E. Harris); Constance Ross (extracts from the papers of A.R. Read); Allan Mott (extracts from the papers of D.J. Polley); Mike Durham (extracts from the memoirs of G.W. Durham); Mrs Louisa Service (extracts from the memories of H.H. Hemming); Rosemary Price (extracts from the diary of S.T. Fuller); John Harlow (extracts from the papers of E.H. Harlow); David Newman (extracts from the memoirs of C.T. Newman); Miss M.A. Johnston (extracts from the papers of J.A. Johnston); Mrs L. Palmer (extracts from the papers of A.E. Lowy); Mrs E.J. Grisenthwaite (extracts from the letters of James Foulis); Mrs Dorothy Kilpin (extracts from the papers of Capt. D.P. Hirsch VC); Eleanor Edwards (extracts from the memoirs of Wilfrid Edwards).

Sources and Credits for Text and Photographs

Text

Imperial War Museum: By kind permission of the Department of Documents, Imperial War Museum, Lambeth Road, London, SE1 6HZ. With grateful thanks to Roderick Suddaby, Anthony Richards and Simon Offord from the Departments of Documents. S.T. Fuller – 86/32/1; A.G.P. Hardwick MC – 98/14/1; Lt E.C. Allfree – 77/14/1; Lt Col H.M. Dillon DSO – 82/25/1; M.R. Evans – P473; P.A. Glock – 99/84/1; F.E. Harris – 06/29/1; C.T. Newman – 03/5/1; A.R. Read – 06/86/1; Capt. J.B. Foulis – 85/15/1; D.J. Polley – 80/35/1; G.W. Durham – 90/7/1; Lt Col H.H. Hemming OBE MC – PP/MCR/155; E.H. Harlow – 03/15/1; J.A. Johnston – 02/29/1; A.E. Lowy – 06/54/1; Capt. J.D. Mackie – 06/109/1; Capt. A. McCormick – 02/6/1; G. Buckeridge – 04/39/1; A.V. Conn – 81/41/1; F.J. Field – 85/39/1; Lt J.W. Gamble – PP/MCR/82; Capt. L. Gameson – PP/MCR/C47 & P395–396 & Con Shelf; Brig. E.E. Mockler-Ferryman CB CBE MC – P323; Lady Londonderry – 06/128/1; Lt Col C.E.L. Lyne – 80/14/1; T.S. Williams – Misc 40 (702).

Every effort has been made to trace copyright holders, and the author and the Imperial War Museum would be grateful for any information which might help to trace those whose identities or addresses are not currently known.

The Liddle Archive: By kind permission of the Liddle Collection, Leeds University Library, Woodhouse Lane, Leeds LS2 9JT, www.leeds.ac.uk. With thanks to Richard Davies.

Capt. D.P. Hirsch VC – GS0770; Pte W.N. Edwards – GS0506;

Lt G.L. Reid – GS1337; 2nd Lt L.W. Pratt – GS1294; Capt. J.W. Tibbles – GS1603; Driver W.M. Peto – GS1256; 2nd M. Webb-Peploe – GS1699; Sgt W.A. Rigden – GS1358; 2nd Lt C.W. Walker – GS1672.

Soldiers of Gloucestershire Museum: By kind permission of the Soldiers of Gloucestershire Museum, Custom House, Gloucester Docks, Gloucester, GL1 2HE, www.glosters.org.uk. With thanks to George Streatfield, David Read and Graham Gordon.

The letters of 2/Lt C.W. Winterbotham, 1/5th Bttn, Gloucestershire Rgt.

Somerset Record Office: By kind permission of the Duty Archivist, Somerset Record Office, Obridge Road, Taunton TA2 7PU, www.somerset.gov.uk/archives/, and Lt Col Mike Motum, Somerset Military Museum Trust, 14 Mount Street, TA1 3QB. Arthur Cook diary – Ref: DD/SLI/17/1/40.

King's Own Scottish Borderers Regimental Museum: By kind permission of the King's Own Scottish Borderers Regimental Museum, The Barracks, The Parade, Berwick-upon-Tweed, TD15 1DG, www.kosb.co.uk/museum. With thanks to the Regimental Secretary and Ian Martin.

Capt. A.J.M. Shaw, 1st Bttn, Ref – KOSB T/1/13.

Royal Engineers Museum: By kind permission of the Royal Engineers Museum, Prince Arthur Road, Gillingham, Kent ME4 4UG, www.remuseum.org.uk. With thanks to Rebecca Nash and her staff.

Lt F.J. Mulqueen; Col Logan: Memorandum on Gas Poisoning in Mines.

The Regimental Museum of the Royal Welsh: By kind permission of the Regimental Museum of the Royal Welsh (formerly South Wales Borderers & Monmouthshire Regimental Museum), The Barracks, Watton, Brecon, Powys LD3 7EB, www.rrw.org.uk. With many thanks to Martin Everett and Celia Green.

Pte C.P. Heare, 1/2nd Monmouthshire Rgt – unpublished diary, July 1913–March 1919, Acc. No. 1997.139.

The Fusiliers Museum of Northumberland: By kind permission of the Fusiliers Museum of Northumberland, The Abbott's Tower, Alnwick Castle, Alnwick, NE66 1NG, www.northumberlandfusiliers.org.uk. With thanks to staff at the Fusiliers Museum of Northumberland.

Diary and letter of A.O. Terry, 23rd Bttn, Northumberland Fusiliers (4th Tyneside Scottish) January 1916–July 1918 [34th Division].

The King's Own Royal Border Regiment Museum: By kind permission of Border Regiment & King's Own Royal Border Regiment Museum, Queen Mary's Tower, The Castle, Carlisle, CA3 8UR, www.kingsownbordermuseum.btik.com. With thanks to Stuart Eastwood and Tony Goddard.

Lt C.H.M Whiteside, 7th Bttn, Ref: 11/G2/001/29A.

The National Archives, Kew, Richmond, Surrey, TW9 4DU, www.nationalarchives.gov.uk.

In the 1920s the following officers corresponded with the official historian (Cab45), and extracts from their letters have been used in this book:

2nd Lt Eric Anderson, 108 Batt. RFA; Maj. George Walker, 59th Field Coy, REs; Maj. Percy Hastings, 1st Queens Own Royal West Kent Rgt; Capt. Charles Norman, 9th (Queen's Royal) Lancers; Capt. and Quartermaster W.W. Finch, 1st Royal Scots Fusiliers.

Bibliography
Memoirs

Adams, Bernard, *Nothing of Importance*, Methuen & Co. Ltd, 1917

Barnett, D.O., *In Happy Memory*, privately printed, 1915

Bolwell, F.A., *With a Reservist in France*, George Routledge, n.d.

Bridges, Sir Tom, *Alarms and Excursions: Reminiscences of a Soldier*, Longmans, Green & Co., 1938

Butler, Partick, *A Galloper at Ypres*, T. Fisher Unwin Ltd, 1920

Buxton, Andrew, *The Rifle Brigade: A Memoir*, Robert Scott, 1918

Clouting, Benjamin, *Tickled to Death to Go: Memoirs of a Cavalryman in the First World War*, Spellmount, 1996

Corbett-Smith, A., *The Marne and After*, Cassell & Co. Ltd, 1917

Crouch, Lionel, *Duty and Service: Letters from the Front*, privately published, 1917

Cuddeford, Douglas, *And All For What? Some War Time Experiences*, Heath Cranton Ltd, 1933

Douie, Charles, *The Weary Road*, John Murray, 1929

Dunn, J.C., *The War the Infantry Knew, 1914–1919*, Jane's Publishing Co. Ltd, 1987

Edwards, H.N., *I Did My Duty*, Cloverleaf Publications, 1998

Empey, Arthur, *Over the Top*, G.P. Putnam & Sons, 1917

Ewart, Wilfrid, *Scots Guard on the Western Front, 1915–1918*, Strong Oak, 2001

Fielding, Rowland, *War Letters to a Wife*, Spellmount Classics, 2001

Fildes, G.P.A., *Iron Times with the Guards*, John Murray, 1918

Fraser-Tytler, Neil, *Field Guns in France*, The Naval and Military Press, n.d.

Gillespie, Alexander, *Letters from Flanders*, Smith, Elder & Co., 1916

Gosse, Philip, *Memoirs of a Camp Follower*, Longmans, Green & Co., 1934

Gyde, Arnold, *Contemptible by 'Casualty'*, William Heinemann, 1916

Hancock, Reginald, *Memoirs of a Veterinary Surgeon*, Macgibbon & Kee, 1952

Harvey, Harold, *Soldiers' Sketches Under Fire*, Sampson Low, Marston & Co. Ltd, n.d.

Haworth, Haworth, *March to Armistice 1918*, William Kimber, 1968

Hodges, Frederick James, *Men of 18 in 1918*, Arthur H. Stockwell Ltd, 1988

Hope, T.S., *The Winding Road Unfolds*, Putnam, 1937

Hutchison, Graham Seton, *Footslogger*, Hutchinson & Co. Ltd, 1933

Lawson, Henry, *Vignettes of the Western Front*, Positif Press, 1979

Living, Edward, G.D., *Attack on the Somme: An Infantry Subaltern's Impressions of July 1st 1916*, Spa Books, 1986

Lloyd, R.A., *A Trooper in the 'Tins': Autobiography of a Lifeguardsman*, Hurst & Blackett, 1938

Lucy, John, *There's a Devil in the Drum*, The Naval and Military Press, 1993

Mack, Isaac Alec, *Letters from France,* privately printed, n.d.

Martin, Sapper, *The Secret War Diary of Jack Martin*, Bloomsbury, 2009

Massie, Christopher, *Red and Khaki, or Impressions of a Stretcher-Bearer*, The Blackfriars Press Ltd, n.d.

McQueen, James, *Our War*, privately published, n.d.

Mitchell, F., *Tank Warfare*, Thomas Nelson & Sons Ltd, n.d.

Munro, H.H., 'Birds on the Western Front' (article), *Westminster Gazette*, 1916

Osburn, Arthur, *Unwilling Passenger*, Faber & Faber, 1932

Patch, Harry, *The Last Fighting Tommy*, Bloomsbury, 2007

Quigley, Hugh, *Passchendaele and the Somme: A Diary of 1917*, The Naval and Military Press, n.d.

Raven, Charles E., *In Praise of Birds*, George Allen & Unwin Ltd, 1950

Richards, Frank, *Old Soldiers Never Die*, Faber & Faber, 1933

Smith, Aubrey, *Four Years on the Western Front*, Odhams Press, 1922

Talbot Kelly, R.B., *A Subaltern's Odyssey: A Memoir of the Great War 1915–1917*, William Kimber, 1980

Tiplady, Thomas, *The Cross at the Front: A Chaplain's Experiences*, Epworth Press, 1939

Vernede, Robert, *Letters to His Wife*, Collins, 1917

Vivian, Alfred, *The Phantom Brigade*, Ernest Benn Ltd, 1930

Voigt, F.A., *Combed Out,* Jonathan Cape, 1929

Watson, W.H.L., *Adventures of a Despatch Rider*, Blackwood, 1915

Other Reading

Baker, Peter Shaw, *Animal War Heroes*, A&C Black Ltd, 1933

Baynes, Ernest Harold, *Animal Heroes of the Great War*, Macmillan, 1926

Cooper, Jilly, *Animals in War*, Corgi Books, 2000

Fairholme, Edward G., Wellesley Pain, *A Century of Work for Animals*, John Murray, 1924

Gardiner, Juliet, *The Animals' War: Animals in Wartime from the First World War to the Present Day*, Portrait, 2006

Goring, Alan, 2nd Lt, 6th The Yorkshire Regt, extract taken from Lyn Macdonald's *They Called It Passchendaele*, Papermac, 1978

Owen, Thomas, L/Cpl, 1st South Wales Borderers, extract from *True World War I Stories*, Robinson, 1999

Wycliffe and the Great War: A School Record, 1923. Extract of letters taken from the following former pupils: Pte Cyril Baker, A/Capt. Kenneth Jones, Lt Melville Hastings.

Interviews conducted by the author with the following Great War veterans:

Andrew Bowie

Ben Clouting

Frank Deane

Norman Dillon

Alfred Finnigan

George Gadsby

William Golightly

Fred Hodges

Fred Lloyd

Harry Patch

Robert Renwick

Dick Trafford

Photographs

Imperial War Museum, London: By kind permission of the picture library of the Imperial War Museum, Lambeth Road, London, SE1 6HZ.

Q53386; Q26623; Q1629; Q3223; Q1451; Q448; CO1414; Q10958; Q11517; Q3210; Q11269; Q6400; Q11250; Q10949; Q3249; Q8715.

First Plate Section

Page

1. Full page– Stephen Chambers (*hereafter* SC)
2. All photos – author's collection (*hereafter* AC)
3. All photos – AC
4. Top – AC; bottom – Imperial War Museum (*hereafter* IWM)
5. Top left – IWM; top right – SC; bottom left and right – AC
6. & 7. Double-page spread – Stewart Simpson
8. Top – AC; middle and bottom – Stuart Arrowsmith (*hereafter* SA)
9. All photos – SA
10 & 11 All images – AC
12. Top left – AC; top right – Andrew Read (*hereafter* AR); bottom – IWM
13. All photos – AC
14. All images – AC
15. Top – IWM; bottom left – AC; bottom right – AR
16. Full page – SC

Second Plate Section

Page

1. Full page – IWM
2. Top – SC; bottom – IWM
3. All photos – AC
4. Top – IWM; bottom – AR
5. Top and middle – IWM; bottom – AR

6. All images – AC
7. All photos – IWM
8. & 9. Double-page spread – IWM
10. All images – AC
11. All photos – IWM
12. Top – AC; bottom – IWM
13. Top – AC; bottom – IWM
14. Top – AC; bottom – AR
15. Top – AC; middle and bottom – AR
16. Full page – AC

Index

A NOTE ON THE TYPE

Linotype Garamond Three — based on seventeenth-century copies of Claude Garamond's types, cut by Jean Jannon. This version was designed for American Type Founders in 1917, by Morris Fuller Benton and Thomas Maitland Cleland, and adapted for mechanical composition by Linotype in 1936.

ALSO AVAILABLE BY RICHARD VAN EMDEN

THE LAST FIGHTING TOMMY
THE LIFE OF HARRY PATCH, LAST VETERAN OF THE TRENCHES, 1898-2009

(Written with Harry Patch)

'An extraordinary biography by the very last witness of a devastating four years in British history'
DAILY MAIL

Harry Patch was the last British soldier alive to have fought in the trenches of the First World War. From his vivid memories of an Edwardian childhood, the horror of the Great War and fighting in the mud during the Battle of Passchendaele, working on the home front in the Second World War and fame in later life as a veteran, *The Last Fighting Tommy* is the story of an ordinary man's extraordinary life...

*

'Patch was not unique among millions of his comrades who endured that prolonged and supreme test of nerve and courage. But, uniquely, as the last survivor, he embodies them all'
SUNDAY EXPRESS

This articulate, modest and outspoken man not only remains one of the last living links with a traumatic event that has become part of the national consciousness, but is an unassailable witness of what the war was like for'
DAILY TELEGRAPH

*

ISBN: 9780747593362 / PAPERBACK / £7.99

BLOOMSBURY

THE SOLDIER'S WAR
THE GREAT WAR THROUGH VETERANS' EYES

'Thousands of books have been written about the Great War, but perhaps none so vividly evocative as The Soldier's War ... an extraordinary homage to a lost generation'
DAILY MAIL

The Great War ended more than ninety years ago yet still haunts and fascinates us today. In *The Soldier's War*, Richard van Emden traces a history of the fighting month by month and year by year, using original diaries, letters and as-yet-unseen photographs taken by the soldiers themselves. We follow the British Tommy through devastating battles and trench warfare from the outbreak of war in 1914 to the armistice four years later, guided by Richard van Emden's sure explanations. This is a history of the war as seen from the trenches that is shockingly intimate, sometimes heartbreaking, often wryly amusing, but always compelling.

✳

'In *The Soldier's War*, Richard van Emden has toiled in archives and hunted down caches of letters to tell the story of the war chronologically through the eyes of the Tommies who fought it'
THE TIMES

'Van Emden manages to establish in an immediate empathy with these ordinary men of Britain, thrown into such horrendous conditions. They hope, moan, laugh, grieve, despair and pray their way through the four years of the "war to end all wars"'
TIME OUT

✳

ISBN: 9780747598732 / PAPERBACK / £8.99

B L O O M S B U R Y

EDITED BY RICHARD VAN EMDEN

SAPPER MARTIN
THE SECRET GREAT WAR DIARY OF JACK MARTIN

'Honest, insightful and full of humour ... Richard Van Emden's editing of the diaries is sensibly unobtrusive and self-effacing, largely allowing Martin's words to speak for themselves'
SUNDAY TIMES

Jack Martin was a thirty-two-year-old clerk at the Admiralty when he was called up to serve in the army in September 1916. These diaries, written in secret, hidden from his colleagues and only discovered by his family after his return home, present the Great War with heartbreaking clarity, written in a voice as compelling and distinctive as Wilfred Owen or Siegfried Sassoon and all the more extraordinary given that it is not an officer's but that of a private. From his arrival in France and his participation in the Somme, through offensives at Ypres and eventual demobilisation after the Armistice, we see wartime life as it really was for the ordinary Tommy

*

'Extraordinary. Beautifully written, it reveals a cheerful man with a sharp eye and a gift for description that's unforgettable. Through his eyes we see wartime life as it really was for the ordinary Tommy'
CHOICE

*

ISBN: 9780747503110 / PAPERBACK / £7.99